Prais

Why Budd

"I have been waiting all my life for a readable, lucid explanation of Buddhism by a tough-minded, skeptical intellect. Here it is. This is a scientific and spiritual voyage unlike any I have taken before."

—Martin Seligman, professor of psychology at Penn
and bestselling author of *Authentic Happiness*

"A wry, self-deprecating, and brutally empirical guide to the avoidance of suffering.... It constantly made me smile a little, and occasionally chuckle."

—Andrew Sullivan, *New York Magazine*

"Robert Wright brings his sharp wit and love of analysis to good purpose, making a compelling case for the nuts and bolts of how meditation actually works. This book will be useful for all of us, from experienced meditators to hardened skeptics who are wondering what all the fuss is about."

—Sharon Salzberg, cofounder of the Insight Meditation
Society and bestselling author of *Real Love*

"[*Why Buddhism Is True*] will become the go-to explication of Buddhism for modern western seekers."

—*Scientific American*

"What happens when someone steeped in evolutionary psychology takes a cool look at Buddhism? If that person is, like Robert Wright, a gifted writer, the answer is this surprising, enjoyable, challenging, and potentially life-changing book."

—Peter Singer, professor of philosophy at Princeton
and author of *Ethics in the Real World*

"What a terrific book. The combination of evolutionary psychology, philosophy, astute readings of Buddhist tradition, and personal meditative experience is absolutely unique and clarifying."

—Jonathan Gold, professor of religion at Princeton
and author of *Paving the Great Way:
Vasubandhu's Unifying Buddhist Philosophy*

"Delightfully personal, yet broadly important."

—Adam Frank, NPR.org

"Joyful and insightful . . . both entertaining and informative."

—*Publishers Weekly* (starred review)

"Rendered in a down-to-earth and highly readable style, with witty quips and self-effacing humility that give the book its distinctive appeal and persuasive power."

—*America* magazine

"Cool, rational, and dryly cynical, Robert Wright is an unlikely guide to the Dharma and 'not-self.' But in this extraordinary book, he makes a powerful case for a Buddhist way of life and a Buddhist view of the mind. With great clarity and wit, he brings together personal anecdotes with insights from evolutionary theory and cognitive science to defend an ancient yet radical worldview. This is a truly transformative work."

—Paul Bloom, professor of psychology at Yale
and author of *How Pleasure Works*

Why
Buddhism
Is True

The Science and Philosophy of
Meditation and Enlightenment

Robert Wright

Simon & Schuster Paperbacks

New York   London   Toronto   Sydney   New Delhi

Simon & Schuster Paperbacks
An Imprint of Simon & Schuster, Inc.
1230 Avenue of the Americas
New York, NY 10020

First Simon & Schuster paperback edition May 2018

SIMON & SCHUSTER PAPERBACKS and colophon are registered
trademarks of Simon & Schuster, Inc.

For information about special discounts for bulk purchases, please contact
Simon & Schuster Special Sales at 1-866-506-1949 or business@simonandschuster.com.

The Simon & Schuster Speakers Bureau can bring authors to your live event.
For more information or to book an event, contact the Simon & Schuster Speakers Bureau
at 1-866-248-3049 or visit our website at www.simonspeakers.com.

Interior design by Ruth Lee-Mui

Manufactured in the United States of America

20   19   18   17   16   15   14   13

Library of Congress Cataloging-in-Publication Data is available.

ISBN 978-1-4391-9545-1
ISBN 978-1-4391-9546-8 (pbk)
ISBN 978-1-4391-9547-5 (ebook)

For Terri, Mike, Becki, and Linda

WRITER: But tell me before you go. What was the worst thing about being down here?

AGNES: Just existing. Knowing my sight was blurred by my eyes, my hearing dulled by my ears, and my bright thought trapped in the grey maze of a brain. Have you seen a brain?

WRITER: And you're telling me that's what's wrong with us? How else can we be?

—*A Dream Play* by August Strindberg, as adapted by Caryl Churchill

Contents

A Note to Readers

Any book with a title like *Why Buddhism Is True* should have some careful qualification somewhere along the way. We might as well get that over with:

1. I'm not talking about the "supernatural" or more exotically metaphysical parts of Buddhism—reincarnation, for example—but rather about the naturalistic parts: ideas that fall squarely within modern psychology and philosophy. That said, I *am* talking about some of Buddhism's more extraordinary, even radical, claims—claims that, if you take them seriously, could revolutionize your view of yourself and of the world. This book is intended to get you to take these claims seriously.

2. I'm of course aware that there's no one Buddhism, but rather various Buddhist traditions, which differ on all kinds of doctrines. But this book focuses on a kind of "common core"—fundamental ideas that are found across the major Buddhist traditions, even if they get different degrees of emphasis, and may assume somewhat different form, in different traditions.

3. I'm not getting into super-fine-grained parts of Buddhist psychology and philosophy. For example, the *Abhidhamma Pitaka,* a collection of early Buddhist texts, asserts that there are eighty-nine

kinds of consciousness, twelve of which are unwholesome. You may be relieved to hear that this book will spend no time trying to evaluate that claim.

4. I realize that *true* is a tricky word, and asserting the truth of anything, certainly including deep ideas in philosophy or psychology, is a tricky business. In fact, one big lesson from Buddhism is to be suspicious of the intuition that your ordinary way of perceiving the world brings you the truth about it. Some early Buddhist writings go so far as to raise doubts about whether such a thing as "truth" ultimately exists. On the other hand, the Buddha, in his most famous sermon, lays out what are commonly called "The Four Noble Truths," so it's not as if the word *true* has no place in discussions of Buddhist thought. In any event, I'll try to proceed with appropriate humility and nuance as I make my argument that Buddhism's diagnosis of the human predicament is fundamentally correct, and that its prescription is deeply valid and urgently important.

5. Asserting the validity of core Buddhist ideas doesn't necessarily say anything, one way or the other, about other spiritual or philosophical traditions. There will sometimes be logical tension between a Buddhist idea and an idea in another tradition, but often there won't be. The Dalai Lama has said, "Don't try to use what you learn from Buddhism to be a better Buddhist; use it to be a better whatever-you-already-are."

—Robert Wright

1

Taking the
Red Pill

At the risk of overdramatizing the human condition: Have you ever seen the movie *The Matrix*?

It's about a guy named Neo (played by Keanu Reeves), who discovers that he's been inhabiting a dream world. The life he thought he was living is actually an elaborate hallucination. He's having that hallucination while, unbeknownst to him, his actual physical body is inside a gooey, coffin-size pod—one among many pods, rows and rows of pods, each pod containing a human being absorbed in a dream. These people have been put in their pods by robot overlords and given dream lives as pacifiers.

The choice faced by Neo—to keep living a delusion or wake up to reality—is famously captured in the movie's "red pill" scene. Neo has been contacted by rebels who have entered his dream (or, strictly speaking, whose avatars have entered his dream). Their leader, Morpheus (played by Laurence Fishburne), explains the situation to Neo: "You are a slave, Neo. Like everyone else, you were born into bondage, into a prison that you cannot taste or see or touch—a prison for your mind." The prison is called the Matrix, but there's no way to explain to Neo what the Matrix ultimately is. The only way to get the whole picture, says Morpheus, is "to see it for yourself." He offers Neo two pills, a red one and a blue one. Neo can take the blue pill and return to his dream world, or take the red pill and break through the shroud of delusion. Neo chooses the red pill.

That's a pretty stark choice: a life of delusion and bondage or a life of insight and freedom. In fact, it's a choice so dramatic that you'd think a Hollywood movie is exactly where it belongs—that the choices we really get to make about how to live our lives are less momentous than this, more pedestrian. Yet when that movie came out, a number of people saw it as mirroring a choice they had actually made.

The people I'm thinking about are what you might call Western Buddhists, people in the United States and other Western countries who, for the most part, didn't grow up Buddhist but at some point adopted Buddhism. At least they adopted a *version* of Buddhism, a version that had been stripped of some supernatural elements typically found in Asian Buddhism, such as belief in reincarnation and in various deities. This Western Buddhism centers on a part of Buddhist practice that in Asia is more common among monks than among laypeople: meditation, along with immersion in Buddhist philosophy. (Two of the most common Western conceptions of Buddhism—that it's atheistic and that it revolves around meditation—are wrong; most *Asian* Buddhists do believe in gods, though not an omnipotent creator God, and don't meditate.)

These Western Buddhists, long before they watched *The Matrix*, had become convinced that the world as they had once seen it was a kind of illusion—not an out-and-out hallucination but a seriously warped picture of reality that in turn warped their approach to life, with bad consequences for them and the people around them. Now they felt that, thanks to meditation and Buddhist philosophy, they were seeing things more clearly. Among these people, *The Matrix* seemed an apt allegory of the transition they'd undergone, and so became known as a "dharma movie." The word *dharma* has several meanings, including the Buddha's teachings and the path that Buddhists should tread in re sponse to those teachings. In the wake of *The Matrix*, a new shorthand for "I follow the dharma" came into currency: "I took the red pill."

I saw *The Matrix* in 1999, right after it came out, and some months later I learned that I had a kind of connection to it. The movie's directors, the Wachowski siblings, had given Keanu Reeves three books to read in preparation for playing Neo. One of them was a book I had written a few years earlier, *The Moral Animal: Evolutionary Psychology and Everyday Life.*

I'm not sure what kind of link the directors saw between my book and *The Matrix.* But I know what kind of link I see. Evolutionary psychology can be described in various ways, and here's one way I had described it in my book: It is the study of how the human brain was designed by natural selection—to mislead us, even enslave us.

Don't get me wrong: natural selection has its virtues, and I'd rather be created by it than not be created at all—which, so far as I can tell, are the two options this universe offers. Being a product of evolution is by no means *entirely* a story of enslavement and delusion. Our evolved brains empower us in many ways, and they often bless us with a basically accurate view of reality.

Still, ultimately, natural selection cares about only one thing (or, I should say, "cares"—in quotes—about only one thing, since natural selection is just a blind process, not a conscious designer). And that one thing is getting genes into the next generation. Genetically based traits that in the past contributed to genetic proliferation have flourished, while traits that didn't have fallen by the wayside. And the traits that have survived this test include mental traits—structures and algorithms that are built into the brain and shape our everyday experience. So if you ask the question "What kinds of perceptions and thoughts and feelings guide us through life each day?" the answer, at the most basic level, isn't "The kinds of thoughts and feelings and perceptions that give us an accurate picture of reality." No, at the *most* basic level the answer is "The kinds of thoughts and feelings and perceptions that helped our ancestors get genes into the next generation." Whether those thoughts and feelings and perceptions give us a true view of reality is, strictly speaking, beside the point. As a result, they sometimes don't. Our brains are designed to, among other things, delude us.

Not that there's anything wrong with that! Some of my happiest moments have come from delusion—believing, for example, that the Tooth Fairy would pay me a visit after I lost a tooth. But delusion can also produce bad moments. And I don't just mean moments that, in retrospect, are obviously delusional, like horrible nightmares. I also mean moments that you might not think of as delusional, such as lying awake at night with anxiety. Or feeling hopeless, even depressed, for days on end. Or feeling bursts of hatred toward people, bursts that may actually feel good for a moment but slowly corrode your character. Or feeling bursts of hatred toward yourself. Or feeling greedy, feeling a compulsion to buy things or eat things or drink things well beyond the point where your well-being is served.

Though these feelings—anxiety, despair, hatred, greed—aren't delusional the way a nightmare is delusional, if you examine them closely, you'll see that they have elements of delusion, elements you'd be better off without.

And if you think *you* would be better off, imagine how the whole *world* would be. After all, feelings like despair and hatred and greed can foster wars and atrocities. So if what I'm saying is true—if these basic sources of human suffering and human cruelty are indeed in large part the product of delusion—there is value in exposing this delusion to the light.

Sounds logical, right? But here's a problem that I started to appreciate shortly after I wrote my book about evolutionary psychology: the exact value of exposing a delusion to the light depends on what kind of light you're talking about. Sometimes understanding the ultimate source of your suffering doesn't, by itself, help very much.

An Everyday Delusion

Let's take a simple but fundamental example: eating some junk food, feeling briefly satisfied, and then, only minutes later, feeling a kind of crash and maybe a hunger for more junk food. This is a good example to start with for two reasons.

First, it illustrates how subtle our delusions can be. There's no point in the course of eating a six-pack of small powdered-sugar doughnuts when you're believing that you're the messiah or that foreign agents are conspiring to assassinate you. And that's true of many sources of delusion that I'll discuss in this book: they're more about illusion—about things not being quite what they seem—than about delusion in the more dramatic sense of that word. Still, by the end of the book, I'll have argued that all of these illusions do add up to a very large-scale warping of reality, a disorientation that is as significant and consequential as out-and-out delusion.

The second reason junk food is a good example to start with is that it's fundamental to the Buddha's teachings. Okay, it can't be *literally* fundamental to the Buddha's teachings, because 2,500 years ago, when the Buddha taught, junk food as we know it didn't exist. What's fundamental to the Buddha's teachings is the general dynamic of being powerfully drawn to sensory pleasure that winds up being fleeting at best. One of the Buddha's main messages was that the pleasures we seek evaporate quickly and leave us thirsting for more. We spend our time looking for the next gratifying thing—the next powdered-sugar doughnut, the next sexual encounter, the next status-enhancing promotion, the next online purchase. But the thrill always fades, and it always leaves us wanting more. The old Rolling Stones lyric "I can't get no satisfaction" is, according to Buddhism, the human condition. Indeed, though the Buddha is famous for asserting that life is pervaded by suffering, some scholars say that's an incomplete rendering of his message and that the word translated as "suffering," *dukkha*, could, for some purposes, be translated as "unsatisfactoriness."

So what exactly is the illusory part of pursuing doughnuts or sex or consumer goods or a promotion? There are different illusions associated with different pursuits, but for now we can focus on one illusion that's common to these things: the overestimation of how much happiness they'll bring. Again, by itself this is delusional only in a subtle sense. If I asked you whether you thought that getting that next promotion, or getting an A on that next exam, or eating that next powdered-sugar doughnut would bring you eternal bliss, you'd say no, obviously not. On the other hand, we do often pursue such things with, at the very least, an unbalanced view of the future. We spend more time envisioning the perks that a promotion will bring than envisioning the headaches it will bring. And there may be an unspoken sense that once we've achieved this long-sought goal, once we've reached the summit, we'll be able to relax, or at least things will be enduringly better. Similarly, when we see that doughnut sitting there, we immediately imagine how good it tastes, not how intensely we'll want another doughnut only moments after eating it, or how we'll feel a bit tired or agitated later, when the sugar rush subsides.

Why Pleasure Fades

It doesn't take a rocket scientist to explain why this sort of distortion would be built into human anticipation. It just takes an evolutionary biologist—or, for that matter, anyone willing to spend a little time thinking about how evolution works.

Here's the basic logic. We were "designed" by natural selection to do certain things that helped our ancestors get their genes into the next generation—things like eating, having sex, earning the esteem of other people, and outdoing rivals. I put "designed" in quotation marks because, again, natural selection isn't a conscious, intelligent designer but an unconscious process. Still, natural selection does create organisms that look as if they're the product of a conscious designer, a designer who kept fiddling with them to make them effective gene propagators. So, as a kind of thought experiment, it's legitimate to think of natural selection as a "designer" and put yourself in its shoes and ask: If you were designing organisms to be good at spreading their genes, how would you get them to pursue the goals that further this cause? In other words, granted that eating, having sex, impressing peers, and besting rivals helped our ancestors spread their genes, how exactly would you design their brains to get them to pursue these goals? I submit that at least three basic principles of design would make sense:

1. Achieving these goals should bring pleasure, since animals, including humans, tend to pursue things that bring pleasure.
2. The pleasure shouldn't last forever. After all, if the pleasure didn't subside, we'd never seek it again; our first meal would be our last, because hunger would never return. So too with sex: a single act of intercourse, and then a lifetime of lying there basking in the afterglow. That's no way to get lots of genes into the next generation!
3. The animal's brain should focus more on (1), the fact that pleasure will accompany the reaching of a goal, than on (2), the fact that the pleasure will dissipate shortly thereafter. After all, if you focus on (1), you'll pursue things like food and sex and social status with unalloyed gusto, whereas if you focus on (2), you could start feeling ambivalence. You might, for example, start asking what the point is of so fiercely pursuing pleasure if the pleasure will wear off shortly after you get it and leave you hungering for

more. Before you know it, you'll be full of ennui and wishing you'd majored in philosophy.

If you put these three principles of design together, you get a pretty plausible explanation of the human predicament as diagnosed by the Buddha. Yes, as he said, pleasure is fleeting, and, yes, this leaves us recurrently dissatisfied. And the reason is that pleasure is designed by natural selection to evaporate so that the ensuing dissatisfaction will get us to pursue more pleasure. Natural selection doesn't "want" us to be happy, after all; it just "wants" us to be productive, in its narrow sense of *productive*. And the way to make us productive is to make the anticipation of pleasure very strong but the pleasure itself not very long-lasting.

Scientists can watch this logic play out at the biochemical level by observing dopamine, a neurotransmitter that is correlated with pleasure and the anticipation of pleasure. In one seminal study, they took monkeys and monitored dopamine-generating neurons as drops of sweet juice fell onto the monkeys' tongues. Predictably, dopamine was released right after the juice touched the tongue. But then the monkeys were trained to expect drops of juice after a light turned on. As the trials proceeded, more and more of the dopamine came when the light turned on, and less and less came after the juice hit the tongue.

We have no way of knowing for sure what it felt like to be one of those monkeys, but it would seem that, as time passed, there was more in the way of *anticipating* the pleasure that would come from the sweetness, yet less in the way of pleasure actually coming from the sweetness.[†] To translate this conjecture into everyday human terms:

If you encounter a new kind of pleasure—if, say, you've somehow gone your whole life without eating a powdered-sugar doughnut, and

---

[†]This and all subsequent daggers refer to elaborative notes that can be found in the Notes section at the end of the book.

somebody hands you one and suggests you try it—you'll get a big blast of dopamine after the taste of the doughnut sinks in. But later, once you're a confirmed powdered-sugar-doughnut eater, the lion's share of the dopamine spike comes before you actually bite into the doughnut, as you're staring longingly at it; the amount that comes after the bite is much less than the amount you got after that first, blissful bite into a powdered-sugar doughnut. The pre-bite dopamine blast you're now getting is the promise of more bliss, and the post-bite drop in dopamine is, in a way, the breaking of the promise—or, at least, it's a kind of biochemical acknowledgment that there was some overpromising. To the extent that you bought the promise—anticipated greater pleasure than would be delivered by the consumption itself—you have been, if not deluded in the strong sense of that term, at least misled.

Kind of cruel, in a way—but what do you expect from natural selection? Its job is to build machines that spread genes, and if that means programming some measure of illusion into the machines, then illusion there will be.

Unhelpful Insights

So this is one kind of light science can shed on an illusion. Call it "Darwinian light." By looking at things from the point of view of natural selection, we see why the illusion would be built into us, and we have more reason than ever to see that it is an illusion. But—and this is the main point of this little digression—this kind of light is of limited value if your goal is to actually liberate yourself from the illusion.

Don't believe me? Try this simple experiment: (1) Reflect on the fact that our lust for doughnuts and other sweet things is a kind of illusion—that the lust implicitly promises more enduring pleasure than will result from succumbing to it, while blinding us to the letdown that may ensue. (2) As you're reflecting on this fact, hold a powdered-sugar doughnut six inches from your face. Do you feel the lust for it magically weakening? Not if you're like me, no.

This is what I discovered after immersing myself in evolutionary psychology: knowing the truth about your situation, at least in the form that evolutionary psychology provides it, doesn't necessarily make your life any better. In fact, it can actually make it worse. You're still stuck in the natural human cycle of ultimately futile pleasure-seeking—what psychologists sometimes call "the hedonic treadmill"—but now you have new reason to see the absurdity of it. In other words, now you see that it's a treadmill, a treadmill specifically designed to keep you running, often without really getting anywhere—yet you keep running!

And powdered-sugar doughnuts are just the tip of the iceberg. I mean, the truth is, it's not all that uncomfortable to be aware of the Darwinian logic behind your lack of dietary self-discipline. In fact, you may find in this logic a comforting excuse: it's hard to fight Mother Nature, right? But evolutionary psychology also made me more aware of how illusion shapes other kinds of behavior, such as the way I treat other people and the way I, in various senses, treat myself. In these realms, Darwinian self-consciousness was sometimes very uncomfortable.

Yongey Mingyur Rinpoche, a meditation teacher in the Tibetan Buddhist tradition, has said, "Ultimately, happiness comes down to choosing between the discomfort of becoming aware of your mental afflictions and the discomfort of being ruled by them." What he meant is that if you want to liberate yourself from the parts of the mind that keep you from realizing true happiness, you have to first become aware of them, which can be unpleasant.

Okay, fine; that's a form of painful self-consciousness that would be worthwhile—the kind that leads ultimately to deep happiness. But the kind I got from evolutionary psychology was the worst of both worlds: the painful self-consciousness without the deep happiness. I had *both* the discomfort of being aware of my mental afflictions *and* the discomfort of being ruled by them.

Jesus said, "I am the way and the truth and the life." Well, with evolutionary psychology I felt I had found the truth. But, manifestly, I had not found the way. Which was enough to make me wonder about another thing Jesus said: that the truth will set you free. I felt I had seen the basic truth about human nature, and I saw more clearly than ever how various illusions imprisoned me, but this truth wasn't amounting to a Get Out of Jail Free card.

So is there another version of the truth out there that would set me free? No, I don't think so. At least, I don't think there's an *alternative* to the truth presented by science; natural selection, like it or not, is the process that created us. But some years after writing *The Moral Animal*, I did start to wonder if there was a way to *operationalize* the truth—a way to put the actual, scientific truth about human nature and the human condition into a form that would not just identify and explain the illusions we labor under but would also help us liberate ourselves from them. I started wondering if this Western Buddhism I was hearing about might be that way. Maybe many of the Buddha's teachings were saying essentially the same thing modern psychological science says. And maybe meditation was in large part a different way of appreciating these truths—and, in addition, a way of actually doing something about them.

So in August 2003 I headed to rural Massachusetts for my first silent meditation retreat—a whole week devoted to meditation and devoid of such distractions as email, news from the outside world, and speaking to other human beings.

The Truth about Mindfulness

You could be excused for doubting that a retreat like this would yield anything very dramatic or profound. The retreat was, broadly speaking, in the tradition of "mindfulness meditation," the kind of meditation that was starting to catch on in the West and that in the years since has gone mainstream. As commonly described, mindfulness—the thing mindfulness meditation aims to cultivate—isn't very deep or exotic. To live mindfully is to pay attention to, to be "mindful of" what's happening in the here and now and to experience it in a clear, direct way, unclouded by various mental obfuscations. Stop and smell the roses.

This is an accurate description of mindfulness as far as it goes. But it doesn't go very far. "Mindfulness," as popularly conceived, is just the beginning of mindfulness.

And it's in some ways a misleading beginning. If you delve into ancient Buddhist writings, you won't find a lot of exhortations to stop and smell the roses—and that's true even if you focus on those writings that feature the word *sati*, the word that's translated as "mindfulness." Indeed, sometimes these writings seem to carry a very different message. The ancient Buddhist text known as *The Four Foundations of Mindfulness*—the closest thing there is to a Bible of Mindfulness— reminds us that our bodies are "full of various kinds of unclean things" and instructs us to meditate on such bodily ingredients as "feces, bile, phlegm, pus, blood, sweat, fat, tears, skin-oil, saliva, mucus, fluid in the joints, urine." It also calls for us to imagine our bodies "one day, two days, three days dead—bloated, livid, and festering."

I'm not aware of any bestselling books on mindfulness meditation called *Stop and Smell the Feces.* And I've never heard a meditation teacher recommend that I meditate on my bile, phlegm, and pus or on the rotting corpse that I will someday be. What is presented today as an ancient meditative tradition is actually a selective rendering of an ancient meditative tradition, in some cases carefully manicured.

There's no scandal here. There's nothing wrong with modern interpreters of Buddhism being selective—even, sometimes, creative—in what they present as Buddhism. All spiritual traditions evolve, adapting to time and place, and the Buddhist teachings that find an audience today in the United States and Europe are a product of such evolution.

The main thing, for our purposes, is that this evolution—the evolution that has produced a distinctively Western, twenty-first-century version of Buddhism—hasn't severed the connection between current practice and ancient thought. Modern mindfulness meditation isn't exactly the same as ancient mindfulness meditation, but the two share a common philosophical foundation. If you follow the underlying logic of either of them far enough, you will find a dramatic claim: that we are, metaphorically speaking, living in the Matrix. However mundane mindfulness meditation may sometimes sound, it is a practice that, if pursued rigorously, can let you see what Morpheus says the red pill will let you see. Namely, "how deep the rabbit hole goes."

On that first meditation retreat, I had some pretty powerful experiences—powerful enough to make me want to see just how deep the rabbit hole goes. So I read more about Buddhist philosophy, and talked to experts on Buddhism, and eventually went on more meditation retreats, and established a daily meditation practice.

All of this made it clearer to me why *The Matrix* had come to be known as a "dharma movie." Though evolutionary psychology had already convinced me that people are by nature pretty deluded, Buddhism, it turned out, painted an even more dramatic picture. In the Buddhist view, the delusion touches everyday perceptions and thoughts in ways subtler and more pervasive than I had imagined. And in ways that made sense to me. In other words, this kind of delusion, it seemed to me, could be explained as the natural product of a brain that had been engineered by natural selection. The more I looked into Buddhism, the more radical it seemed, but the more I examined it in the light of modern psychology, the more plausible it seemed. The real-life Matrix, the one in which we're actually embedded, came to seem more like the one in the movie—not quite as mind-bending, maybe, but profoundly deceiving and ultimately oppressive, and something that humanity urgently needs to escape.

The good news is the other thing I came to believe: if you want to escape from the Matrix, Buddhist practice and philosophy offer powerful hope. Buddhism isn't alone in this promise. There are other spiritual traditions that address the human predicament with insight and wisdom. But Buddhist meditation, along with its underlying philosophy, addresses that predicament in a strikingly direct and comprehensive way. Buddhism offers an explicit diagnosis of the problem and a cure. And the cure, when it works, brings not just happiness but clarity of vision: the actual truth about things, or at least something way, way closer to that than our everyday view of them.

Some people who have taken up meditation in recent years have done so for essentially therapeutic reasons. They practice mindfulness-based stress reduction or focus on some specific personal problem. They may have no idea that the kind of meditation they're practicing can be a deeply spiritual endeavor and can transform their view of the world. They are, without knowing it, near the threshold of a basic choice, a choice that only they can make. As Morpheus says to Neo, "I can only show you the door. You're the one that has to walk through it." This book is an attempt to show people the door, give them some idea of what lies beyond it, and explain, from a scientific standpoint, why what lies beyond it has a stronger claim to being real than the world they're familiar with.

2

Paradoxes of
Meditation

I'm not supposed to tell you about my first big success at meditating. The reason is that there isn't supposed to *be* success at meditating. As any good meditation teacher will tell you, if you talk about meditation in terms of success or failure, you're misunderstanding what meditation is.

Here I must depart from orthodoxy. I wouldn't advocate meditation if I didn't think there was something people could achieve by it. And if people don't achieve that something, well, that would constitute failure, right? As in: the opposite of success.

Granted, it may be best for people who are meditating to not *think* about succeeding, but that's because thinking about succeeding gets in the way of success! And, granted, if you do achieve meditative "success," that may lead to a new frame of mind that is less caught up in the pursuit of success than your old frame of mind—less relentlessly focused on achieving certain kinds of distant material goals, more aware of the here and now.

In sum: you can best achieve success at meditation by not pursuing success, and achieving this success may mean caring less about success, at least as success is conventionally defined. If this sounds unbearably paradoxical, maybe you should quit reading here, because this won't be the last time we find paradox in Buddhist practice or Buddhist teachings. Then again, there's paradoxical stuff in modern physics (an electron is both a particle and a wave), and modern physics works fine. So you might as well keep reading.

Anyway, before I violate protocol by telling you about my first big "success" as a meditator, I have to commit another violation of protocol by noting what a naturally bad meditator I am. That you shouldn't talk about how bad you are at meditating is a straightforward corollary of the axiom that there's no such thing as succeeding or failing at meditating. And if I'm violating the axiom, I might as well violate its corollary, so here goes.

Suppose you ranked all the people in the world in terms of their likelihood of picking up mindfulness meditation easily—sitting down, focusing on the breath, and slowly sinking into a state of calm, dispassionate observation. At one end of the spectrum you'd have Bobby Knight—the college basketball coach famous for his red, furious face and for once flinging a chair onto a basketball court. At the other end you'd have, I don't know, the Dalai Lama or maybe the late Mister Rogers. On this spectrum, I would be much closer to Bobby Knight than to the Dalai Lama or Mister Rogers. I've never thrown a chair onto a basketball court, but I threw a chicken leg at a dinner guest when I was four and a baseball bat at a brother-in-law when I was twelve. Happily, my penchant for throwing things at people has waned with age, but the underlying volatility hasn't entirely disappeared. And volatility doesn't smooth the path toward mindfulness.

Plus (and perhaps relatedly) there's my attitude toward other human beings, which could get in the way of the *metta*, or loving-kindness, that you're supposed to deploy during a certain kind of meditation. Michael Kinsley, who was editor of the *New Republic* when I worked there many years ago, suggested, not even half-jokingly, that I should write a column called "The Misanthrope."

Actually, I think that oversimplifies my problem. I don't have a hostile disposition toward humankind per se. In fact, I feel quite warmly toward humankind. It's individual humans I have trouble with. I'm prone to a certain skepticism about people's motives and character, and this critical appraisal can harden into enduringly harsh judgment. I'm particularly tough on people who disagree with me on moral or political issues that I consider important. Once I place these people on the other side of a critical ideological boundary, I can have trouble thinking generous and sympathetic thoughts about them.

On top of all this, there's my attention-deficit disorder. Meditation is hard enough even if you have normal skills of concentration. I don't.

Here's an interesting thing about this hypothetical spectrum of people ranked from most likely meditators to least likely meditators: the least likely meditators are the people who seem to most need the benefits of meditation! Personally, I think that if the Dalai Lama had never started meditating, he'd still be a pretty easy guy to get along with. I don't think he was born with a lot of rough edges that needed sanding down. So too with Mister Rogers. Bobby Knight and I are another story altogether.

Hence another paradox of meditation: the problems that meditation can help you overcome often make it hard to meditate in the first place. Yes, meditation may help you lengthen your attention span, dampen your rage, and view your fellow human beings less judgmentally. Unfortunately, a short attention span, a hot temper, and a penchant for harsh judgment may slow your progress along the meditative path. This is bad news for me.

But there's an upside to my possessing this rich array of impediments to meditation. They make me a good laboratory rat, a kind of stand-in for the rest of humankind. After all, even if I score higher on these scales than the average person, most people score much higher on them than is optimal. And it may well be that the average person scores higher on them than used to be the case. Technologies of distraction have made attention deficits more common. And there's something about the modern environment—something technological or cultural or political or all of the above—that seems conducive to harsh judgment and ready rage. Just look at all the tribalism—the discord and even open conflict along religious, ethnic, national, and ideological lines. More and more, it seems, groups of people define their identity in terms of sharp opposition to other groups of people.

I consider this tribalism the biggest problem of our time. I think it could undo millennia of movement toward global integration, unravel the social web just when technology has brought the prospect of a cohesive planetary community within reach. Given that the world is still loaded with nuclear weapons and that biotechnology is opening a Pandora's box of new weaponry, you can imagine our tribalistic impulses ushering in a truly dark age.

Or maybe I'm getting carried away. Anyway, I'll spare you the full-length, high-volume version of my sermon about our imperiled planet. You don't have to share my apocalyptic fears to think that it would be good for the world if meditation could help more people overcome the mental tendencies that sustain the more belligerent forms of tribalism. And if it can help *me* overcome them—help me tamp down rage and contemplate my enemies, real and imagined, more calmly—it can help just about anyone overcome them. That's what makes me such an exemplary laboratory rat. I am a walking embodiment of what I consider to be the biggest problem facing humanity. I am, in microcosm, what's wrong with the world.

My career as a laboratory rat began in earnest when I went to that retreat in rural Massachusetts in August 2003. I had decided that meditation was worth exploring, but I had learned that casual experimentation wouldn't get a person like me very far. Boot camp was in order. So I signed up for a seven-day retreat at the Insight Meditation Society, auspiciously located on Pleasant Street in the town of Barre. There, every day, I would do sitting meditation for a total of five and a half hours and walking meditation for about that long. As for the rest of the day, when you add three (silent) meals, a one-hour "yogi job" in the morning (vacuuming hallways, in my case), and listening to one of the teachers give a "dharma talk" in the evening, you've pretty much exhausted the day. Which is good, because if there was time you needed to waste, the traditional means of wasting it wouldn't be available. There was no TV, no internet, no news from the outside world. And you're not supposed to bring books to read or do any writing. (That last rule I secretly broke so that I'd have a record of events. I wasn't planning to write this book at that point, but I'm a writer, and I consider pretty much everything I do grist for my mill.) And, of course, no talking.

This daily regimen may not sound taxing, since, aside from the yogi job, it doesn't involve anything we normally call work. But the first couple of days were pretty excruciating. Have you ever tried sitting on a cushion with your legs crossed, focusing on your breath? It's no picnic, especially if you're as bad at focusing on your breath as I am. Early in the retreat, I could go a whole forty-five-minute meditation session without ever sustaining focus for ten consecutive breaths. And I know, because I was counting! Time and again, after I counted three or four breaths, my mind would wander, and then eventually I'd realize that I had lost count—or, in some cases, that I was still going through the motions of counting but was in fact thinking about something else and not consciously feeling the breaths.

It didn't help that I got mad at myself every time this happened—madder and madder as the first couple of days wore on. Naturally, my anger then extended to all the people who seemed to be doing better than I was. Which was around eighty people—that is, everybody.

Imagine being stuck for a week with eighty people who are doing better than you! People who succeed while you fail—or at least "succeed" while you "fail."

My Big Breakthrough

My big breakthrough came on the fifth morning of the retreat. After breakfast I consumed a bit too much of the instant coffee I had brought, and as I tried to meditate I felt the classic symptom of overcaffeination: a very unpleasant tension in my jaw that made me feel like grinding my teeth. This feeling kept intruding on my focus, and, after trying for a while to fight the intrusion, I finally just surrendered to it and shifted my attention to the tension in my jaw. Or maybe it wasn't so much a shifting of attention as an expansion of attention—staying conscious of my breath but letting it recede into the background as this annoying jaw sensation moved to center stage.

This sort of readjustment of attention, by the way, is a perfectly fine thing to do. In mindfulness meditation as it's typically taught, the point of focusing on your breath isn't just to focus on your breath. It's to stabilize your mind, to free it of its normal preoccupations so you can observe things that are happening in a clear, unhurried, less reactive way. And "things that are happening" emphatically includes things happening inside your mind. Feelings arise within you—sadness, anxiety, annoyance, relief, joy—and you try to experience them from a different vantage point than is usual, neither clinging to the good feelings nor running away from the bad ones, but rather just experiencing them straightforwardly and observing them. This altered perspective can be the beginning of a fundamental and enduring change in your relationship to your feelings; you can, if all goes well, cease to be their slave.

After devoting some attention to the overcaffeinated feeling in my jaw, I suddenly had an angle on my interior life that I'd never had before. I remember thinking something like, "Yes, the grinding sensation is still there—the sensation I typically define as unpleasant. But that sensation is down there in my jaw, and that's not where I am. I'm up here in my head." I was no longer identifying with the feeling; I was viewing it objectively, I guess you could say. In the space of a moment it had entirely lost its grip on me. It was a very strange thing to have an unpleasant feeling cease to be unpleasant without really going away.

There is a paradox here. (Don't say I didn't warn you!) When I first expanded my attention to encompass the obnoxiously intrusive jaw-grinding sensation, this involved relaxing my resistance to the sensation. I was, in a sense, accepting, even embracing a feeling that I had been trying to keep at a distance. But the result of this closer proximity to the feeling was to acquire a kind of distance from it—a certain degree of detachment (or, as some meditation teachers prefer, for somewhat technical reasons, to put it, "nonattachment"). This is something that can happen again and again via meditation: accepting, even embracing, an unpleasant feeling can give you a critical distance from it that winds up diminishing the unpleasantness.

In fact, one thing I occasionally do when I'm feeling very sad—and this is something you can experiment with even if you've never meditated—is sit down, close my eyes, and study the sadness: accept its presence and just observe how it actually makes me feel. For example, it's kind of interesting that, though I may not be close to actually crying, the feeling of sadness does have a strong presence right around the parts of my eyes that would get active if I did start crying. I'd never noticed that before meditating on sadness. This careful observation of sadness, combined with a kind of acceptance of it, does, in my experience, make it less unpleasant.

Now, here is a question that is fundamental: Which, if either, of my two perceptions was "truer"—when the feeling felt unpleasant, or when the unpleasantness subsided and the feeling became, for practical purposes, neutral? To put it another way: Was the initial unpleasantness in any sense an illusion? Certainly, by adopting another perspective, I made it disappear—and that's something that's often true of what we call illusions: shifting your perspective dispels them. But are there any additional grounds for thinking of it as an illusion?

This question goes way beyond my own little episodes of transcending overcaffeination and melancholy. It applies, in principle, to all negative feelings: fears, anxieties, loathing, self-loathing, and more. Imagine if our negative feelings, or at least lots of them, turned out to be illusions, and we could dispel them by just contemplating them from a particular vantage point.

Pain That Doesn't Hurt

There's no doubt that meditation training has allowed some people to become essentially indifferent to what otherwise would have been unbearable pain. In June of 1963 a monk named Thich Quang Duc staged a public protest of the South Vietnamese government's treatment of Buddhists. On a cushion placed in a Saigon street, he assumed the lotus position. After another monk poured gasoline over him, Duc said, "Before closing my eyes and moving towards the vision of the Buddha, I respectfully plead to President Ngo Dinh Diem to take a mind of compassion towards the people of the nation and implement religious equality to maintain the strength of the homeland eternally." Then he lit a match. The journalist David Halberstam, who witnessed the event, wrote, "As he burned he never moved a muscle, never uttered a sound, his outward composure in sharp contrast to the wailing people around him."

Now, you might argue that Duc, far from liberating himself from an illusion, was actually *suffering* from an illusion. After all, the fact is that he *was* burning to death. So if he lacked the sensation we normally associate with burning to death—a sensation that carries intense pain and triggers alarm that would strike most of us as appropriate—then isn't there some sense in which he wasn't getting the picture?

The question I'm circling around—which of our "normal" feelings, thoughts, and perceptions are in some sense illusions—is important for two reasons. One reason is simple and practical: obviously, if many unpleasant feelings—feelings of anxiety, fear, self-loathing, melancholy, and so on—are in some sense illusions, and we can use meditation to dispel them or at least weaken their grip on us, that's news you can use. The other reason is at first glance more academic, but it ultimately has a kind of practical value as well. Figuring out when our feelings mislead us will help shed light on the question of whether the Buddhist view of the mind, and of the mind's relationship to reality, is as crazy as it sometimes sounds. Is perceived reality, or a sizable chunk of it, really an illusion?

This question takes us into depths of Buddhist philosophy that aren't often plumbed in popular accounts of meditation. Naturally enough, these accounts tend to focus on things with a near-term payoff—stress reduction, boosting self-esteem, and so on—without getting deeply into the philosophical context in which Buddhist meditation arose and within which it has flourished. Using meditation this way, as a purely therapeutic device that doesn't deeply change your view of reality, is a perfectly fine thing to do. It's good for you, and it will probably be good for the world.

Still, using meditation this way isn't, by itself, taking the red pill. Taking the red pill means asking basic questions about the relationship of the perceiver to the perceived and examining the underpinnings of our normal view of reality. If you're thinking seriously about taking the red pill, you'll be curious as to whether the Buddhist view of the world "works" not just in a therapeutic sense but in a more philosophical sense. Does this Buddhist perspective, with its seemingly topsy-turvy conception of what's real and what's not, make any sense in light of modern science? That's the question I'll take up in the next chapter—and, indeed, in much of the rest of this book. As we'll see, this question, though important on sheerly philosophical grounds, also has implications for how we live our lives—implications that, though in a sense practical, are probably better described as "spiritual" than as "therapeutic."

But first a word of caution. Strictly speaking, there is no "Buddhist view of the world." Buddhism began to split into different schools of interpretation not long after it arose, around the middle of the first millennium BCE. As a result, just as there are Catholic and Protestant Christians and Sunni and Shia Muslims, there are distinct branches of Buddhist thought that differ on particular points of doctrine.

The most basic division in Buddhism is between the Theravada school and the Mahayana school. My own meditative tradition, Vipassana, derives from the Theravada lineage. It is within the Mahayana lineage (to which Quang Duc belonged) that you find the most radically broad conception of illusion. Some Mahayana Buddhists even subscribe to a "mind-only" doctrine that, in its more extreme incarnations, dismisses the things we "perceive" via consciousness as, pretty literally, figments of our imagination. This strand of Buddhist thought—the strand that most obviously resonates with the movie *The Matrix*—isn't dominant within Mahayana Buddhism, much less within Buddhism at large. But even mainstream Buddhist thinkers accept some version of the concept of emptiness, a subtle idea that is hard to capture in a few words (or in many words) but certainly holds, at a minimum, that the things we see when we look out on the world have less in the way of distinct and substantial existence than they seem to have.

And then there is the famous Buddhist idea that the self—you know, your self, my self—is an illusion. In this view, the "you" that you think of as thinking your thoughts, feeling your feelings, and making your decisions doesn't really exist.*

---

*In Mahayana Buddhism, for reasons I'll touch on in chapter 13, the term *emptiness* is often taken to *include* the concept of not-self. But in Theravada Buddhism, not-self is typically treated separately from any broader notion of emptiness (a notion that is less prominent in Theravada thinking anyway). Throughout this book, I use the terms *not-self*

If you put these two fundamental Buddhist ideas together—the idea of not-self and the idea of emptiness—you have a radical proposition: neither the world inside you nor the world outside you is anything like it seems.

Both of these ideas would strike most people as dubious, if not crazy. Then again, since the premise of these ideas is that people are naturally deluded, it would seem perverse to let people's natural reactions to them keep us from exploring them. This book is in no small part an exploration of these two ideas, and what I hope to show is that they make a lot of sense. Both our natural view of the world "out there" and our natural view of the world "in here"—the world inside our heads—are deeply misleading. What's more, failing to see these two worlds clearly does lead, as Buddhism holds, to a lot of suffering. And meditation can help us see them more clearly.

When I say we're going to be exploring the scientific foundation of a Buddhist worldview, I don't mean "scientific foundation" in the sense of scientific evidence that meditation can reduce suffering. If you want such evidence, there are lots of studies, readily available and widely reported, that seem to show as much. And I don't mean "scientific foundation" only in the sense of what's going on in the brain when you're meditating and starting to change your view of reality—though I will, to be sure, get into some of the more important brain-scan studies.

I mean "scientific foundation" in the sense of using all the tools of modern psychology to look at such questions as these: Why, and in what particular ways, are human beings naturally deluded? How exactly does the delusion work? How does delusion make us suffer? How does it make us make other people suffer? Why would the Buddhist prescription for dispelling the delusion—in particular, the meditative part of that prescription—work? And what would it mean for it to work

---

and *emptiness* in a nonoverlapping way; *emptiness* will be used more narrowly than in the Mahayana tradition, referring only to the world "out there."

fully? In other words, does the elusive state that is said to lie at the culmination of the meditative path—sometimes called enlightenment—really qualify for that term? What would it be like to see the world with perfect clarity?

And speaking of the world: Is saving the world—keeping the psychology of tribalism from covering the planet in chaos and bloodshed—really a matter of just clarifying the vision of the world's people? I shouldn't say "just," because, obviously, if delusion is deeply ingrained in us, then dispelling it will take work. Still, it would be nice to know if the struggle for enduring peace is also the struggle for truth; as long as we're undertaking a task as Herculean as saving the world, it would be great to kill two birds with one stone! It would also be nice to think that when people pursue the path to liberation—use meditation to try and see the world more clearly, and in the process reduce their suffering—they are helping humanity broadly, that the quest for individual salvation advances the quest for social salvation.

The first step in this epic inquiry is to take a closer look at our feelings: pain, pleasure, fear, anxiety, love, lust, and so on. Feelings play a very big role in shaping our perceptions and guiding us through life—bigger than most people realize. Are they reliable guides? That's a question we'll start to examine in the next chapter.

3

When Are Feelings
Illusions?

Hovering over the question posed by the title of this chapter is a larger question: What the hell are we talking about here? Illusions are things that seem to be true but aren't—and what would it even mean to say that feelings are "true" or "false"? Feelings just are. If we feel them, then they're feelings—real feelings, not imagined feelings. End of story.

There's something to be said for this point of view. In fact, one of the take-home lessons of Buddhist philosophy is that feelings just are. If we accepted their arising and subsiding as part of life, rather than reacting to them as if they were deeply meaningful, we'd often be better off. Learning to do that is a big part of what mindfulness meditation is about. And there are lots of satisfied customers who attest that it works.

Still, saying that it works isn't the same as saying that it's intellectually valid. Just because being less reactive to some of your feelings makes you happier doesn't mean it brings a truer apprehension of the world. Maybe this less reactive stance is like a narcotic: it dulls the pain by insulating you from the real-world feedback that your feelings provide. Maybe it's meditation, not your ordinary consciousness, that puts you in a dream world.

If we want to see whether meditation does, in fact, bring you closer to the truth, it helps to ask whether some of the feelings it can liberate you from would otherwise have carried you away from the truth. So we need to try to get a handle on this admittedly unwieldy question: Are our feelings in some sense "false"? Or "true"? Are some false and some true? And which are which?

One way to approach these questions is to go back in evolutionary time. Way back. Back to when feelings first arose. Sadly, no one knows exactly when that was, or even approximately when that was. Was it back when mammals appeared? Reptiles? Squishy blobs floating in the sea? One-celled creatures such as bacteria?

One reason it's hard to say is that feelings have an odd property: you can never be absolutely, positively sure that anyone or anything other than you has them. Part of the definition of a feeling is that it's private, not visible from the outside. So I don't know for sure that, say, my dog Frazier has feelings. Maybe that wagging tail is just a wagging tail!

But just as I seriously doubt that I'm the only human with feelings, I seriously doubt that my species is the only species with feelings. I suspect that when my cousin the chimpanzee writhes in seeming pain, it is writhing in actual pain. And if, from chimpanzees, you go down the ladder of behavioral complexity—down to wolves, lizards, even jellyfish, and (what the hell) bacteria—I don't see an obvious place to *stop* assuming that there are feelings.

Anyway, regardless of when feelings first arose, there is a rough consensus among behavioral scientists on what the original function of good feelings and bad feelings was: to get organisms to approach things or avoid things that are, respectively, good for them or bad for them. Nutrients, for example, keep organisms alive, so natural selection favored genes that gave organisms feelings that led them to approach things containing nutrients—that is, food. (You may be familiar with such feelings.) Things that harm or kill organisms, in contrast, are best avoided, so natural selection gave organisms feelings that inclined them to avoid such things—feelings of aversion. To approach or to avoid is the most elemental behavioral decision there is, and feelings seem to be the tool natural selection used to get organisms to make what, by natural selection's lights, was the right decision.

After all, your average animal isn't smart enough to think, "Hmm, that substance is rich in carbohydrates, which give me energy, so I'll make a habit of approaching and ingesting it." In fact, your average animal isn't even smart enough to think, "Food good for me, so I approach." Feelings arose as proxies for this kind of thinking. The inviting warmth of a campfire on a freezing night means that staying warm is better for us than freezing. The pain caused by actual contact with the fire means that there's such a thing as too much warmth. The job of these and other feelings is to convey to the organism what's good for it and what's bad for it. As the biologist George Romanes put it in 1884, twenty-five years after Darwin's *The Origin of Species* appeared, "Pleasures and pains must have been evolved as the subjective accompaniment of processes which are respectively beneficial or injurious to the organism, and so evolved for the purpose or to the end that the organism should seek the one and shun the other."

This suggests one way to think about whether feelings are true or false. Feelings are designed to encode *judgments about things in our environment.* Typically these judgments are about whether these things are good or bad for the survival of the organism doing the feeling (though sometimes they're about whether these things are good or bad for close kin—notably offspring—since close kin share so many of our genes). So we could say that feelings are "true" if the judgments they encode are accurate—if, say, the things they attract the organism to are indeed good for it, or if the things they encourage the organism to avoid are indeed bad for it. We could say feelings are "false" or perhaps "illusory" if they lead the organism astray—if following the feelings leads to things that are bad for the organism.[†]

This isn't the only way you could define *true* and *false* in a biological context, but it's one approach, so let's see how far we get with it.

Obsolete Urges

Take powdered-sugar doughnuts. I personally have very warm feelings toward them—so warm that, if I were guided only by my feelings, I would eat them for breakfast, lunch, dinner, and between-meal snacks. Yet I'm told that, actually, eating that many doughnuts each day would be bad for me. So I guess my feeling of attraction to powdered-sugar doughnuts could be called false: these doughnuts *feel* good, but this is an illusion because they're not really good for me. This is of course hard news to take; it calls to mind the plaintive lyrics of that old Luther Ingram song: "If loving you is wrong, I don't want to be right."

It also calls to mind a question: How could natural selection let something like this happen? Shouldn't our feelings direct us toward things that are good for the organism? They should, yes. But here's the thing: natural selection designed our feelings in a particular environment—an environment with no junk food, an environment in which the sweetest thing available was fruit. So a sweet tooth served us well; it gave us feelings that, you might say, were "true" in the sense that they steered us toward things that were good for us. But in a modern environment, which features the achievement of culinary science known as "empty calories," these feelings become "false," or at least not reliably true; they sometimes tell us something is good when it's not good for us.

There are quite a few feelings like this—feelings that, back when they entered our lineage, served our ancestors' interests but that don't always serve our interests now. Take road rage. The desire to punish people who treat you unfairly or show you disrespect is deeply human. And admit it: though there's something unpleasant about being made angry, there's something pleasing about the feeling of anger itself—the feeling that you're *rightfully* enraged. The Buddha said anger has a "poisoned root and honeyed tip."

And you can see why natural selection would have made righteous rage attractive: in a small hunter-gatherer village, if someone took advantage of you—stole your food, stole your mate, or just generally treated you like dirt—you needed to teach him a lesson. After all, if he learns he can get away with abusing you, he may do it again and again. Worse still, others in your social universe will see that you can be thus exploited, so *they* may start treating you badly. In such an intimate, unchanging social environment, it would be worth your while to get so angry over exploitation that you would confront your exploiter and be willing to come to blows. Even if you lost the fight—even if you got battered pretty badly—you'd have sent the message that there's a cost for disrespecting you, and this message would pay dividends over time.

You may already be pondering the absurdity of the way this feeling can play out on a modern highway. The disrespectful driver you feel like punishing is someone you'll never see again, and so are all the drivers who might witness any revenge you wreak. So there's no benefit whatsoever that comes from indulging your rage. As for the cost: I'd guess that chasing somebody in a car at eighty miles per hour is more likely to get you killed than was starting a fistfight in a hunter-gatherer society.

So you could call road rage "false." It *feels* good, but the aura of goodness is illusory, because succumbing to its attraction leads to behavior that will not, on average, be good for the organism.

There are lots of instances of off-road rage as well that are "false"—bursts of anger that are at best unproductive and at worst counterproductive. So if meditation did liberate you from obedience to these feelings, it would be, in a certain sense, dispelling an illusion—the illusion you implicitly subscribe to when you follow the feeling, the illusion that the rage, and for that matter the revenge it inspires, is fundamentally "good." It turns out the feeling isn't even good in the basic sense of self-interest.

So that's one way to define *true* and *false* as they apply to feelings: if they feel good but lead us to do things that aren't really good for us, then they're false feelings. But there's another sense in which feelings can be true or false. Some feelings, after all, are more than feelings; they don't just *imply* judgments about whether doing certain things will be good for the organism; they come with actual, explicit beliefs about things in the environment and how they relate to the organism's welfare. Obviously, such beliefs can be true or false in a pretty straightforward sense.

False Positives

Suppose you're hiking through what you know to be rattlesnake terrain, and suppose you know that only a year ago, someone hiking alone in this vicinity was bitten by a rattlesnake and died. Now suppose there's a stirring in the brush next to your feet. This stirring doesn't just give you a surge of fear; you feel the fear *that* there is a rattlesnake near you. In fact, as you turn quickly toward the disturbance and your fear reaches its apex, you may be so clearly envisioning a rattlesnake that, if the culprit turns out to be a lizard, there will be a fraction of a second when the lizard looks like a snake. This is an illusion in a literal sense: you actually believe there is something there that isn't there; in fact, you actually "see" it.

These kinds of misperceptions are known as "false positives"; from natural selection's point of view, they're a feature, not a bug. Though your brief conviction that you've seen a rattlesnake may be wrong ninety-nine times out of a hundred, the conviction could be lifesaving the other one time in a hundred. And in natural selection's calculus, being right 1 percent of the time in matters of life or death can be worth being wrong 99 percent of the time, even if in every one of those ninety-nine instances you're briefly terrified.

So there are actually *two* differences between the snake illusion, on the one hand, and the doughnut and road rage illusions, on the other: (1) in the case of the snake, the illusion is explicit—it's an actual false perception about the physical world and, for a moment, a false belief; (2) in the case of the snake, your emotional machinery is working exactly as designed. In other words, the snake illusion isn't a result of "environmental mismatch"; it's not a case where a feeling designed by natural selection to be in some sense "true" in a hunter-gatherer environment was rendered "false" by circumstances of modern life. Rather, natural selection designed this feeling to be *almost always* illusory in a literal sense; the feeling fills you with a conviction—a judgment about what's in your immediate environment—that is pretty reliably untrue. This is a reminder that natural selection didn't design your mind to see the world clearly; it designed your mind to have perceptions and beliefs that would help take care of your genes.

Which brings us to a third difference between the doughnut and road rage illusions and the snake illusion: the snake illusion, in the long run, may well be good for you; it may keep you safe from harm that would otherwise befall you. The same goes for comparable illusions that, depending on where you live, might be more likely to visit you than a snake illusion. You might, while walking home at night, fear that the footsteps behind you belong to a mugger; and, though you're probably wrong, crossing the street is a precaution that, over the course of your whole life, may prevent a crime that otherwise would have victimized you.

I have a fear that all this may be sounding more clear-cut than it is. It may seem as if there are two kinds of false feelings—the unnatural, "environmental mismatch" kind and the natural, "false positive" kind—and you should always ignore the former, whereas obeying the latter makes sense. In the real world, it turns out, these lines can get blurry.

For example: Have you ever been visited by the fear that something you said to someone had offended her? And has this person ever been someone you weren't going to see for a while? And has it been the case that, because you didn't know her very well, it would have been awkward to call her or send her an email to make sure you hadn't offended her or to clarify that no offense was meant?

The feeling itself—the concern that you've offended someone—is perfectly natural; staying on good terms with people boosted our ancestors' chances of surviving and reproducing. Also natural, perhaps, is the fact that in some cases you're exaggerating the chances that you've offended the person, even feeling bursts of certainty that you've done so. This may be another one of nature's false positives; the sense that you've erred may be "designed" to be so powerful that you'll take remedial action more often than it's really called for.

What's *not* natural is that remedial action is so hard to take. In a hunter-gatherer village, the person you feared you'd offended would live, oh, fifty feet away from you and you'd see her again in, oh, twenty minutes or so. At that point you could gauge her demeanor and perhaps be reassured that no offense was taken or conclude that she was in fact miffed and try to rectify the situation.

In other words, the initial feeling—even if illusory—is probably natural, designed to appear on occasions like this. What's not natural are features of the modern world that make it hard to find out whether the feeling was or wasn't an illusion. So the feeling lasts longer than is likely to be of any practical value. And, unfortunately, the feeling is unpleasant.

Another unpleasant product of environmental mismatch is painful self-consciousness. We're designed by natural selection to care—and care a lot—about what other people think of us. During evolution, people who were liked, admired, and respected would have been more effective gene propagators than people who were the opposite. But in a hunter-gatherer village, your neighbors would have had a vast database on your behavior, so you'd be unlikely, on any given day, to do anything that radically revised their opinion of you, for better or worse. Social encounters wouldn't typically have been high-pressure events.

In the modern world, we often find ourselves in the unnatural position of meeting someone who knows little or nothing about us. That can add a little pressure to the occasion, and it may add more if your mother was prone to saying "You get only one chance to make a good first impression!" You may find yourself scanning the person for feedback so intensively that you start seeing things that aren't there.

A social psychology experiment from the 1980s makes the point. A makeup artist put realistic-looking "scars" on the faces of the subjects, who had been told that the purpose of the experiment was to see how a scar affected the way people reacted to them. The subjects were to have a conversation with someone, and the experimenters would observe the reaction. The subjects were shown their scars in a mirror, but then, right before their social encounter, they were told that the scar needed a bit of work; moisturizer would be added to keep it from cracking. In fact, though, the scar was removed. Then the subjects headed out to their social encounters with a warped idea of what they looked like.

After the encounters, they were debriefed: Had they noticed their conversation partner reacting to the scar? Oh yes, many of them said. In fact, when they were shown video of the conversation partner, they could point to these reactions. Sometimes, for example, the person would look away from them—obviously averting their eyes from the scar. So again, a feeling—an uncomfortable feeling of self-consciousness—sponsors a kind of perceptual illusion, a basic misreading of the behavior of others.

Modern life is full of emotional reactions that make little sense except in light of the environment in which our species evolved. You may be haunted for hours by some embarrassing thing you did on a public bus or an airplane, even though you'll never again see the people who witnessed it and their opinions of you therefore have no consequence. Why would natural selection design organisms to feel discomfort that seems so pointless? Maybe because in the environment of our ancestors it wouldn't have been pointless; in a hunter-gatherer society, you're pretty much *always* performing in front of people you'll see again and whose opinions therefore matter.

My mother used to say, "We wouldn't spend so much time worrying about what other people think of us if we realized how seldom they do." She was right; our assumption that people give much thought to us one way or the other is often an illusion, as is our unspoken sense that it matters what pretty much everyone we see thinks of us. But these intuitions were less often illusory in the environment of our evolution, and that's one reason they're so persistent today.

Public Speaking and Other Horrors

If there's anything more unnatural than being in the presence of a bunch of people you've never seen before, it's speaking to all of them at once. The mere thought of such an event can give us terrifying illusions about the future. Suppose you're giving some kind of presentation tomorrow—maybe it's a PowerPoint talk, maybe it's a presentation in some looser sense. Now suppose one further thing: that you're like me. If you're like me, as the time approaches, you may feel anxiety. What's more, this anxiety may feature bursts of conviction that things are going to go badly; you may even envision specific disaster scenarios. And, pretty reliably, these visions will turn out to be wrong; in retrospect, these anxiety-sponsored bursts of apocalyptic conviction were false positives.

Of course, it's possible that the anxiety is the reason things wound up going well; maybe it spurred you to prepare a great presentation.

If so, these "false PowerPoint apocalypse positives" are different from "false rattlesnake positives." After all, your momentary fear that a rattlesnake was afoot had no bearing on whether or not a rattlesnake would in fact turn out to be afoot. In contrast, your PowerPoint-apocalypse anxiety may conceivably have headed off a PowerPoint apocalypse.

Conceivably. But let's face it: though anxiety is sometimes productive in this sense, people do a lot of worrying that serves no good purpose. There are people who are beset by images of themselves projectile-vomiting while talking to a crowd—even though, come to think of it, they've never projectile-vomited while talking to a crowd.

In a particularly perverse twist on PowerPoint-apocalypse anxiety, I've been known to lie awake the night before a big presentation *worrying that if I don't get to sleep I'll do a bad job the next day.* Actually, that's an oversimplification. I don't just worry about not getting to sleep. For the sake of variety, I periodically interrupt that worry with bouts of self-loathing for being the kind of person who would worry so much about not getting to sleep that he'd be unable to get to sleep. Then, after my rage has subsided, I get back to the important business of worrying so much about not getting to sleep that I can't get to sleep.

I'm proud to say that this doesn't happen before most of my public speaking events. But it's happened, and I defy anyone to argue that it is natural selection's way of increasing my chances of surviving and reproducing. So too with lots of other anxieties related to human social interaction: a sense of dread before going to a cocktail party that, in fact, is very unlikely to lead to anything that is worth dreading; worrying about how your child is doing at her first slumber party, something you're powerless to influence; or worrying about your PowerPoint presentation *after* you've given it—as if fretting over whether people liked it will change whether they did.

I'd guess that all three of these examples have at least something to do with the way our environment has changed since the human species evolved. Our ancestral environment didn't feature cocktail parties, slumber parties, or PowerPoint. Our hunter-gatherer ancestors didn't have to navigate roomfuls of people they'd never met, or send their children off to sleep in homes they'd never seen, or give presentations to an audience consisting largely of people they didn't know very well, if at all.

By the way, this mismatch between our evolved nature and the environment in which we find ourselves isn't just a modern phenomenon. For thousands of years, there have been human social environments that weren't the ones we were designed for. The Buddha was born to a royal family, which means he lived in a society with clusters of population much bigger than a hunter-gatherer village. And though PowerPoint hadn't been invented, there is evidence that people were being called on to speak before large audiences and that something like PowerPoint-apocalypse anxiety had taken shape. In one discourse the Buddha listed as one of the "five fears" the "fear of embarrassment in assemblies." This fear remains in the top five today; some polls, in fact, show public speaking to be the most dreaded activity of all.

Just to be clear (and at the risk of repeating myself), I'm not saying that social anxiety isn't in any sense a product of natural selection. The ancestral environment—the environment of our evolution—featured lots of social interaction, and this interaction had great consequence for our genes. If you had low social status and few friends, that cut your chances of spreading your genes, so impressing people mattered, even if PowerPoint wasn't the thing you impressed them with. Similarly, if your offspring didn't thrive socially, that boded ill for their reproductive prospects, and hence for your genes. So genes inclining us toward anxiety about our social prospects and our progeny's social prospects seem to have become part of the human gene pool.

In this sense our social anxieties can be considered "natural." But they're operating in a very different environment from the environment they were "designed" for, and this fact may explain why they're often unproductive, sponsoring illusions that are of no value at all.

Thus can we have beliefs—about, for example, the near-certainty of impending disaster—that are false both in the literal and the pragmatic sense: they aren't true, and they aren't good for us.

If you accept the idea that many of our most troublesome feelings are in one sense or another illusions, then meditation can be seen as, among other things, a process of dispelling illusions.

Here's an example.

In 2003, a couple of months after my first meditation retreat, I traveled to Camden, Maine, to give a talk at an annual conference called Poptech. The night before my talk I woke up at 2 or 3 a.m. with one of my little bouts of anxiety. After a few minutes of staying awake pondering the grave implications of staying awake pondering grave implications, I decided to sit up in my bed and meditate. I focused on my breathing for a while, but I also focused on the anxiety itself: the tight feeling in my gut. I tried to look at it, as I'd been taught to do at my meditation retreat, nonjudgmentally. It wasn't necessarily a bad thing, and there was no reason to run away from it. It was just a feeling, so I sat there feeling it and watching it. I can't say that the feeling felt great, but the more I accepted it, observing it nonjudgmentally, the less unpleasant it got.

And then something happened that was much like my big over-caffeination breakthrough at the meditation retreat. The anxiety now seemed like something removed from me, something I was just looking at, in my mind's eye, the way I might look at an abstract sculpture in a museum. It looked like a kind of thick, knotted rope of tightness, occupying the part of my abdomen where anxiety is felt, but it didn't *feel* like tightness anymore. My anxiety, which had been painful only minutes earlier, now felt neither good nor bad. And not long after it attained this neutral status, it dissolved entirely. After a few minutes of this pleasant relief from suffering, I lay down and went to sleep. The next day my talk went—I'll pause here to let the suspense build—fine.

It's possible, in principle, to attack anxiety from another angle.

Rather than focus on the feeling itself, as I did that night, you investigate the thoughts associated with it. This is the way cognitive-behavioral therapy works: your therapist asks questions like "*Is* there much likelihood of screwing up that presentation, judging by your history of giving presentations?" and "If you did screw it up, *would* your career really vaporize on the spot?" Then, if you see that the thoughts are lacking in logic, the attendant feelings may weaken.

So cognitive-behavioral therapy is very much in the spirit of mindfulness meditation. Both in some sense question the validity of feelings. It's just that with cognitive-behavioral therapy, the questioning is more literal. By the way, if you're thinking about combining these two approaches and becoming famous as the founder of a whole new school of therapy, I have bad news: mindfulness-based cognitive-behavioral therapy—MCBT—already exists.

Levels of Delusion: A Recap

If I've done my job, you should be feeling a bit deceived—not by me, but by your feelings. And I haven't even gotten to the deepest, subtlest deceptions perpetrated by your feelings. I'll save those for later in the book. Meanwhile, let's review several senses in which feelings can be misleading:

1. *Our feelings weren't designed to depict reality accurately even in our "natural" environment.* Feelings were designed to get the genes of our hunter-gatherer ancestors into the next generation. If that meant deluding our ancestors—making them so fearful that they "see" a snake that isn't actually there, say—so be it. This class of illusions, "natural" illusions, helps explain a lot of distortions in our apprehension of the world, especially the social world: warped ideas about ourselves, about our friends, our kin, our enemies, our casual acquaintances, and even strangers. (Which about covers it, right?)

2. *The fact that we're not living in a "natural" environment makes our feelings even less reliable guides to reality.* Feelings that are designed to create illusions, such as seeing a snake that isn't there, may at least have the virtue of increasing the organism's prospects for surviving and reproducing. But the modern environment can take various kinds of feelings that served our ancestors in this Darwinian sense and render them counterproductive in the same sense—they may actually lower a person's life expectancy. Violent rage and the yearnings of a sweet tooth are good examples. These feelings were once "true" at least in the pragmatic sense of guiding the organism toward behaviors that were in some sense good for it. But now they're likely to mislead.

3. *Underlying it all is the happiness delusion.* As the Buddha emphasized, our ongoing attempts to feel better tend to involve an overestimation of how long "better" is going to last. What's more, when "better" ends, it can be followed by "worse"—an unsettled feeling, a thirst for more. Long before psychologists were describing the hedonic treadmill, the Buddha saw it.

What he couldn't have seen is its source. We were built by natural selection, and natural selection works to maximize genetic proliferation, period. In addition to not caring about the truth per se, it doesn't care about our long-term happiness. It will readily delude us about what does and doesn't bring lasting happiness if that delusion has propelled our ancestors' genes forward. In fact, natural selection doesn't even care about our *short-term* happiness. Just look at the price of all those false positives: being terrified by a snake that isn't there ninety-nine times in a row could take a toll on a person's psychological well-being. The good news, of course, is that on the hundredth time the fear may have helped keep our ancestors alive and thus led ultimately to the creation of us. Still, we are the heirs of this tendency toward false positives—not just in the realm of snakes but in the realm of other fears and everyday anxieties. As Aaron Beck, who is sometimes called the founder of cognitive-behavioral therapy, has written, "The cost of survival of the lineage may be a lifetime of discomfort." Or, as the Buddha would have put it, a lifetime of *dukkha*. And the Buddha might have added: But this cost is avoidable, if you address the psychological causes of it head-on.

Obviously, this chapter hasn't been a blanket indictment of human feelings. Some, maybe most, of our feelings serve us reasonably well; they don't much distort our view of reality, and they help keep us alive and flourishing. My attraction to apples, my aversion to grasping knife blades and scaling skyscrapers—all to the good. Still, I hope you can see the virtue of subjecting your feelings to investigation—inspecting them to see which ones deserve obedience and which ones don't, and trying to free yourself from the grip of the ones that don't.

And I hope you can see why this is difficult. It's in the nature of feelings to make it hard to tell the valuable ones from the harmful ones, the reliable from the misleading. One thing all feelings have in common is that they were originally "designed" to convince you to follow them. They feel right and true almost by definition. They actively discourage you from viewing them objectively.

Maybe this helps explain why it took me so long to get the hang of mindfulness meditation—why it never "worked" for me until I took the full-immersion approach and went on a one-week silent meditation retreat. But it's not the only reason. There are other things about the way feelings influence us that make it hard to turn the tables on them and reverse the servant-master relationship. And there are other things about the way the mind works that make it hard to sink into a meditative state in the first place. Indeed, it was only after I went on that first retreat that I started to realize how challenging it can be—and *why* it can be so challenging—to get to the point where mindfulness meditation is really working.

Then again, rewarding things often require work. And another thing I started to realize on that retreat is how great the rewards of mindfulness meditation can be. Indeed, those rewards go so far beyond the ones hinted at in this chapter that I fear I may have trivialized the meditative experience. Sure, starting to get a grip on a few of your more troublesome feelings is great—and if knowing that these feelings are in one sense or another "false" helps you do that, so much the better. But the taming of troublesome feelings can be just the beginning. There are other dimensions of mindfulness, and there are insights much deeper and subtler than the realization that maybe surrendering to road rage isn't such a great idea.

4

Bliss, Ecstasy, and
More Important Reasons to Meditate

Strictly speaking, "silent meditation retreat" is a misnomer. On my first weeklong retreat, back in the summer of 2003, there were two times when students spoke with a meditation teacher. On one of those occasions, a group of eight or nine of us "yogis" assembled in a room near the meditation hall. There, for forty-five minutes, we could air any problems we were having.

Which was good, because I was having a problem: *I couldn't meditate!* I hadn't yet had my big meditation breakthrough, that moment when I viewed my overcaffeination mindfully and transcended it. All I had done was spend a day and a half failing to concentrate on my breath. I tried and tried, but I just couldn't stop *thinking* about stuff.

So when my turn came to speak, I gave voice to this frustration. The ensuing dialogue with my teacher went something like this:

So you notice that your mind keeps wandering?
Yes.
That's good.
It's good that my mind keeps wandering?
No. It's good that you notice that your mind keeps wandering.
But it happens, like, all the time.
That's even better. It means you're noticing a lot.

This didn't have the uplifting effect that my teacher had perhaps intended. I felt a bit patronized. It was kind of like those times when one of my daughters, back in the toddler stage, would fail abjectly at something and I'd strain to find an encouraging word. Maybe she would fall down while trying to get on a tricycle, and I'd say, "You got back up! What a big girl!"   neglecting to note that, actually, big girls don't fall down while trying to get on tricycles in the first place.

But I've since come to realize that this first bit of feedback I ever got from a meditation teacher wasn't just strained encouragement. My teacher was right: by frequently noticing that my mind was wandering, I was breaking new ground. In my ordinary, workaday life, when my mind wandered I would follow it over hill and dale, not even aware that I was being led. Now I was following it for only short stretches before breaking free—at least, briefly free, free for long enough to realize it had been leading me, a realization that would then give way to its leading me some more.

To put this in more scientific-sounding terminology: I was beginning to observe the workings of what psychologists call the "default mode network." This is a network in the brain that, according to brain-scan studies, is active when we're doing nothing in particular—not talking to people, not focusing on our work or any other task, not playing a sport or reading a book or watching a movie. It is the network along which our mind wanders when it's wandering.

As for where the mind wanders to: well, lots of places, obviously, but studies have shown that these places are usually in the past or the future; you may ponder recent events or distant, strong memories; you may dread upcoming events or eagerly anticipate them; you may strategize about how to head off some looming crisis or fantasize about romancing the attractive person in the cubicle next to yours. What you're generally *not* doing when your mind is wandering is directly experiencing the present moment.

In one sense it's not hard to quiet your default mode network: just do something that requires concentration. Do a crossword puzzle or try to juggle three tennis balls. Until you get to a point where juggling is second nature, you probably won't be fantasizing about the attractive person in the cubicle next to yours.

What's hard is to abandon the default mode network when you're not doing much of anything—like, say, when you're sitting in a meditation hall with your eyes closed. That's why you try to focus on the breath: the mind needs *some* object of focus to wean it from its habitual meandering.

But even with this crutch available, you may find yourself in the position I was in during the early part of that retreat: being repeatedly, frequently, helplessly carried away from experiential mode into default mode. Every time you realize you've been carried away, it's tempting to feel frustration or anger or (my personal favorite) self-loathing. But the standard instruction is to not waste time on that; instead just note the fact that your mind was wandering, and perhaps even note what kind of wandering it was doing (dreading work, looking forward to lunch, lamenting a bad golf shot), and then return your focus to the breath. My teacher, in highlighting the silver lining surrounding my cloud of diffuse attention, was no doubt trying to encourage me to do just that.

This turned out to be good guidance. By interrupting the workings of my default mode network, by "snapping out of it" and realizing that my mind was wandering and then returning to my breath, I was diluting the network's dominance. As I got better at focusing on my breath for longer periods, this network would become less and less active. At least, that's a pretty fair guess. Brain-scan studies have shown this happening in novice meditators. Such studies have also shown that highly adept meditators, people who have meditated for tens of thousands of hours and are in a whole 'nother league from me, exhibit dramatically subdued default mode networks while meditating.

When the default mode network subsides—when the mind stops wandering—it can be a good feeling. There can be a sense of liberation from your chattering mind, a sense of peace, even deep peace. You may not get this feeling every time you meditate, but for some people it happens often enough that it's one of the main inducements to get back on the cushion the next day, part of the positive reinforcement that sustains the practice.

But once you get to this point, once you've used your breath to gain some measure of escape from your wandering mind, you're at a cross-roads. There are two different paths you can follow, corresponding to two different types of meditation.

Concentration and Mindfulness

One path is to sustain the focus on your breath, the focus it felt good to establish in the first place, for a long, long time; and try to tighten and deepen the focus, becoming more immersed in the breath. Then just keep going. You may find yourself feeling better and better and better. This is called concentration meditation, and the object of concentration doesn't have to be breath. Depending on the meditation tradition, the object can be a mantra, an imagined visual image, a recurring sound, whatever.

Concentration meditation is sometimes referred to as serenity meditation—which makes sense, because the concentration can bring serenity. Indeed, the concentration can bring more than serenity.

Sometimes, if sustained for long enough, it can bring powerful feelings of bliss or ecstasy.

And I mean *powerful feelings of bliss or ecstasy.* On the fifth night of my first retreat, I had been experimenting with a modified version of the standard focus-on-your-breath technique. I was focusing on my breath during the inhale but on sounds during the exhale. Focusing on sounds was easy, because it was a hot summer night in rural Massachusetts, and the windows of the meditation hall were open, and a chorus of insects—cicadas, I assume—was chanting loudly. As I meditated I got more tightly focused on my breath and the chanting, both of which seemed to grow in intensity as they absorbed my attention more and more fully. At some point, after twenty-five or thirty minutes of meditation, I had a dramatic and powerful experience that's hard to describe. Later in this book I'll do my best to describe it, but for now I'll just say that it was very, very vivid.

In fact, I'd like to add another "very" to that last sentence. I don't know from firsthand experience what it would be like to take LSD and follow it with a heroin chaser, but I'd guess it's something like the experience I had that night: intensely visual, bordering on hallucinatory, and intensely blissful. I remember feeling as if my jaw, in particular, had been injected with some powerful narcotic. My whole being buzzed with joy and vision, and I felt as if I had crossed some threshold and entered another realm.

If the experience I had that night sounds appealing, I have some bad news. The kind of meditation that gave me this peak experience—concentration meditation—isn't the kind of meditation this book is about. And it's not the kind of meditation that the retreat I was on was supposed to be about. When, at the end of the retreat, I proudly told Michael Grady, one of the retreat's two teachers, about my peak experience, he said, with a nonchalance that I found a bit dispiriting, "Sounds nice. But don't get attached to it." This retreat was supposed to be about mindfulness meditation, the second of the two basic meditative paths you can take.

Mindfulness and concentration are such important Buddhist aspirations that each constitutes one of the eight parts of the Eightfold Path that a deeply committed Buddhist is supposed to tread. In fact, they are the seventh and eighth parts, respectively. But that doesn't mean they are the culminating parts, because the term *Eightfold Path* is misleading in its suggestion of sequence. The idea isn't that you completely master the first of these eight factors, "right view," and then move on to the second and third—"right intention" and "right speech"—and so on. There is too much interdependence among the eight factors for such linear progress. So, for example, progress in the seventh and eighth factors—"right mindfulness" and "right concentration"—will help foster a deeply experiential understanding of core Buddhist principles and hence strengthen "right view."

What's more—and what's more relevant to this chapter—although right mindfulness comes before right concentration on the Eightfold Path, cultivating mindfulness may require first cultivating concentration. That's why the early part of a mindfulness meditation session typically involves focusing on your breath or on something else. Mustering some concentration is what liberates you from the default mode network and stops the mental chatter that normally preoccupies you.

Then, having used concentration meditation to stabilize your attention, you can shift your attention to whatever it is you're now going to be mindful of—usually things that are happening inside you, such as emotions or bodily sensations, though you can also focus on things in the outside world, such as sounds. Meanwhile the breath recedes to the background, though it may remain your "anchor," something you're fuzzily aware of even as you examine other things, and something you may return your attention to from time to time. The key thing is that, whatever you're experiencing, you experience it mindfully, with that ironic combination of closeness and critical distance that I mentioned in describing how I had viewed the feeling of overcaffeination.

I realize that mindfully viewing some feeling you're having—anxiety or restlessness, for example—may not sound as exotically appealing as the psychedelic ecstasy that concentration meditation brought me on that summer night in Massachusetts. But there are several consolations of pursuing mindfulness meditation, and some of them have their exotic aspects.

Mindfulness in Real Life

First, mindfulness meditation is good training. Viewing your feelings mindfully while on a meditation cushion can make you better at viewing them mindfully in everyday life, which means your life will be less governed by misleading or unproductive feelings. You spend less time fuming at drivers who (inexcusably oblivious to the important appointment you're late for) take a couple of seconds to hit the accelerator after the light turns green; less time yelling at your kids or your spouse or yourself or whoever you're inclined to yell at; less time pointlessly resenting indignities inflicted on you; less time having revenge fantasies about the inflicters (not that such fantasies are without their pleasures!); and so on.

Another virtue of mindfulness meditation is that it can make you more attuned to beauty. This effect is especially dramatic on a retreat, when you're doing so much meditating and when your isolation from the "real world" is limiting the number of things for you to worry about, eagerly anticipate, or bitterly regret. With your default mode network deprived of fresh fuel, it's easier to stay in experiential mode.

This deepened absorption in everyday sensations can change your consciousness dramatically. Birdsong can sound surreally pretty. Textures of all kinds—the surface of bricks, of asphalt, of wood—can be enthralling. During a mid-retreat walk in the forest, I once found myself caressing—yes, pretty literally caressing—the intricately sculpted trunk of a tree. And believe me when I tell you I'm not the tree-hugging type.

More generally, I'm not the stop-and-smell-the-roses type. On a typical workday, here is the way I eat lunch: open a can of sardines, get a fork, eat the sardines directly out of the can while standing in front of the kitchen sink, throw the can away. There: done with lunch.

But after a few days on my first retreat I found myself taking the opposite approach to eating. Which is all the more surprising given how spartan the food was by conventional standards: strictly vegetarian, no store-bought snacks, and, most disturbing of all, chocolate on a less-than-daily basis.

The first time I entered the dining hall at mealtime, I was puzzled as to why so many people were eating with their eyes closed. Before long I got the picture: shuttering the visual field brought absorption in taste closer to 100 percent. The result was sublime. A single bite of salad—chewed slowly, savored not just for flavor but for texture—could bring fifteen seconds of near bliss. So imagine the buttered cornbread!

On retreat, common visual experiences can assume a kind of drama. I remember reaching to open an aged screen door and suddenly feeling as if I were watching a movie—one of those scenes where an ultra-close-up shot of something ordinary signals something momentous to come. Of course, nothing momentous came, unless you count the next dramatic visual experience, which tended to come soon. Once, on that first retreat, I was in my dorm room, jotting observations on index cards, when I looked up at the drawn window shade and recorded this: "While writing this card, get dazed by beauty of mottled pattern—sun hitting it through trees and screen. Feels like a narcotic."

Speaking of pharmaceuticals: if I'm going to sing the praises of meditation retreats, I'm obliged to mention possible side effects. The very silence and seclusion that frees you from workaday concerns can also give you time to get immersed in other concerns—notably personal or family issues that in everyday life might visit you, and even revisit you, but not settle in for a long stay. What's more, being in closer-than-usual contact with the actual workings of your mind can lead you to confront issues with a new and perhaps unsettling honesty. Which is just as well, when you think about it. Isn't much of the point of Buddhism to confront suffering rather than evade it, and by confronting it, by looking at it unflinchingly, undermine it?

In my experience, this usually works. I tend to "work through" issues that haunt me on a retreat, gaining a new and healthy perspective on them. Still, the working-through part can take a while and can get intense. I sometimes tell people that going on a long meditation retreat is like doing extreme sports for the mind: it features both the sublime and the harrowing. I'm happy to say that in my experience the ratio is about 4 to 1.

When I'm not on retreat, and my morning meditation is confined to thirty minutes (perhaps followed by a shorter sitting later in the day), the rewards are less dramatic. None of my neighbors has ever dialed 911 to report that I was caressing their trees. Still, so long as I keep up my daily meditation, I am more likely to stop while walking my dogs and *look* at the bark of a tree. And I'm more inclined to savor my sardines, or, while eating them, actually *see* the trees through the kitchen window.

At this point I will refrain from delivering an extended sermon on "living in the moment" or "being in the present" or "staying in the now" or any other combination of those three verbs and those three nouns. With everyone from evangelical ministers to professional golfers singing the praises of present-mindedness, this theme needs no assistance from me.

Besides, to put too much emphasis on living in the now would be to give short shrift to the potential of mindfulness meditation, and, in a sense, to mislead you about the heart of Buddhist teaching. As I suggested in the first chapter, the *Satipatthana Sutta*—the ancient text known as *The Four Foundations of Mindfulness*—contains no injunction

to live in the now. In fact, there is no term in the entire text that is translated as "now" or "the present."[†] This doesn't mean that "staying in the
present" wasn't part of the experience of Buddhist meditators two millennia ago. If you focus on your breathing or on bodily sensations, as
prescribed in ancient mindfulness texts, the present is where you will
be. Still, if you want to go full-on Buddhist—if you want to take the red
pill—you need to understand that staying in the present, though an
inherent part of mindfulness meditation, isn't the point of the exercise.
It is the means to an end, not the end itself.

Approaches to Enlightenment

Which brings us to the subject of enlightenment. Becoming enlightened, in the Buddhist sense of the term, would entail wholly ridding
yourself of the twin illusions from which people tend to suffer: the illusion about what's "in here"—inside your mind—and about what's "out
there" in the rest of the world.[†] Just in case this state of perfect understanding doesn't sound appealing, I should add that another term used
to describe it is *liberation*, as in liberation from suffering (or at least
from *dukkha*, however you choose to translate that multifaceted word).
And yet another term for this state is *nirvana*. Surely you've heard of
nirvana?

There is some controversy over how accessible enlightenment is.
Some people think it's a realistic goal for all of us. Some people think
it's so elusive that to find it you'll have to head off to a forest in Asia and
work on the project 24/7 for months, if not years. And some people say
it's not really attainable at all. True, pure enlightenment, in this view,
is like what mathematicians call an asymptote: something you can get
closer and closer to but never quite reach.

How many people there are who have attained enlightenment,
and for that matter whether there are any, are questions I'm not quali-
fied to answer. But there do seem to be people who so thoroughly

dispel illusions about what's "in here" and what's "out there" that they cross some sort of threshold. They attain and then more or less sustain a state of consciousness that is radically different from ordinary consciousness—and that, by their account, is exceedingly pleasant.

Which leads to the obvious question: How did they do it? How exactly would you go about getting enlightened—or, at least, getting close enough to enlightenment to feel genuinely transformed, to feel that you've entered a whole new world?

There's a natural tendency to think of these transformations as sudden and powerful. After all, isn't that the way the great spiritual apprehensions happen? Moses and the burning bush, Muhammad in the cave, Paul on the road to Damascus? Even the Buddha is said to have seen the light in a single, epic episode of meditation. And if you doubt how vividly dramatic this moment was, just check out the enlightenment scene in the movie *Little Buddha* (which, like *The Matrix*, features Keanu Reeves in the lead role). Talk about great visuals!

If you think of meditation this way—think of its aim as being a dramatic and overwhelming experience of revelation, of enlightenment— you might conclude that, of the two meditative paths I've described, concentration meditation would be the surer route. Certainly my own inadvertent experiment with extended concentration meditation during that first retreat suggested as much; I did have the sense that I was suddenly getting a radically truer view of things and that I had made some kind of big breakthrough. And, though I don't think this experience brought me anywhere near actual enlightenment, I do think that some people get into or at least near that rare territory in sudden and dramatic ways via concentration meditation.

But since that first retreat, I've come to believe that, as dramatic and profound as that experience felt, and as unspectacular as mindfulness meditation may sound by comparison, mindfulness meditation can in fact lead to the same kind of place, a place of sharply and vividly altered perspective. The routine business of mindfulness—observing the world inside you and outside you with inordinate care—can do more than tone down troublesome feelings and enhance your sense of beauty. It can, in a slow, incremental, often uneven yet ultimately systematic way, transform your view of what's really "out there" and what's really "in here." What begins as a modest pursuit—a way to relieve stress or anxiety, cool anger, or dial down self-loathing just a notch—can lead to profound realizations about the nature of things, and commensurately profound feelings of freedom and happiness. An essentially therapeutic endeavor can turn into a deeply philosophical and spiritual endeavor. This is the third virtue of mindfulness meditation: it offers a path to liberation from the Matrix.

I wish I could say that the entire preceding paragraph is based on my own experience, that I walk around seeing things with near-perfect clarity, having undergone an enduring and momentous shift of perspective, and that I live in the general vicinity of bliss. Sadly, no. But I've now talked to enough highly adept meditators, who have traveled much farther along the path than I have, to feel confident that the preceding paragraph is true. We'll be hearing testimony from some of them that I hope will give you the same kind of confidence.

What's more, I've personally experienced *pretty* dramatic, if sometimes fleeting, shifts of perspective. I've already mentioned some of these—notably my moments of suddenly transformed relationship to my anxiety and, earlier, to my overcaffeination. And one thing I've noticed in talking to those highly adept meditators is that, almost invariably, they recognize these and other kinds of experiences I've had as the kinds of experiences they too had somewhere along the path. Indeed, in many cases these experiences seem to have paved the way for their more encompassing illuminations. Though I haven't seen the whole edifice of enlightenment, apparently I've seen some of the building blocks.

Insight Meditation

Strictly speaking, it isn't just mindfulness meditation that has let me see these building blocks. The mindfulness meditation I've done has been within a particular school of meditation known as Vipassana (pronounced *vih PAW suh nuh*). *Vipassana* is an ancient word that denotes clear vision and is usually translated as "insight." The name of the place where I did that meditation retreat in 2003, the Insight Meditation Society, could be rendered as the Society for Vipassana Meditation, which in fact is what it is.

Vipassana teaching puts so much emphasis on mindfulness that some people use the two terms interchangeably. But the distinction is important. Mindfulness meditation is a technique you can use for various purposes, beginning with simple stress reduction. But if you are doing mindfulness meditation within a traditional Vipassana framework, the ultimate purpose is more ambitious: to gain *insight*. And not just insight in the everyday sense of understanding some new stuff. The idea is to see the true nature of reality, and Buddhist texts going back more than a millennium spell out what that means. They define *vipassana* as apprehending what are known as "the three marks of existence."

Two of the three marks of existence sound as if, actually, they wouldn't be too hard to apprehend. The first is impermanence. Who could deny that nothing lasts forever? The second mark of existence is *dukkha*—suffering, unsatisfactoriness. And who among us hasn't suffered and felt unsatisfied? With these two marks of existence, the point of Vipassana meditation isn't so much to comprehend them—since basic comprehension is easy enough—as to comprehend them with new subtlety, to see them at such high resolution that you deeply appreciate their pervasiveness. But the third mark of existence, "not-self," is different. With not-self, comprehension itself is a challenge.[†] Yet according to Buddhist doctrine, it is crucially important to grasp not-self if your goal is *vipassana*: seeing reality with true clarity, such clarity as to pave the path to enlightenment.

My own progress toward grasping not-self began on that first meditation retreat. In fact, in retrospect, it began around the time I told my teacher that my wandering mind was keeping me from focusing on my breath. Noticing that your mind is wandering doesn't seem like a very profound insight; and in fact it isn't one, notwithstanding my teacher's kind insistence on giving it a standing ovation. But it's not without significance. What I was saying in that session with my teacher was that I—that is, my "self," the thing I had thought was in control—don't readily control the most fundamental aspect of my mental life: what I'm thinking about.

As we'll see in the next chapter, this absence of control is part, though by no means all, of what the Buddha had in mind when he emphasized the importance of grasping not-self. And later in the book we'll see that, however ironic it sounds, grappling with the sense in which you don't exist is a step toward putting you—or at least "you"— in charge.

5

The Alleged Nonexistence of Your Self

Ajahn Chah, a twentieth-century Thai monk who did much to spread awareness of Vipassana meditation in the West, used to warn about the difficulty of grasping the Buddhist idea of *anatta*, or "not-self." The basic idea is that the self—your self, my self—in some sense doesn't exist. "To understand not-self, you have to meditate," he advised. If you try to grasp the doctrine through "intellectualizing" alone, "your head will explode."

I'm happy to report that he was wrong about the exploding head. You can try to fathom not-self without meditating and without fear of detonation. I'm not saying you'll *succeed* in fathoming not-self. I'll try to help you get as close to success as possible, but if at the end of this chapter you feel you still don't have a crystal-clear understanding of the idea, don't worry: you're not alone.

Anyway, Ajahn Chah wasn't just making a point about the difficulty of grasping this idea intellectually. He was also underscoring the importance, in Buddhism, of grasping key ideas experientially, through meditation. There's a big difference between seeing the not-self doctrine in the abstract and really seeing—or, in a way, feeling—what it means firsthand. And that's particularly true if you want to not just apprehend the idea of not-self but actually put it to use, harness it to become a happier person and even a better person: to feel a new sense of connection with your fellow creatures and a new sense of generosity toward them. According to Buddhism, truly, deeply realizing that you are selfless—in the sense of not having a self—can make you selfless in the more familiar sense of the term.

Listen to how dramatically Walpola Rahula, a Buddhist monk who in 1959 published an influential book called *What the Buddha Taught*, put the matter: "According to the teaching of the Buddha, the idea of self is an imaginary, false belief which has no corresponding reality, and it produces harmful thoughts of 'me' and 'mine,' selfish desire, craving, attachment, hatred, ill-will, conceit, pride, egoism, and other defilements, impurities, and problems. It is the source of all the troubles in the world from personal conflicts to wars between nations. In short, to this false view can be traced all the evil in the world."

Kind of makes you wish more people would realize they don't have a self! But here we run into a problem: experiencing full-fledged not-self is typically reported only by meditators who have done a whole, whole lot of meditating—certainly more than I've done. If saving the world depends on a big chunk of the human race having this experience, we may be in for a long wait.

But we have to start somewhere! And here there is good news. The not-self experience isn't strictly binary. You don't have to think of it as a threshold that you either manage to finally cross, to transformative effect, or forever fall short of, getting no edification whatsoever. As strange as it may sound, you can, with even a fairly modest daily meditation practice, experience a little bit of not-self. Then, as time goes by, maybe a little more. And—who knows—maybe someday you'll have the full-on, transformative version of the experience. But even if you don't, important and lasting progress can be made, and benefits, for you and for humankind, can accrue along the way.

And, actually, I'd say that what Ajahn Chah called "intellectualizing"—trying to understand not-self conceptually, in the abstract—can help a person get on this path of meditative progress. Particularly worthwhile, I think, is pondering the argument that the Buddha himself made about not-self.

Before we start the pondering, maybe I should put a warning label on top of Ajahn Chah's warning label, because the Buddha's argument has quirks that in some ways steepen the inherent challenge of grasping the concept. He analyzes the human mind in ways that the average psychologist, and for that matter you and I, probably wouldn't analyze it. But after this chapter we'll be back on the firmer-feeling terrain of modern science, and in the meanwhile there is real practical value in trying to look at the whole thing the way the Buddha looked at it.

The Seminal Not-Self Sermon

The logical place to begin is with the primordial text, *Discourse on the Not-Self*, which is said to be the Buddha's earliest utterance on the subject. The occasion for the discourse is an encounter with five monks. Events follow a pattern that's common in such encounters: the Buddha takes the monks through the logic behind some aspect of his teaching, and they are instantly persuaded. In fact, in this case they are instantly *enlightened*. By the end of the discourse they've all transitioned from being mere monks to being *arhats*, truly enlightened beings. These monks are said to be the first five people to have attained that rank aside from the Buddha himself.

That this historic milestone was reached via the grasping of not-self tells you something about the importance of the doctrine in Buddhist thought. And the fact that this particular discourse on not-self is the one that did the trick gives it a special place in the Buddhist canon. Like lots of doctrines in lots of ancient philosophies and religions, not-self is subject to varying interpretations, and when people argue about its true meaning, they can point to various Buddhist texts for support. But this particular text is foundational.

The Buddha's strategy in this discourse is to shake the monks' confidence in their traditional ideas about the self by asking them where exactly, in a human being, we would find anything that warrants the label *self*. He conducts this search systematically; he goes through what are known as the five "aggregates" that, according to Buddhist philosophy, constitute a human being and that human's experience. Describing these aggregates precisely would take a chapter in itself, but for present purposes we can label them roughly as (1) the physical body (called "form" in this discourse), including such sense organs as eyes and ears; (2) basic feelings; (3) perceptions (of, say, identifiable sights or sounds); (4) "mental formations" (a big category that includes complex emotions, thoughts, inclinations, habits, decisions); and (5) "consciousness," or awareness—notably, awareness of the contents of the other four aggregates. The Buddha runs down this list and asks which, if any, of these five aggregates seem to qualify as *self*. In other words, which of the aggregates evince the qualities you'd expect self to possess?

Which in turn raises the question: What qualities *would* you expect self to possess? More fundamentally, what did the word *self* mean to the Buddha? Unfortunately, the Buddha didn't spend a lot of time defining his terms. Still, if you pay close attention to his arguments *against* the self, you can get some sense of what he meant by *self*—a sense of what particular properties he'd expect something worthy of the name *self* to have.

For starters, he links the idea of self to the idea of *control*. Listen to what he says about the aggregate of "form," the physical body: "If form were self, then form would not lead to affliction, and it should obtain regarding form: 'May my form be thus, may my form not be thus.' " But, he notes, our bodies *do* lead to affliction, and we *can't* magically change that by saying "May my form be thus." So form—the stuff the human body is made of—isn't really under our control. Therefore, says the Buddha, it must be the case that "form is not-self." We are not our bodies.

He then goes through the other four aggregates, one by one. "If feeling were self, then feeling would not lead to affliction," and you'd be able to change your feelings by saying "May my feeling be thus, may my feeling not be thus." But, of course, we *don't* ordinarily have this kind of control over our feelings—hence the tendency of unpleasant feelings to linger even though we'd rather they didn't.[†] So feeling, the Buddha concludes, "is not-self." So too with perceptions, mental formations, and consciousness. Are any of these things really under control—so completely under control that they never lead to suffering? And if they're not under control, then how can we think of them as part of the self?

At this point some readers may be puzzled and feel a question welling up that goes something like this: "Wait, is the Buddha saying that the self is something that's *under* control? I personally would be more inclined to think of my self as the thing that's *in* control, kind of like the CEO of my being." Of course, you may not be one of these readers, and in fact you may not understand why any reader would ask such a question. One problem with talking about the self is that different people have different intuitions about what the word *self* means. But if you do feel that question welling up within you, here is an answer of sorts:

This idea of the self as a kind of CEO, as the thing that runs the show, does appear more clearly in other Buddhist texts, where the existence of such a self is denied. And one could mount an argument that in this discourse the Buddha is *implicitly* denying the existence of such a self.[†] In any event, we'll get into the existence—or lack thereof—of the CEO self in the next chapter. For now, my advice is to not worry about following every nuance of the argument the Buddha is making here. The main thing is to get a feel for the texture of it. It's the texture of the argument, the way the Buddha does this item-by-item inventory of a human being as he searches for signs of self, that will come in handy when we start thinking about how a meditator—even a beginning meditator—can make use of the not-self idea.

Control isn't the only property that people tend to associate with the self, and it's not the only property the Buddha examines in this discourse. When I think of my self, I think of something that *persists through time*. I've changed a lot since I was ten years old, but hasn't some inner essence—my identity, my self—in some sense endured? Isn't that the one constant amid the flux?

The Buddha would naturally be skeptical of this claim, since he holds that everything is in flux and nothing is permanent. In the *Discourse on the Not-Self*, he applies this skepticism to each of the five aggregates. "What do you think of this, O monks? Is feeling permanent or impermanent?" Obligingly, the monks reply, "Impermanent, O Lord." He continues, "Is perception permanent or impermanent?" And so on—mental formations, the body, consciousness: none of the aggregates is permanent, the monks agree.

So two of the properties commonly associated with a self—control and persistence through time—are found to be absent, not evident in any of the five components that seem to constitute human beings. This is the core of the argument the Buddha makes in this first and most famous discourse on not-self, and it's commonly taken as the core Buddhist argument that the self doesn't exist.

Does Not-Self Really Mean *No* Self?

But this landmark argument that the self doesn't exist has one odd feature: an occasional tendency to suggest that the self exists.

Near the end of the discourse, delivering the take-home lesson, the Buddha instructs the monks to go through each of the aggregates and say, "This is not mine, this I am not, this is not my self." He says that a monk who follows this guidance unswervingly "becomes passion-free. In his freedom from passion, he is emancipated."

Okay, fine. But if there's no self, then what is the nature of the "he" that is liberated after all the things that aren't self have been disowned? Who is doing the disowning? If you don't exist, then how can you say of each aggregate, "This is not mine, this I am not"? If it makes sense to say that there's something you don't possess and that there's something you are not, then there must be a you in the first place, right? How can the Buddha, on the one hand, insist that the self doesn't exist, and, on the other hand, keep using terms like *I* and *you* and *he* and *she*?

One common Buddhist response to these kinds of questions is this: Though in the deepest sense the self doesn't exist, human language isn't very good at describing reality at the deepest level. So as a practical matter—as a linguistic convention—we have to talk about there being an *I* and a *you* and a *he* and a *she*. In other words, the self doesn't exist in an "ultimate" sense, but it exists in a "conventional" sense.

There, did that clear things up? No, right? Then how about this less formal formulation of the same basic idea from a Buddhist teacher: "You're real. But you're not really real."

Still confused? Then maybe you should try another approach to resolving the paradox: consider the possibility that in this famous sermon, the Buddha *didn't really mean to be denying the existence of the self.* If you're wondering why the last half of the previous sentence is italicized, it's to underscore what a radical idea this is, at least among mainstream Buddhist thinkers. Still, it's an idea that has been taken seriously by a few maverick scholars. It's worth exploring.

A Heresy Examined

One point these mavericks tend to make is that nowhere in that first, foundational discourse on not-self does the Buddha actually say that the self doesn't exist. He does say that each of the five aggregates is not-self, but he doesn't claim that examining the five aggregates constitutes an exhaustive search for the self. Maybe there's more to a person than five aggregates!

Well, maybe, but if you raise this possibility, you'll get blowback from the many non-maverick Buddhist scholars who insist that, no, according to Buddhist philosophy, the five aggregates are all there is to a person, even if the Buddha didn't say that in this particular discourse. And it's true that the exhaustiveness of the five aggregates did become a tenet of Buddhist philosophy. Then again, so did the idea that the self doesn't exist. But we're not asking whether these things are part of Buddhist philosophy; we're asking whether they were *originally* part of Buddhist philosophy—whether the Buddha himself held them. And the point is just that neither of them is explicit in what is said to be the Buddha's first big statement on the subject.

Anyway, this is one possible way to explain what the Buddha had in mind when he talked as if there is a "you" that abandons the five aggregates and is liberated after the abandonment: maybe, in the Buddha's view, there was more to you than the five aggregates in the first place.

There's a second, related scenario that might explain where we find the "you" that is liberated after the aggregates have been abandoned: maybe not all aggregates are created equal. Maybe one of them—consciousness—is special. Maybe, after "you" let go of all five aggregates, it's this one aggregate that is liberated, released from entanglement with the other four. And maybe that's what "you" are after letting go of the idea of the self: a kind of purified form of consciousness.

There's an obvious problem with this scenario that non-mavericks would be quick to point out: The Buddha does, in this first discourse on the not-self, talk as if "you" abandon consciousness just as thoroughly as you abandon the other aggregates—as if, in other words, the "you" that is left after liberation is no more closely associated with consciousness than with the other aggregates.

It's a valid point. On the other hand, there are discourses—not many, but some—in which the Buddha seems to sing a slightly different tune. In one discourse, describing what happens after you take the not-self teaching seriously and abandon your attachment to the five aggregates, he says that consciousness itself is "liberated." What's more, as he describes the state of this liberated consciousness, he shifts almost seamlessly to describing the state of the person who has been liberated. He says of consciousness: "By being liberated, it is steady; by being steady, it is content; by being content, he is not agitated. Being unagitated, he personally attains nirvana."

When the Buddha puts it like this—speaks of consciousness itself as being liberated—he frames the relationship between consciousness and the other four aggregates in an interesting way. In its ordinary form—the form with which all of us unenlightened beings are familiar—consciousness is "engaged" with the other four aggregates, the Buddha says; it is engaged with feeling, with mental formations, with perception, with the body.

This doesn't just mean that consciousness has *access* to perceptions, bodily sensations, and so on; after all, even the consciousness of a fully enlightened being would have *access* to these things; otherwise—if there weren't access even to perceptions, for example—there wouldn't be much, if anything, for enlightened beings to be conscious *of*. "Engagement" refers, rather, to a stronger connection between consciousness and the other aggregates. Engagement is the product of a "lust," as the Buddha puts it, that people have for the aggregates; there is a clinging to them, a possessive relationship to them. In other words, the "engagement" persists so long as the person fails to realize that the aggregates are "not-self." The person clings to emotions, thoughts, and other elements of the aggregates as if they were personal belongings. But they're not.†

This discourse—the Buddha's discourse on engagement—suggests an appealingly simple model: liberation consists of changing the relationship between your consciousness and the things you normally think of as its "contents"—your feelings, your thoughts, and so on. Once you realize that these things are "not-self," the relationship of your consciousness to them becomes more like contemplation than engagement, and your consciousness is liberated. And the "you" that remains—the you that, in that first discourse on the not-self, the Buddha depicts as liberated—*is* this liberated consciousness.

I wish I could say this scenario cleanly and definitively answers the riddle I set out to answer. Namely, if the five aggregates are all there are to a person, where do you find the "he" who, in that first discourse on the not-self, is said to be liberated? Unfortunately, the more deeply you delve into the discourse on engagement—confront its ambiguities and seeming inconsistencies, ponder translation issues, and weigh ancient commentaries on it—the harder it is to confidently extract any such simple scenario.† Besides, there's no denying that the Buddha repeatedly, in that first not-self discourse and elsewhere, *does* say that consciousness is not-self, something that "you" have to let go of for liberation to happen—which seems quite at odds with the prospect that "you" can happily inhabit the consciousness aggregate once it is disengaged from the other four aggregates.

But don't give up on this prospect quite yet. Some philosophers of Buddhism have suggested that maybe there are two kinds of consciousness—or two modes of consciousness, or two layers of consciousness, or however you want to think of them. One is the kind of consciousness you're liberated *from*, and the other is the kind of consciousness that stays with "you"—that *is* you—after the liberation. The first kind of consciousness is deeply entangled with—fully engaged with—the contents of the other aggregates, and the second kind is a more objective awareness of those contents, a more contemplative consciousness that persists after the engagement has been broken.

Advanced meditators sometimes report experiencing a "witness consciousness" that seems to roughly fit this description of the second kind of consciousness, and some of them experience it for a long time. Maybe if it lasted forever they could claim to be enlightened. Maybe this "witness consciousness" is where the "you" that is left over after liberation resides.[†]

Maybe. Or maybe we should just acknowledge that Ajahn Chah was onto something: trying to understand the idea of not-self by "intellectualizing" could make your head explode. And maybe, in light of this possibility, we should stop the intellectualizing right here.

Of course, your head, though intact, may still be in a somewhat confused state. But I have good news: you don't have to dispel your confusion right now; you can wait a few years, until you've meditated so much that you become fully enlightened. Then, having directly apprehended not-self, you can explain it to me.

Meanwhile, here's what I recommend:

Continue to entertain the proposition you've probably been entertaining your whole life, that somewhere within you there's something that deserves the name *I*. And don't feel like you're committing a felony-level violation of Buddhist dogma just because you think of yourself as being a self. *But* be open to the radical possibility that your self, at the deepest level, is not at all what you've always thought of it as being. If you followed the Buddha's guidance and abandoned the massive chunks of psychological landscape you've always thought of as belonging to you, you would undergo a breathtaking shift in what it means to be a human. If you attained the state he's recommending, this would be very different from having a self in the sense in which you've always had one before.

What exactly would it feel like? I'm not the best person to ask, since I've never abandoned *massive* chunks of psychological landscape. But I did have that experience I described in chapter 2—my first "success" at meditating. The tension I felt in my jaw, the overcaffeinated feeling that made me want to grind my teeth, suddenly ceased to seem like part of me. And at that moment it ceased to feel unpleasant. I was still *conscious* of the feeling in my jaw, but my consciousness was no longer *engaged* with it in the sense of having possessive feelings toward it. I hadn't let go of my attachment to all feelings, as the Buddha recommends, but I had let go of my attachment to this one feeling. I had realized, you might say, that this feeling didn't have to be part of my self; I had redefined my self in a way that excluded it.

Obviously, the feeling was still in some sense part of my consciousness, but now my consciousness was contemplating it in the way that it contemplates the trees that are swaying in the breeze beyond my window as I write this sentence. I had no sense of ownership toward the tension that had made me want to grind my teeth, so I could view it with dispassion and calm.

Taking the Ache out of Toothache

Speaking of teeth, here's something Edward Conze, an eminent twentieth-century scholar of Buddhism, wrote about the Buddhist conception of the self: "If there is a tooth, and there is decay in that tooth, this is a process in the tooth, and in the nerve attached to it. If now my 'I' reaches out to the tooth, convinces itself that this is 'my' tooth—and it sometimes does not seem to need very much convincing—and believes that what happens to the tooth is bound to affect *me*, a certain disturbance of thought is likely to result." In that sense, "the belief in a 'self' is considered by all Buddhists as an indispensable condition to the emergence of suffering." In other words, pain in your tooth can hurt you only if you own the tooth in the first place.

I actually know a guy who has put in many, many hours of meditation and once tested this proposition. Before having a cavity filled, he

decided, as a kind of experiment, to tell the dentist to skip the Novo-
cain. He didn't report *loving* the experience, but he said he preferred it
to the typical post-dentist experience of walking around for hours with
a partly paralyzed face.

Personally, I'll take the partly paralyzed face. I don't think I could
enter a state of profound mindfulness in a dentist's chair. However,
once, about ten days into a two-week meditation retreat, I did something kind of like that. A tooth—which turned out to require a root
canal—had started hurting me whenever I drank anything. The pain
was sharp and could be excruciating, even if what I was drinking was
at room temperature. So, just to see what would happen, I sat down in
my room and meditated for thirty minutes and then took a giant swig
of water and made a point of bathing the tooth in it.

The result was dramatic and strange. I felt a throbbing so powerful
that I got absorbed in its waves, but the throbbing didn't consistently
feel bad; it was right on the cusp between bitter and sweet and just
teetered between the two. At times it was even awesome in the old-
fashioned sense of actually inspiring awe—breathtaking in its power
and, you might even say, its grandeur and its beauty. Maybe the simplest way to describe the difference between this and my ordinary experience with tooth pain is that there was less "youch!" than usual and
more "whoa!" than usual.

I wouldn't have been able to do this if not on retreat. Thirty minutes of my workaday meditation doesn't put me in a position to view
acute tooth pain so objectively as to take much of the suffering out of it.
Still, this experience was testament to the fact that ownership of even
serious pain is, strictly speaking, optional.

Of course, tooth pain isn't as big a problem as it was in the Buddha's day, thanks to modern dentistry. What *is* a big problem is anxiety.
And, as I noted earlier, I did manage to disown some of that the night
before the talk I gave in Camden, Maine. The anxiety came to seem

like something I was observing as much as feeling, something I was experiencing with dispassion. Maybe the Buddha would say that my consciousness had ceased to be "engaged" with the anxiety.

To look at this from a slightly different angle: the key to letting go of a chunk or two of my self was to separate the act of observation from the act of evaluation. I still experienced the anxiety, but I no longer experienced it as either good or bad. As we saw in chapter 2, feelings are designed by natural selection to represent *judgments* about things, evaluations of them; natural selection "wants" you to experience things as either good or bad. The Buddha believed that the less you judge things—including the contents of your mind—the more clearly you'll see them, and the less deluded you'll be.

Taking Charge by Letting Go

One lesson I take away from my experience disowning these various unpleasant feelings—the tension in my jaw from overcaffeination, the tooth pain, the anxiety—is the paradox of control. All three feelings, in their initial, annoying persistence, proved that they were not under my control—indeed, if anything, they were controlling me! And, according to the Buddha's conception of "self," my lack of control over them in turn proved that they were not part of my self. But once I followed that logic—quit *seeing* these things I couldn't control as part of my self—I was liberated from them and, in a certain sense, back in control. Or maybe it would be better to put it this way: my lack of control over them ceased to be a problem.

Note how many times the words *I*, *me*, and *my* appear in the previous paragraph—proof, perhaps, of how far I am from realizing not-self. At no time, either in the course of having these experiences or in the course of thinking about them later, did I come close to abandoning the concept of self altogether. But hanging on to some notion of self didn't keep me from experiencing a pretty significant redefinition of my self—a redefinition that, who knows, may be the first step toward someday experiencing full-on not-self!

Maybe it's actually *useful* to hang on to some conception of self for a while; maybe hanging on to it could help you get to the point where you no longer believe it exists. The scholar Peter Harvey has written, "One can, then, perhaps see the Self idea as fulfilling a role akin to a rocket which boosts a payload into space, against the force of gravity. It provides the force to drive the mind out of the 'gravity field' of attachment to the personality-factors [the aggregates]. Having done so, it then 'falls away and is burnt up,' as itself a baseless concept."

In any event, Harvey believes, the not-self teaching "is not so much a thing to be thought about as to be *done*." And who knows, maybe that was the Buddha's view of the matter. Maybe he wasn't really trying to articulate a doctrine but rather to draw you down a path. And that path involves showing you how many things there are that you think of as part of your self but that don't have to be thought of that way. In this view, the Buddha, in that first discourse on the not-self, wasn't delivering a lecture about metaphysics or the mind-body problem or anything else so purely philosophical; he was just trying to get the monks to think about their minds in a way that would lead them toward liberation.

This might explain that feature of the discourse that people who think of the self as a CEO find odd: that the Buddha's criterion for labeling a part of you *not-self* is that it's not *under* control rather than that it's not *in* control. Maybe by *not-self* the Buddha just meant something like "not usefully considered part of your self" or "not to be identified with." In which case he was basically saying, "Look, if there's part of you that isn't under your control and therefore makes you suffer, then do yourself a favor and quit identifying with it!" This interpretation meshes well with the guidance he offers near the end of the discourse, when he says that the proper attitude toward each of the five aggregates is "This is not mine, this I am not, this is not my self."

In a way we're back to square one, Ajahn Chah's opening advice about the not-self doctrine: Don't *think* about it so much—just *do* it. But I hope you think that thinking about it has been useful. Later we'll hear from someone who seems to have not just thought about it but done it—someone who says that, after abandoning ownership of larger and larger chunks of what we traditionally think of as the self, he finally let go of all of it. But for now my advice to beginning meditators is this: *Don't take the idea of not-self too seriously*. Maybe the contemplative path will eventually lead you to the experience of full-on not-self, and you'll come to believe that, in a profound and hard-to-describe sense, there's no "I" in there.

Until then, just be guided by the less dramatic lessons from the Buddha's not-self discourse. Think of yourself as having, in principle, the power to establish a different relationship with your feelings and thoughts and impulses and perceptions—the power to disengage from some of them; the power to, in a sense, disown them, to define the bounds of your self in a way that excludes them. Think of some degree of liberation as being possible—and don't worry about the fact that this would seem to imply that there's a self to be liberated. There are worse things than being a self that gets liberated.

By the way, at the risk of draining this whole subject of some drama, in my own view these arguments over what the Buddha actually believed about the self are in one sense pointless. There's roughly no chance that all the sayings attributed to him in Buddhist texts were uttered by him. In fact, some scholars will tell you that there is little or nothing in these texts that we can confidently attribute to him. Like the "historical Jesus," the "historical Buddha" is hard to discern through the mists of history. Just as the gospel accounts of Jesus are products of evolution, of oral and textual accretion over time, so are ancient accounts of the Buddha's utterances. Even assuming that most of these accounts were originally grounded in things he actually said, they were subject to amendment, intentional or not, as they passed through the generations. In this light, it's hardly surprising that there should be inconsistencies and outright contradictions within the Buddhist canon.

Still, amid all the disagreement over what the Buddha said and what the Buddha meant, there are some themes that everyone agrees are part of the Buddhist tradition from early on. And one of these is that our conception of our selves is, at best, wildly off the mark. We associate the self with control and with firm persistence through time, but on close inspection we turn out to be much less under control, and much more fluid, with a much less fixed identity, than we think.

In the next chapter, we'll start to see what modern psychology has to say about all of this. Does psychology tend to corroborate the Buddhist view? Does it suggest that our commonsense conception of the self—as a solid, enduring core that keeps the system under control—is actually an illusion? Does it lend credibility to the Buddhist idea that "disowning" large chunks of the self—and maybe, someday, disowning the whole thing—could actually bring you closer to the truth? In my view, the answers are yes, yes, and yes.

6

Your CEO Is MIA

Apparently the Buddha's famous discourse on the not-self didn't immediately convert everyone to his way of thinking. Sometime after delivering it, according to Buddhist scripture, he runs into a man named Aggivessana, a braggart who has assembled a large audience to watch him vanquish the Buddha in a debate about the self. Aggivessana begins the proceedings by challenging the Buddha's claim that the self can't be found in any of the five aggregates. He declares, "Form is my self, feeling is my self, perception is my self, mental formations are my self, consciousness is my self."

This is a pretty blatant provocation, a direct assault on the Buddha's worldview. But the Buddha, being the Buddha, remains calm. He says, "Very well then, Aggivessana, I will cross-question you on this matter."

If you've read many of the Buddha's discourses, you know that

Aggivessana's convictions will not survive the ensuing dialogue in good shape. The only question is which rhetorical tool the Buddha will use to dispel his interlocutor's confusion. Turns out the answer is the "king" metaphor.

The Buddha asks, "Would a consecrated, noble-warrior king— such as King Pasendai of Kosala or King Ajatasattu Vedehiputta of Magadha—wield the power in his own domain to execute those who deserve execution, to fine those who deserve to be fined, and to banish those who deserve to be banished?"

"Yes, Master Gotama," answers Aggivessana. "He would wield it, and he would deserve to wield it."

The Buddha then says, "What do you think, Aggivessana? When you say, 'Form is my self,' do you wield power over that form: 'May my form be thus, may my form not be thus'?" Aggivessana says nothing. The Buddha repeats the question. Aggivessana remains silent.

Now the Buddha pulls out the big guns. He reminds Aggivessana that "when anyone doesn't answer when asked a legitimate question by the Tathagata [the Buddha] up to three times, his head splits into seven pieces right here." At that point Aggivessana looks up and, ominously, sees a spirit with an iron thunderbolt in hand. (The spirit is aptly named "Thunderbolt-in-hand.") The spirit speaks up, warning that if Aggivessana "doesn't answer when asked a legitimate question by the Blessed One up to three times, I will split his head into seven pieces right here."

Thus incentivized, Aggivessana answers the Buddha's question: "No, Master Gotama," he doesn't, he admits, have complete power over his body. The Buddha then runs through the other aggregates— feeling, perception, and so on. Aggivessana sees that, no, he doesn't have the power over any of these things that a king has over his domain.

So the Buddha has made his point. You—the "you" that experiences feelings and perceptions and entertains thoughts—isn't really in complete control of these things. If you think that somewhere inside your head there's a kind of supreme ruler, a chief executive, well, there's some question as to where exactly you would find it.

Twenty-five hundred years later, the science of psychology is talking the Buddha's language. Well, not *exactly* his language; psychologists don't often assert that you're not the king of your personal domain, since these days there aren't many kings who wield actual power over their own domains. Psychologists use more modern terminology. As Robert Kurzban, a professor of psychology at Penn, puts it, " 'You' aren't the president, the central executive, the prime minister."

This is a matter of nearly unanimous agreement among psychologists: the conscious self is not some all-powerful executive authority. In fact, according to modern psychology, the conscious self has even less power than Aggivessana attributed to it after the Buddha clarified his thinking. Aggivessana was just acknowledging that, on reflection, the various aggregates aren't under *complete* control. After all, if they were, then, as the Buddha was known to ask, why would they cause so much suffering? Modern psychology is making a stronger point. It's basically saying: You know how, on reflection, you conclude, along with Aggivessana, that you're not in total control? Well, you're actually in even less control than you conclude on reflection.

Unless, maybe, by "on reflection" you mean "upon doing the kind of reflection you're doing as you approach the end of a one-week silent meditation retreat." If the retreat works as intended, by that point your mind is much calmer than usual, and you are viewing its contents much more objectively than usual. And some of the contents of your consciousness that you normally think of yourself as generating seem to be getting generated by something other than you. More than once I've heard a meditation teacher say, "Thoughts think themselves." By the end of a retreat, oddly, that can start to make sense.

So if the conscious mind isn't in control, what *is* in control? As we'll see, the answer may be: nothing in particular. The closer we look at the mind, the more it seems to consist of a lot of different players,

players that sometimes collaborate but sometimes fight for control, with victory going to the one that is in some sense the strongest. In other words, it's a jungle in there, and you're not the king of the jungle. The good news is that, paradoxically, realizing you're not king can be the first step toward getting some real power.

Of course, it's hard to admit you're not king, and that's not just because king seems like a great thing to be. It's because we *feel* like we're king; we feel that our conscious self is in charge of our behavior, deciding what to do and when. But a number of experiments over the past few decades have cast doubt on this intuition.

Of Two Minds

Among the most dramatic are the famous "split-brain" experiments. These were done with people whose left and right brain hemispheres had been separated via surgery that severed the bundle of fibers connecting them. (Typically, the purpose of the surgery was to control seizures in cases of severe epilepsy.) It turns out that this surgery has little effect on behavior; under normal circumstances, people with split brains act normally. But back in the 1960s the neuroscientists Roger Sperry and Michael Gazzaniga devised clever experiments that led split-brain patients to behave strangely.

The key was to confine information to a single hemisphere by presenting it to only half of the patient's visual field. If, for example, a word is presented only to the left visual field, which is processed by the right hemisphere, it won't enter the left hemisphere at all, since the hemispheres have been surgically separated.

It's the left hemisphere that, in most people, controls language. Sure enough, patients whose right hemisphere is exposed to, say, the word *nut* report no awareness of this input. Yet their left hand—which is controlled by the right hemisphere—will, if allowed to rummage through a box containing various objects, choose a nut.

That finding alone could make you start questioning traditional notions of the conscious "self." Now consider this one: when the left hemisphere is asked to explain behavior initiated by the right hemisphere, it tries to generate a plausible story. If you send the command "Walk" to the right hemisphere of these patients, they will get up and walk. But if you ask them where they're going, the answer will come from the left hemisphere, which wasn't privy to the command. And this hemisphere will come up with what, from its point of view, is a reasonable answer. One man replied, plausibly enough, that he was going to get a soda. And the person who comes up with the improvised explanation—or, at least, the person's left hemisphere, the part of the person that's doing the talking—seems to believe the story.

In one experiment, an image of a chicken claw was shown to the patient's left hemisphere and a snow scene was shown to the right hemisphere. Then an array of pictures was made visible to both hemispheres, and the patient was asked to choose a picture. The patient's left hand pointed to a shovel, presumably because a snow scene had been seen by the hemisphere that controls the left hand, and snow is something that gets shoveled. The right hand pointed to a chicken. Gazzaniga recounts what happened next: "Then we asked why he chose those items. His left-hemisphere speech center replied, 'Oh, that's simple. The chicken claw goes with the chicken,' easily explaining what it knew. It had seen the chicken claw. Then, looking down at his left hand pointing to the shovel, without missing a beat, he said, 'And you need a shovel to clean out the chicken shed.'" Again, the part of the brain that controls language had generated a coherent, if false, explanation of behavior—and apparently had convinced itself of the truth of the explanation.

The split-brain experiments powerfully demonstrated the capacity of the conscious self to convince itself that it's calling the shots when it's not. However, this demonstration was done with people who don't have normal brains. How about the rest of us, whose two hemispheres aren't separated? Do our brains actually make use of this capacity for self-deception?

There is good reason to believe the answer is yes. In one much-cited experiment, the psychologists Richard Nisbett and Timothy Wilson asked shoppers to appraise four pairs of pantyhose and choose the best pair. It turned out people had a strong tendency to choose the pair on the far right. But when asked why they had chosen that pair, they didn't say "Because it's on the far right." They tended to explain their choices in terms of the quality of the pantyhose, sometimes going into detail about the fabric, the feel, and so on. Unfortunately for these explanations, the four pairs of pantyhose were identical.

Psychologists have devised various ways to get people to do things without being aware of why they're doing them. A common technique is to present information subliminally—for example, to flash a word or an image on a screen for a small fraction of a second, not long enough for conscious awareness to set in.

In one study done in Britain, subjects were told they would be given a monetary reward according to how hard they squeezed a hand grip in a series of trials, and that the stakes would vary from trial to trial. As they awaited a trial, watching the screen that would tell them how hard they had managed to squeeze the grip, an image of a coin was flashed on the screen, either a penny or a pound. Even when the image was shown subliminally, the stakes influenced how hard the subjects squeezed the grip.

This experiment had a second dimension. These subjects were having their brains scanned. The scientists paid special attention to a brain region that is associated with motivation and emotion and is thought to encode information about rewards. This part of the brain was more active when the monetary reward was higher—and that was true regardless of whether the information about the reward had been presented subliminally or had been left on the screen long enough to enter consciousness. The scientists wrote, "Consistently, the same basal forebrain region underpinned subliminal and conscious motivation."

But is "conscious motivation" really the right term? That could be taken to mean that the motivation *originates* with conscious volition. And this experiment suggests a different scenario: the actual brain machinery that translates incentive into motivation is the same regardless of whether you're consciously aware of the incentive and consciously experiencing the translation; so maybe the conscious awareness doesn't really add anything to the process. In other words, maybe it's not so much "conscious motivation" as "consciousness *of* motivation." With or without conscious awareness, the same physical motivational machinery seems to be doing the heavy lifting.[†]

Sure, you might *feel* as if your awareness of the incentive is what led you to strengthen your grip. But what this experiment suggests is that maybe this is an illusion. That's not the only possible interpretation, but it's a salient one, and it's one the Buddha would probably warm to: you think you're directing the movie, but you're actually just watching it. Or, at the risk of turning this into a metaphor that's impossible to wrap your mind around, the movie is directing you—unless you manage to liberate yourself from it.

Questions about how in control the conscious mind really is have now been raised from a lot of experimental angles. In a famous series of experiments first done in the early 1980s by Benjamin Libet, researchers monitored the brains of subjects while they "chose" to initiate an action. The researchers concluded that the brain was initiating the action before the person became aware of "deciding" to initiate it.

This body of research is still coalescing. Not all the findings will hold up in the long run, as the experiments are repeated. And in some cases, including the Libet studies, there are unsettled questions of interpretation. Still, at a minimum it seems fair to say that the role of our conscious selves in guiding behavior is not nearly as big as was long thought. And the reason this role was exaggerated is that the conscious mind *feels* so powerful; in other words, the conscious mind is naturally deluded about its own nature.

The Darwinian Benefits of Self-Delusion

So if you're a Buddhist philosopher, you may feel vindicated. But you may also feel puzzled. Why would natural selection design a brain that leaves people deluded about themselves? One answer is that if we believe something about ourselves, that will help us convince other people to believe it. And certainly it's to our benefit—or, more precisely, it would have been to the benefit of the genes of our hunter-gatherer ancestors—to convince the world that we're coherent, consistent actors who have things under control.

Remember the guy whose right hemisphere was told to walk, and whose left hemisphere, when asked where he was going, said he was going to get a soda? His answer wasn't really true, but it does inspire a kind of confidence in him. He seems like a guy who is in charge of himself, who doesn't go around doing things for no good reason. Compare him with a guy who offers a more truthful account: "I don't really know why I got up or where I'm going. Sometimes I just do stuff for reasons that make no sense to me." If those two guys were your neighbors in a hunter-gatherer village, which one would you want to go hunting with? Which one would you want to become friends with? During human evolution, the answers to such questions mattered: if you were thought unworthy of collaboration and friendship, your genes were in trouble.

In short, from natural selection's point of view, it's good for you to tell a coherent story about yourself, to depict yourself as a rational, self-aware actor. So whenever your actual motivations aren't accessible to the part of your brain that communicates with the world, it would make sense for that part of your brain to generate stories about your motivation.

Of course, coherence of motivation, though a desirable quality in a friend or collaborator, isn't by itself decisive. If someone has clear and consistent goals but always fails to reach them, or fails to contribute much to team endeavors, or doesn't keep promises, he or she won't be overloaded with friends and collaborators. So you would expect us to tell (and believe) not just coherent stories about ourselves but flattering stories about ourselves.

And by and large we do. In 1980 the psychologist Anthony Greenwald invented the term *beneffectance* to describe the way people naturally present themselves to the world—as beneficial and effective. Lots of experiments since then have shown that people not only put out this kind of publicity about themselves but actually believe it.

And they could be right! There *are* beneficial and effective people in the world. But one thing that can't be the case is that *most* people are above average in these regards. Yet study after study has shown that most people do think they're above average along various dimensions, ranging from athletic ability to social skills. And this sort of self-appraisal can firmly resist evidence. One study of fifty people found that on average they rated their driving skill toward the "expert" end of the spectrum—which would be less notable were it not for the fact that all fifty had recently been in car accidents, and two-thirds of them had been deemed responsible for the accidents by police.

If there is anything we're more impressed by than our competence, it's our moral fiber. One finding among many that drive this point home is that the average person believes he or she does more good things and fewer bad things than the average person. Nearly half a millennium after Montaigne died, science has validated the logic behind his perhaps too modest remark: "I consider myself an average man except for the fact that I consider myself an average man."

And we don't just consider ourselves above average compared to a vaguely envisioned population of human beings at large. When put on a very small team, we tend to convince ourselves that we're more valuable than the average team member. In one study, academics who had worked on jointly authored research papers were asked what fraction of the team's output their own work accounted for. On the average four-person team, the sum of the claimed credit was 140 percent. The key word in the previous sentence is *credit*. When team efforts fail, our perceived contribution to the outcome shrinks.

People are often aware of these forms of self-delusion—at least, they're aware of them in other people. In one American study, experimenters described eight different kinds of biases that are common in people, such as "they tend to take credit for success but deny responsibility for failure; they see their successes as the result of personal qualities, like drive or ability, but their failures as the result of external factors, like unreasonable work requirements or inadequate instruction." In the case of all eight biases, the average person said the average American is more susceptible than they themselves were. As Kurzban has summarized this finding, "We think we're better than average *at not being biased in thinking that we're better than average.*"

Our egocentric biases are aided and abetted by the way memory works. Though certain painful events get seared into our memories— perhaps so we can avoid repeating the mistakes that led to them—we are on balance more likely to remember events that reflect favorably on us than those that don't. And we remember positive experiences in greater detail than negative experiences, as if the positive events are specially primed for sharing with the public in rich detail. No such asymmetry of narrative detail is found in our memory of positive and negative things that happen to other people.

What's more, when we recount an experience to someone, the act of recounting it changes the memory of it. So if we reshape the story a bit each time—omitting inconvenient facts, exaggerating convenient ones—we can, over time, transform our actual belief about what happened. Which presumably makes it easier to convince others that our story is true.

Of course, people don't *always* have inflated conceptions of themselves. There is such a thing as low self-esteem—and there are explanations, speculative but plausible explanations, as to why it would make Darwinian sense for certain experiences to instill it. There are other differences as well among people that can influence the kinds of stories they tell and believe about themselves. In one study, people who ranked high on an extroversion scale and people who ranked high on a neuroticism scale both kept diaries about their everyday emotional experiences. Later the extroverts recalled more positive experiences than they had in fact had, and the neurotics recalled more negative experiences than they had in fact had. This is proof that self-inflation, though the norm in our species, isn't an iron law. But note that both kinds of people were wrong; their particular personalities had steered them toward different kinds of illusions, but in both cases *illusion* is the operative word.

The kinds of stories we tell about ourselves can also vary across cultures. Along some dimensions, Asians, on average, do less self-inflating than Westerners; along other dimensions—notably "collectivist" virtues, such as loyalty to the group—Asians tend to do more self-inflating than Westerners. Still, the basic pattern of self-inflation holds worldwide, and that's particularly true when it comes to ethical virtues such as fairness; on average, people think they're morally above average. This is an especially important piece of self-flattery, because it helps fuel the self-righteousness that starts and sustains conflicts, ranging from quarrels to wars.

So, all told, we're under at least two kinds of illusions. One is about the nature of the conscious self, which we see as more in control of things than it actually is. The other illusion is about exactly what kind of people we are—namely, capable and upstanding. You might call these two misconceptions the illusion about our selves and the illusion about ourselves. They work in synergy. The first illusion helps us convince the world that we are coherent, consistent actors: we don't do things for no reason, and the reasons we do them make sense; if our behaviors merit credit or blame, there is an inner us that deserves that credit or blame. The second illusion helps convince the world that what we deserve is credit, not blame; we're more ethical than the average person, and we're more productive than the average teammate. We have beneffectance.

In other words, if you were to build into the brain a component in charge of public relations, it would look something like the conscious self. The anthropologist Jerome Barkow has written, "It is possible to argue that the primary evolutionary function of the self is to be the organ of impression management (rather than, as our folk psychology would have it, a decision-maker)." The only thing I'd add is that the folk psychology itself may be part of the evolutionary function; our presentation of ourselves as effective, upstanding people involves believing in the power of our selves.

Of Many Minds

If the conscious self isn't a CEO, directing all the behavior it thinks it's directing, how *does* behavior get directed? How do decisions get made?

An increasingly common answer within the field of psychology, especially evolutionary psychology, is that the mind is "modular." In this view, your mind is composed of lots of specialized modules—modules for sizing up situations and reacting to them—and it's the interplay among these modules that shapes your behavior. And much of this interplay happens without conscious awareness on your part.

The modular model of the mind, though still young and not fully fleshed out, holds a lot of promise. For starters, it makes sense in terms of evolution: the mind got built bit by bit, chunk by chunk, and as our species encountered new challenges, new chunks would have been added. As we'll see, this model also helps make sense of some of life's great internal conflicts, such as whether to cheat on your spouse, whether to take addictive drugs, and whether to eat another powdered-sugar doughnut. Perhaps most important for our purposes, thinking of the mind as modular helps make sense of things you hear from Buddhist meditation teachers, such as that "thoughts think themselves" and that appreciating this fact can be liberating.

But the modular model of the mind has one big problem: its name. The word *module* begs to be misinterpreted, so before we get into the workings of the modular mind, let me try to preempt misunderstanding by listing three ways you *shouldn't* conceive of modules:

1. *The modules aren't like a bunch of physical compartments.* You can't point to one part of your brain and say, "This is the module that helps me infer what people are thinking from what they say and from their body language and facial expressions." Psychologists do think there's such a module: the "theory of mind" module. (Autism has been linked to deficiencies in this module.) But when scientists try to sketch out this module via brain scans, they find that it's far-flung, drawing on various regions of the brain, and sometimes drawing more on one region, sometimes more on another.

2. *The different modules aren't like the blades on a Swiss Army knife or the apps on a smartphone.* I say this with some hesitation, because proponents of the modular paradigm sometimes use these very metaphors. But the truth is that there is much more interaction among and overlap between different mental modules than you see in a Swiss Army knife or even a smartphone.

   For example, some psychologists have argued that there is a "cheater detection" module that helps you figure out who you can trust. This module would presumably draw on the "theory of mind" module but probably not on all of it, and it would probably draw on parts of the brain outside of it. It might, say, communicate with some kind of labeling module that gives people a negative or positive rating, depending on whether they pass the cheater test.

   To further complicate things, there are different *kinds* of

cheaters to detect. There are transactional cheaters—the unscru-
pulous used-car salesman—and there are sexual cheaters, mates
who are unfaithful. Does it make sense to think of these two kinds
of detection as being handled by a single module? There is likely
some overlap between them; we might in both cases assess whether
the person can look us in the eye while saying something we suspect is untrue. But the overlap isn't complete because, for one
thing, the motivational systems that drive the cheater-detection
machinery differ in the two cases; jealousy isn't what gets me to
pay extra-close attention to the facial expressions of a used-car
salesman, and if I conclude he's untrustworthy, I don't fly into a
jealous rage (though if I conclude this after the car he sold me dies,
I might fly into a nonjealous rage). All told, the division of labor
among, and delineation among, the modules in our mind is much
less clear-cut than the word *modules* suggests, and the extent of interaction among them is greater than the word suggests. So if you'd
rather use a word like *networks* or *systems*, feel free.

3. *The modules aren't like departments in a company's organization
   chart.* Maybe this goes without saying, given what I've just noted
   about how fluidly interactive and overlapping the modules are, and
   given that the whole context for this discussion is that our minds
   lack a CEO. Still, it's worth dwelling on how utterly unlike the
   idealized working of a corporation the operation of the mind is.
   Among the traits modules often lack are obedience and harmony.
   Yes, the modules may sometimes collaborate, but they sometimes
   compete, and they can compete fiercely. Someone once did a series of jokey organization charts for major corporations, and Microsoft, famous for its infighting, was depicted as a circular firing
   squad. Our minds aren't *that* torn by internal strife, but they're
   sometimes as close to that as to Microsoft's official organization
   chart. Gazzaniga, the split-brain experiment pioneer, has written,
   "While hierarchical processing takes place within the modules, it

is looking like there is no hierarchy among the modules. All these modules are not reporting to a department head—it is a free-for-all, self-organizing system."

There's a little tension in that last sentence. "Free-for-all" and "self-organizing system" have different connotations. Then again, the two terms don't have to be applied to the mind at the same time. Sometimes the mind feels like a free-for-all, and sometimes it feels more organized, as if the free-for-all has been resolved. What's more, the sense of organization is sometimes misleading, because the free-for-alls can happen at a subconscious level and can get resolved at that level. "Whichever notion you happened to be conscious of at a particular moment is the one that comes bubbling up, the one that becomes dominant," writes Gazzaniga. "It's a dog-eat-dog world going on in your brain, with different systems competing to make it to the surface to win the prize of conscious recognition."

When Gazzaniga talks about the "dog-eat-dog world" inside your head, he isn't just talking about the obvious Dr. Jekyll–Mr. Hyde kind of internal struggle between the you who wants to eat a doughnut (or maybe even steal a doughnut!) and the you who counsels restraint. In fact, with *that* kind of struggle, the conflict *itself* is often part of consciousness. We'll get into that kind of intermodular struggle in a later chapter, when I address the problem commonly known as "self-control." Gazzaniga is talking more about struggles that get resolved at an unconscious or barely conscious level. The things I pay attention to, the stories I tell about the things I pay attention to, the stories I tell about myself—all these result from choices getting made, and "I," the conscious "I," the thing I think of as my self, am by and large not making the choices.

It's almost enough to make you wonder whether the thing you think of as your self deserves that label! Kurzban has written, "In the end, if it's true that your brain consists of many, many little modules with various functions, and if only a small number of them are conscious, then there might not be any particular reason to consider some of them to be 'you' or 'really you' or your 'self' or maybe anything else particularly special." When Kurzban wrote that—in a book called *Why Everyone (Else) Is a Hypocrite: Evolution and the Modular Mind*—he wasn't conversant with the Buddhist idea of not-self. But millennia after that idea arose, science had steered him toward it.

I'd take issue with Kurzban's suggestion that the conscious mind isn't "special." The conscious mind is special, I'd argue, because it's, well, conscious. As such, it can feel pleasure and pain, joy and sadness. The capacity for feeling, and for subjective experience in general, is what gives life meaning and what gives valence to moral questions. If you imagine a planet full of humanlike robots, incapable of subjective experience, would there be anything obviously wrong about destroying them, or anything obviously good about creating more of them?

Still, the conscious mind—the conscious "self"—isn't special in the way we commonly assume it's special. It's not calling as many of the shots as we think it is. It's less like a president than like the speaker of the US House of Representatives, who presides over votes and announces the outcome but doesn't control the votes. Of course, the speaker of the House may do some behind-the-scenes nudging and so exert some influence over the votes. And we can't rule out the possibility that the conscious mind gets to do some nudging here and there.

Indeed, you may find it useful to think of meditation as a process that takes a conscious mind that gets to do a little nudging and turns it into something that can do a lot of nudging—maybe even turns it into something more like a president than a speaker of the House. And you may, to that end, find it useful to understand how the brain determines which module is in charge at any given moment. That's the question we'll focus on in the next chapter.

7

The Mental Modules That
Run Your Life

When I was a freshman in college, I learned that I had an intertemporal utility function. This wasn't a diagnosis; "intertemporal utility function" isn't a malady. It's something everybody has. It's an equation that describes, roughly speaking, your willingness to delay gratification—your willingness to forgo something you like in order to have more of that something later.

So, for example, I might be willing to give up $100 in wages today if I could be guaranteed that I'd get $125 a year from now. But my friend, whose intertemporal utility function is calibrated differently, might demand $150 a year from now in exchange for giving up $100 now.

This is also called "time discounting." People tend to "discount" the future in the sense of feeling that getting $100 a year from now isn't as good as getting $100 today. In the example above, my friend discounts the future more steeply than I do.

Anyway, according to the models presented in my economics class, however my intertemporal utility function was calibrated—however steep my time discounting—it would stay that way tomorrow and next week and next month and next year. My discount rate was said to be a firm and enduring feature of my psychology.

I think the Buddha would have been skeptical of this claim. He tended not to see things as enduring—certainly not things that are part of a person's psychology. I think if he had been my college classmate, he would have stood up during an econ lecture and said, "What do you think of this, O monks? Are mental formations permanent or impermanent?"

Actually, he might not have been quite that disruptive. But according to Buddhist scripture, he did say that very thing in another setting. It was during one of his not-self sermons. In fact, it was during his very first and most famous discourse on not-self, the one we looked at in chapter 5. In that chapter and chapter 6, I focused mainly on only one part of the Buddha's basic not-self argument: the idea that the "five aggregates" are not under your control; they do not, as he later put it, bear the relationship to you that a king's domain bears to a king.

The other big part of the Buddha's not-self argument, the part I touched on only lightly, was about flux, impermanence. After he asks the monks "Are mental formations permanent or impermanent?" he gets the predictable reply: "Impermanent, O Lord."

Well, the Buddha goes on to ask, does it make sense to say of impermanent things "they are mine, this I am, this is my self"?

"Indeed, not that, O Lord."

The Buddha then goes through the same drill with the other four aggregates. He insists, in each case, that something subject to change shouldn't be thought of as part of the self. He doesn't explicitly say why.[†] And to provide the fullest explanation, we'd need to delve into ideas about the self that were circulating in his day. But certainly, leaving his intellectual context aside, there's a kind of commonsense appeal to his argument: We do tend to think of the self—the inner, real me—as something enduring, something that persists even as we grow from children to adults to senior citizens.

But in fact, of course, we change. And we don't just change in the sense of changing from children into adults. We change on a moment-by-moment basis. And sometimes we change along dimensions that are commonly thought to be constants.

Which brings us back to my intertemporal utility function. Psychologists have found that if you show men pictures of women they find attractive, their intertemporal utility function, the rate at which they discount the future, changes. They become less willing to forgo cash in the near term—yes, the experimenters offered them real money—for a bigger amount of cash farther down the road.

Why would someone's basic financial philosophy change after looking at pictures of women? We'll get to that. But here's a clue: it seems to involve the mental modules discussed in the previous chapter. More broadly, the psychological flux, the impermanence, that in Buddhist thought calls into question the existence of the self can be described partly as the workings of those modules. Seeing things in these terms helps illuminate a core paradox of Buddhist meditation practice: accepting that your self isn't in control, and may in some sense not even exist, can put your self—or something like it—in control.

This time-discounting experiment belongs to a genre of experiments in which psychologists manipulate people's states of mind and then see how their inclinations change. Often the takeaway is the same as it was in this experiment: something you might have thought was a pretty firm feature of a person's mind is in fact not so firm.

For example: Do you tend to follow the crowd or take the road less traveled? Correct answer: It depends! A study in the *Journal of Marketing Research* suggested ways for advertisers to increase their impact by matching their sales pitch to its media context. The experimenters showed different subjects clips from different movies, either the terrifying movie *The Shining* or the romantic movie *Before Sunrise*. People in each group then saw one of two ads for an art museum. In the first ad the pitch line was "Visited by over a Million People Each Year." In the second the pitch line was "Stand Out from the Crowd."

People who had been watching *The Shining* felt more favorably about the museum, and more inclined to visit it, when given the first pitch, presumably because a state of fear inclines you to see crowds as safe havens. People who had been watching *Before Sunrise* had the opposite reaction, perhaps because feeling romantic inclines you toward a more intimate environment.

This may not seem earthshaking. We all know that we behave differently when in different moods, so it stands to reason that putting us in a romantic mood would change our behavior. But the people who did this study don't think that the "moods" paradigm is the best one to use here. Douglas Kenrick and Vladas Griskevicius, two of the psychologists who collaborated on the study, see us each as having multiple "subselves"—or modules, as Kenrick sometimes calls them—and they think that in this case which movie you watch determines which subself, or module, controls your reaction to the ad. The romantic movie puts your "mate-acquisition" module in charge. The scary movie puts your "self-protection" module in charge.

I can imagine the Buddha liking this kind of language. The alternative way of describing the situation—saying that "I" act differently when in different "moods"—is just a way of evading the question he seems to have been asking: If you have different preferences from one moment to the next, then in what sense is it the same "you" from moment to moment? Isn't this image of you exchanging one mood for another just a way of covering up the fact that today's you and tomorrow's you aren't really the same you?

We could argue that one all day. But it's worth noting that over the past two decades a fair number of psychologists have come to agree with Kenrick and Griskevicius—and Kurzban and Gazzaniga from the previous chapter—that the dynamics of the mind are well captured by a modular model. In this view, if you built a robot whose brain worked like the human brain, and then asked computer scientists to describe its workings, they'd say that its brain consists of lots of partly overlapping modules, and modules within modules, and the robot's circumstances determine which modules are, for the moment, running the show. These computer scientists would have trouble pointing to a part of the robot's programming and saying, "This part is the robot itself."

The closest thing to a self would be the algorithm that determines which circumstances put which modules in charge. And that algorithm can't be what we mean by the "conscious self" in humans—the CEO self—because humans don't consciously decide to go into romantic mode or fearful mode. Indeed, if a psychologist told experimental subjects that they'd responded to a movie by changing their reactions to ad pitches, or that they'd responded to pictures of women by changing their time-discounting rate, they'd probably be surprised.

So if the conscious self isn't the thing that changes our channels, putting a new module in charge, what is? Well, the activation of modules is closely associated with feelings. *The Shining* makes you feel fearful, and this fear seems to have played a role in activating the self-protection module, with its tendency to seek shelter in a crowd. *Before Sunrise* activates feelings of romance, and these feelings seem to have invoked the mate-acquisition module, with its inclination toward intimacy.

This idea—that modules are triggered by feelings—sheds new light on the connection between two fundamental parts of Buddhism: the idea of nonattachment to feelings and the idea of not-self. We've already seen one kind of connection: when you let go of a feeling by viewing it mindfully, you're letting go of something you had previously considered part of your self; you are chipping away at the self, bit by bit. But now we see that calling this a "chipping away" may understate the magnitude of what you're doing. Feelings aren't just little parts of the thing you had thought of as the self; they are closer to its core; they are doing what you had thought "you" were doing: calling the shots. It's feelings that "decide" which module will be in charge for the time being, and it's modules that then decide what you'll actually do during that time. In this light, it becomes a bit clearer why losing attachment to feelings could help you reach a point where there seems to be no self.

Jealousy: Tyrant of the Mind

Sometimes the feeling-module connection is so powerful as to be unmistakable: the feeling itself is overwhelming, and the module it invokes is plainly transformative. Consider sexual jealousy, as analyzed by Leda Cosmides and John Tooby. Cosmides and Tooby, who did as much as anyone to lay the foundations of evolutionary psychology in the 1980s and 1990s, were early and influential advocates of a modular view of the mind. As their thinking developed, they took up the question of how mental modules are connected to emotions. They concluded that what emotions do—what emotions are *for*—is to activate and coordinate the modular functions that are, in Darwinian terms, appropriate for the moment. (This isn't, of course, to say that these functions are appropriate in moral terms, or even that they serve the welfare of the person they steer, but just that they helped our ancestors spread genes.) Tooby and Cosmides used jealousy as an example:

> The emotion of sexual jealousy constitutes an organized mode of operation specifically designed to deploy the programs governing each psychological mechanism so that each is poised to deal with the exposed infidelity. Physiological processes are prepared for such things as violence. . . . The goal of deterring, injuring, or murdering the rival emerges; the goal of punishing, deterring, or deserting the mate appears; the desire

to make oneself more competitively attractive to alternative mates emerges; memory is activated to re-analyze the past; confident assessments of the past are transformed into doubts; the general estimate of the reliability and trustworthiness of the opposite sex (or indeed everyone) may decline; associated shame programs may be triggered to search for situations in which the individual can publicly demonstrate acts of violence or punishment that work to counteract an (imagined or real) social perception of weakness; and so on.

That's a lot of stuff! Indeed, it's so much stuff—so much change in a person's attitude, focus, disposition—that you might say a whole new self has emerged and seized control of the mind. In the seventeenth century, John Dryden wrote a poem titled "Jealousy: Tyrant of the Mind"—and that is indeed the way it works; jealousy is, for a time at least, your mind's unquestioned ruler. Certainly anyone who has been in a jealous rage can attest that, whoever was in charge of your behavior at that moment, it wasn't the ordinary you.

The feeling of jealousy is so powerful that it may be hard to imagine resisting it. But resistance, strictly speaking, isn't the mindful way of dealing with jealousy anyway. Rather the idea would be to observe the feeling mindfully as it begins to emerge and so never become firmly attached to it. If you don't yield to attachment—if you don't, as the Buddha might say, let your consciousness become "engaged" with the feeling—then the jealousy module presumably won't be activated. Observing feelings without attachment is the way you keep modules from seizing control of your consciousness. Easier said than done, I know.

Should you succeed in severing your attachment to jealousy, this needn't leave you incapable of dealing with the situation. You can still reflect on the fact of your mate's infidelity and decide whether it means you should end your relationship. But without surrendering to jealousy, you'll be better able to determine whether the infidelity *is* a fact, better able to decide on a wise course of action, and, in any event, less likely to kill somebody.

Again, jealousy is a particularly dramatic example of a module's seizing control of the mind. Whenever people are throwing things and screaming, that's a tipoff that the brain is under new management. And even when jealousy isn't in its rage phase, it has a conspicuously obsessive quality, compelling your mind to take particular trains of thought over and over.

But even subtler emotions, with less obvious effects, can bring enough little changes to usher in a whole new frame of mind. Consider, again, the experiment in which watching a romantic movie made people crowd-averse. This reaction by itself is hardly transformative, but then again, "by itself" isn't the way it happens; it's one of various changes ushered in by the triggering of what Kenrick and Griskevicius call the "mate-acquisition subself."

Which brings us back to the intertemporal utility function and, specifically, the fact that men who see women they consider attractive tend to discount the future more steeply than they did only moments earlier. What is going on here? Is this another part of the hypothesized mate-acquisition module?

Margo Wilson and Martin Daly, who conducted this time-discounting study (and who, like Tooby and Cosmides, were pioneers in evolutionary psychology), were inspired to do the experiment by their reflections on the history of our species. There is good reason to believe that during evolution men with access to resources (such as food) and with high social status were better able to attract mates. So if there is indeed a mate-acquisition module, you'd expect it to feature the following algorithm: men who see signs of a near-term courtship opportunity take advantage of any near-term resource acquisition opportunities, even if that means forgoing more distant opportunities. They want their resources—which, in a modern environment, means cash—now.

Of course, the men in these experiments didn't see real mating opportunities; they just saw pictures of women. But in the ancestral environment there weren't photographs, so any realistic image of a woman would have signified the actual presence of a woman. That's why the minds of the men in this experiment could be "fooled" by mere pictures, even though the men "knew," at a conscious level, that these women weren't available. So this experiment is, among other things, another reminder that modules can get triggered not only without the conscious self doing the triggering but also without it having a clue as to the Darwinian logic behind the triggering.

Time discounting isn't the only psychological feature that, in mate-acquisition mode, can turn out to be more fluid than you might imagine. You'd think that people's career aspirations, though obviously subject to *some* change over time, wouldn't do a lot of moment-by-moment fluctuating. But apparently they do. In one study, psychologists had men fill out surveys about their career plans; some filled them out in a room where women were also filling out forms, and some filled them out in an all-male room. Men placed in the presence of women, it turned out, were more inclined to rate the accumulation of wealth as an important goal.

This may not have signified an actual shift in their aspirations. Maybe the mate-acquisition module wasn't changing long-term plans but was just briefly activating a "self-advertisement" submodule. In other words, maybe the presence of women prepares the mind of a heterosexual man to wow them by sharing bold plans for future wealth, regardless of how realistic the plans are or how long the boldness will last. But if so, the men's conscious selves don't seem to be privy to this strategic logic. After all, these men were conveying these bold plans via a questionnaire they had no reason to believe the women would read.

We're back to the moral of the split-brain experiments: people are capable of convincing themselves of whatever stories about their own motivation it's in their interest (or their "interest" as defined by natural selection) to tell others. Only these aren't split-brain patients; these are anatomically normal human beings, governed by a mind as it naturally works. Or, at least, governed by the part of the mind that's in charge at that moment.

So we have three things that can change about people who sense a mating opportunity: they can become crowd-averse, suddenly partial to intimate environments; their intertemporal utility function can get recalibrated; and their career goals, at least for the time being, can become more materialistic.[†] These three changes hardly exhaust the list of things that can happen to a person's mind in mating mode. But already you can see why it's tempting to think that a module—or a "subself," as Kenrick and Griskevicius put it—takes control of the mind when people are in the presence of a potential mate who strikes them as attractive.

Messy Modules

At the same time, we should stay mindful of the mind's messiness and not get overly enamored of the modular metaphor. And Kenrick and Griskevicius sometimes sound pretty enamored. They divide the mind neatly into seven "subselves" with the following missions: self-protection, mate attraction, mate retention, affiliation (making and keeping friends), kin care, social status, and disease avoidance. This taxonomy has its virtues; these seven areas of mental functioning no doubt got a lot of emphasis from natural selection as it designed the mind. Still, you don't have to look at this list for long before you are reminded that drawing clean lines between modules is hard.

For example, when the men in that career survey study gilded their career goals, that could be described as trying to attract a mate, but it could also be described as elevating their status in the eyes of a potential mate; moreover, it's the kind of thing they might do to elevate their status in the eyes of someone who *isn't* a potential mate. So should we think of the mate-acquisition module as having a "social status" sub-module? Or should we think of the mate-acquisition module as borrowing some functionality that resides in the separate "social status" module that Kenrick and Griskevicius posit? This kind of conundrum is one reason I warned against thinking of the mind as a Swiss Army knife or a smartphone.

Another problem with the smartphone metaphor is that shifting among modules can be subtler than switching from one app to another. Though "mate-acquisition mode" sounds like a pretty distinct thing, the feeling that triggers it needn't be nearly as dramatic as the feeling that triggers jealousy. There may be no inkling of love or lust; there may be just a sense of heightened attraction and interest. Nor is the ensuing state of mind typically as jarring as a jealous state of mind. Still, it is a distinct state of mind, and it is brought on by a feeling.

If, in light of the misleading neatness of the module metaphor, you prefer the phrase I just used—"state of mind"—to "module that's taken control," that's fine. Either way, two take-home lessons hold: (1) This isn't a state of mind that the conscious "self" "chooses" to enter; rather, the state is triggered by a feeling, and the conscious "self," though it in principle has access to the feeling, may not notice it or notice that a new state *has* been entered. (So much for the idea of the conscious you as CEO.) (2) You can see why the Buddha emphasized how fluid, how impermanent, the various parts of the mind are, and why he considered this flux relevant to the not-self argument; if the self is supposed to be some unchanging essence, it's pretty hard to imagine where exactly that self would be amid the ongoing transitions from state of mind to state of mind.

Indeed, if there is something that qualifies as a constant amid the flux, something that really *does* endure, essentially unchanged, through time, that something is an illusion: the illusion that there is a CEO, a king, and that "I"—the conscious I—am it. We saw in the previous chapter that this illusion makes sense in evolutionary terms. The conscious I is the I that speaks, the I that communicates with the world, so it gets access to perspectives whose purpose is to be shared with the world. These perspectives include the sense that there is an executive self, and that it is a pretty damn effective and upstanding executive self at that! In this chapter we've seen how that conscious mind, in addition to hosting this one persistent illusion, also gets access to other, more transient illusions—about career ambitions, say—depending on which feeling puts which module in charge and what perspective that module wants to share with the world.

It may seem that such illusions aren't worth getting up in arms about. What's wrong with men and women indulging in self-delusion in the course of trying to impress each other? Nothing, I guess. Some illusions are harmless, and some are even beneficial. Far be it from me to try to talk you out of all your illusions. By and large, my philosophy is *Live and let live*: if you're enjoying the Matrix, go crazy.

Except, maybe, when your illusions harm other people in your life or contribute to larger problems in the world. And that can happen. Being in self-protection mode, for example, does more than just give us an attraction to crowds. In one study, men who watched part of a scary film (*The Silence of the Lambs*) and were then shown photos of men from a different ethnic group rated their facial expressions as much angrier than did men who hadn't seen a scary film.

Of course, you can imagine this kind of illusion, this exaggeration of menace, coming in handy. If you're walking through an unfamiliar neighborhood, erring on the side of caution by exiting the neighborhood may conceivably pay off. On the other hand, this tendency to exaggerate the hostility of certain kinds of strangers could keep you from having a constructively friendly interaction with someone of a different ethnicity. What's more, the stakes are sometimes higher than the fate of one person walking through an unfamiliar neighborhood. Politicians activate this same mental tendency to get us to "overread" threats in ways that lead to war or ethnic antagonism.

And as for the mate-acquisition module, it doesn't just encourage us to get away from the crowd and find an intimate bistro; it structures the conversation that takes place in that bistro. It may, for example, encourage us to say unflattering things about any perceived rivals for the affection of the person across the table. And this deflation of rivals is no closer to the truth than the self-inflation that is also high on the agenda for that particular conversation. But the deflation is heartfelt; we tend to believe the bad publicity we give rivals, the better to spread it.

The Buddha seems to have seen this dynamic clearly. A scripture attributed to him reads:

> *The senses' evidence,*
> *And works, inspire such scorn*
> *For others, and such smug*
> *Conviction he is right,*
> *That all his rivals rank*
> *As "sorry, brainless fools."*

So what do we do about all this? If our mind keeps getting seized by different modules, and each module carries with it different illusions, how do we change the situation? The answer isn't simple, but what should already be clear is that getting more control over the situation may have something to do with feelings. A link between feelings and illusion was somewhat apparent back in chapter 3, when I noted that some feelings are in one sense or another "false," so getting some critical distance from them can clarify things. But the case against being enthralled by our feelings only grows when you realize that their connection to illusion can be described in a second way. Feelings don't just bring specific, fleeting illusions; they can usher in a whole mindset and so alter for some time a range of perceptions and proclivities, for better or worse.

Buddhist thought and modern psychology converge on this point:

in human life as it's ordinarily lived, there is no one self, no conscious CEO, that runs the show; rather, there seem to be a series of selves that take turns running the show—and, in a sense, *seizing* control of the show. If the way they seize control of the show is through feelings, it stands to reason that one way to change the show is to change the role feelings play in everyday life. I'm not aware of a better way to do that than mindfulness meditation.

8

How Thoughts Think
Themselves

You know the old saying about Zen meditation, Tibetan meditation, and Vipassana meditation? Well, no, you probably don't. It's a saying that's meant to capture the difference between these three Buddhist contemplative traditions—Vipassana, with its emphasis on mindfulness; Tibetan, which often steers the mind toward visual imagery; and Zen, which sometimes involves pondering those cryptic lines known as koans. Here's the saying: Zen is for poets, Tibetan is for artists, and Vipassana is for psychologists.

Like most stereotypes, this one exaggerates contrasts, but it does contain a valid point: Mindfulness meditation, the main vehicle of Vipassana, is a good way to study the human mind. At least, it's a good way to study *one* human's mind: yours. You sit down, let the mental dust settle, and then watch your mind work.

Strictly speaking, of course, this isn't what psychologists do. Psychology is a science, and sciences, by definition, generate publicly observable data, experimental results that are out there for all to see. In contrast, the things you see when you watch your mind can't be seen by anyone but you. They're not data in the strict sense, so when you're meditating you're not being an experimental psychologist. If you emerge from a meditative state and declare that the self doesn't exist, that's not scientific evidence that the self doesn't exist.

No, if anything, the relationship between science and meditation works the other way around. It's not that meditative observations about your mind validate theories, but more that theories can help validate meditative observations about your mind. If during meditation you see things that are consistent with credible scientific models of how the mind works, that gives you a bit more reason to believe that, indeed, meditation is helping you see the dynamics of your mind clearly.

Take the modular model of the mind, for example. There is good scientific reason to take it seriously. Well, if this modular model is truly an accurate picture of the mind, and if Vipassana meditation—insight meditation—indeed gives us insights into the workings of the mind, then you might expect this kind of meditation to give us glimpses of a modular mind at work.

I think it does. I think some of the experiences people have during mindfulness meditation make particular sense in light of a modular model of the mind. And I'm not just talking about epic experiences—epiphanies you might have after months of seclusion and meditation, such as the sudden realization that there's no self in there. I'm also talking about experiential steps on the meditative path that might eventually lead to such epiphanies but are much more common.

One of these steps is the most widely shared meditative experience of all: finding it really hard to meditate because your mind refuses to stay in one place. As I've already suggested, to see that your mind is wandering is to see part of what the Buddha meant when he challenged conventional conceptions of the self; if a CEO-self existed, then presumably the mind would obey its commands and focus on the breath when told to. Now we're in a position to go further and see that observing your mind in this unruly stage—trying to watch it as the default mode network rages on—can do more than suggest that the conscious "you" isn't running the show; it can shed light on what *is* running the show, revealing a picture of the mind strikingly consistent with the modular model.

To see what I mean, just follow these four easy steps: (1) sit down on a cushion; (2) try to focus on your breath; (3) (this step is the easiest) fail to focus on your breath for very long; (4) notice what *kinds* of thoughts are making you fail. These thoughts can vary depending on your age and other factors, but some good examples of common mind wandering would be:

1. Imagining what it would be like to go on a date with the attractive man or woman you met at your workplace—maybe imagining the witty or endearing things you'd say, the way you'd impress him or her.

2. Reflecting on the encounter you had with him or her yesterday, and wondering if his or her words signified what you hope they signified.

3. Reflecting on an encounter in which a rival subtly dissed you.

4. Briefly indulging in a revenge fantasy in which said rival suffers a public embarrassment that reveals to all his or her baseness and unworthiness.

5. Imagining what it's going to be like when you get home and have the beer you so richly deserve after a hard day of fantasizing about the demise of rivals.

6. Reminiscing about that great approach shot you hit on the eighteenth hole yesterday and recalling how impressed your playing partners rightly were—not to mention the casually witty remark you made afterward and the laughter it elicited.

7. Worrying about the PowerPoint presentation you've got to give tomorrow.

8. Worrying about your daughter in preschool or feeling guilty about not having called your aging mother yesterday.

9. Being annoyed that your so-called friend couldn't do you a favor of the sort you routinely do for him or her.

10. Looking forward to the upcoming dinner with another friend at which you can vent about the first "friend." And so on.

There are three recurring themes here. First, these thoughts involve the past and future, not the present; the one thing you're not doing while having these thoughts is paying attention to what's actually going on in the real world at this moment. Second, all of these thoughts involve you. By default, we think mainly self-referential thoughts. This is unsurprising, given that natural selection designed the brain to focus on our interests (at least, our "interests" as natural selection defined them). Third, most of these thoughts involve other people. This too is unsurprising, given what social animals people are. Indeed, it turns out there's a fair amount of overlap between the default mode network and what brain scans have identified as the "theory of mind network"—the part of the brain involved in thinking about what other people are thinking.

There's also a fourth theme here, a fourth thing that almost all of these mental meanderings have in common. Can you spot it?

Hint: What were the previous two chapters of this book about? Exactly! Modules! Though the trains of thought that carry you away from direct experience can take you to lots of different places, pretty much all of those places seem to lie within the province of one of the sort of mental modules I've already described. Which is to say, modules that make perfect sense in evolutionary terms: modules that deal with attracting mates, keeping them, enhancing your status (which can mean derogating rivals), taking care of kin, tending to your friendships (which includes making sure they are reciprocal and that you're not getting exploited), and so on.

The one glaring exception—the one thought in the list above that doesn't seem to fit naturally into a major module—is number 5: looking forward to that beer you so richly deserve. Presumably, evolution didn't build a "beer-drinking module" into us. But beer, like many other recreational drugs, is an invention that circumvents evolution's logic: it taps directly into the reward center that normally would be activated more arduously, by doing things that helped our ancestors spread their genes.

When your mind is wandering, it may feel like, well, like your mind is wandering—like it's strolling along the landscape of modules and sampling them, indulging one module for a while, then eventually moving on to another one. But another way to describe it is to say that, actually, the different modules are competing for your attention, and when the mind "wanders" from one module to another, what's actually happening is that the second module has acquired enough strength to wrestle control of your consciousness away from the first module.

Far be it from me to insist that you accept one or the other of these ways of looking at mind wandering. For now I'd just make two points: (1) Psychologists who adhere to the modular model of the mind tend toward the second view—the idea that the conscious you isn't choosing modules so much as being commandeered by modules that have prevailed over competing modules and thus, as Gazzaniga put it in chapter 6, "won the prize of conscious recognition." (2) If you do go on a Vipassana meditation retreat and slowly, haltingly, get better at focusing on your breath, you will probably lean increasingly toward the second hypothesis: it will seem more and more like your mind isn't wandering within its own terrain so much as being hijacked by intruders.

And eventually these won't seem so much like hijackings as attempted hijackings. Thoughts will arise, but they won't hold your attention for quite so long before you return to your breath; they'll fail to carry you away; the train will pull into the station, and you'll watch it leave without ever getting on it.

Actually, I shouldn't have written that last sentence with such authority—as if I often watch, with utter detachment, whole trains of thought pull into the station and then leave. My typical experience is more like getting on the train and then, after it's left the station and is picking up speed, realizing I don't want to be on it and jumping off.

This has been something of a frustration for me. On the one hand, I've gotten reasonably good at viewing my *feelings* with some objectivity—actually watching them arise as if I were watching some character walk on stage. (At least, I'm pretty good at this while meditating; in everyday life my record is more mixed.) But I find it harder to view my *thoughts* with such detachment. To put my problem another way: Remember when Gazzaniga said that the thought you're conscious of at any given moment is the thought that comes "bubbling up"? Well, I've had trouble seeing the "bubbling up" part. So if you want a vivid description of that, you should listen to someone other than me. Joseph Goldstein, for example.

In 1975, Goldstein, along with Sharon Salzberg and Jack Kornfield, cofounded the Insight Meditation Society, where I did my first meditation retreat back in 2003. All three had traveled to Asia as young adults; all three encountered Vipassana teachings there; and all three have become important figures in Western Buddhism, teaching and writing prolifically. Goldstein's seminal 1976 book, *The Experience of Insight*, makes him a good person to talk to about, well, the experience of insight. Once I pressed him to describe what it's like to watch your thoughts with detachment (or, as he prefers to put it, with nonattachment).

What It's Like to Watch Your Thoughts

One way to get the idea, Goldstein said, is to "imagine that every thought that's arising in your mind is coming from the person next to you." How would you be relating to these thoughts then? His point was that you wouldn't be identifying with them. "The thought itself is appearing and disappearing like a sound, but being identified with it is something we're adding."

I asked, "So, then, in meditation there can be the sense that thoughts are just kind of coming out of nowhere, so to speak, almost like voices?"

"Yeah," he answered.

I'm always happy to help sane people not sound like they're crazy, so I added, "Although it's not like you're hearing things . . . literally?"

"Yeah, correct."

I liked where this was heading. He seemed to be saying that thoughts, which we normally think of as emanating from the conscious self, are actually directed *toward* what we think of as the conscious self, after which we embrace the thoughts as belonging to that self. This, in turn, seemed consistent with the idea that modules generate thoughts outside of consciousness and somehow inject them into consciousness. So I pressed the point.

"Let me see if I have this right. During meditation, you can begin to see that . . . whereas you might have thought all your life that you're thinking thoughts—the thing you think of as 'you' is thinking thoughts—it's closer to being the case that the thoughts try to capture you, the thing you think of as 'you.'"

"Right."

"They come from somewhere in your body, somewhere in your brain."

"Yes."

So far so good. But then I pressed the point too far for Goldstein's taste. I said, "But whatever part of the brain or body you think of as you is more like the captive of the thoughts; the thoughts try to reach out and grab that—"

"That's kind of an interesting way to describe it, and it certainly feels like that. But I would phrase it a little differently. It's just that the thoughts are arising and there's a strong habit of mind to be identified with them. So it's not so much they have the *intent* to reach out and capture us, but rather there's this very strong habitual identification. This is how we've lived our lives, and it takes practice to try to break this conditioning, to be mindful of the thought rather than be lost in it."

This last point, this idea that identifying with our thoughts is a habit that arose through "conditioning," is one I'd quibble with. I think some of our more generic illusions—including, perhaps, the idea that "we" generate our thoughts—are pretty deeply built into us by natural selection; though they're influenced by life experiences, they're on balance closer to being instincts than bad habits, which explains why uprooting them is so hard.

But I digress. The essence of Goldstein's qualification I accept. I hadn't meant that thoughts literally *try* to capture our attention.

In fact, the modular model of the mind has led me to attribute less agency to thoughts than some meditation teachers do. Though these teachers are inclined to say that "thoughts think themselves," strictly speaking, I'd say *modules* think thoughts. Or rather, modules generate thoughts, and then if those thoughts prove in some sense stronger than the creations of competing modules, they become *thought* thoughts—that is, they enter consciousness. Still, you can see how, while observing the mind during meditation, it could seem like "thoughts think themselves"—because the modules do their work outside of consciousness, so, as far as the conscious mind can tell, the thoughts are coming out of nowhere.

Anyway, the main point these meditation teachers are making is the same as the upshot of the modular-mind model: the conscious self doesn't create thoughts; it *receives* them. And that reception, it seems, is the part of the process Goldstein had observed with much more objectivity and clarity than I'd been able to muster—the part when the thoughts enter conscious awareness, the part when they "bubble up."

After conveying to Goldstein that I hadn't meant that thoughts actually harbor a desire to capture our awareness, I asked whether, nonetheless, they sometimes seem like active things, not passive things. "In other words," I said, "they're actors in your consciousness that you've got to deal with, and you're in the habit of going along with them, but that's not necessary."

"Correct. And they become a lot less active when we see them for what they are. When we're not pulled into the drama of them. It's sort of like going to the movies. We go to the movies and there's a very absorbing story and we're pulled into the story and we feel so many emotions . . . excited, afraid, in love. . . . And then we sit back and see these are just pixels of light projected on a screen. Everything we thought is happening is not really happening. It's the same way with our thoughts. We get caught up in the story, in the drama of them, forgetting their essentially insubstantial nature."

Escaping this drama—seeing your thoughts as passing before you rather than emanating from you—can carry you closer to the not-self experience, to that moment when you "see" that there is no "you" in there doing the thinking or doing anything else, that moment when what seems like a metaphysical truth is unveiled. But, as we saw in chapter 5, some people say that the Buddha's original not-self teaching is best seen not as a metaphysical truth but as a pragmatic strategy: regardless of whether a self exists, by jettisoning parts of what you think of as your self, you clarify your view of the world and become a better and happier person. And this pragmatic strategy of not-self, no less than the metaphysical discovery of not-self, would seem to be furthered by the kind of perspective Goldstein was describing.

As he put it, "When we have that basis of wisdom about the nature of thought, then we have more power to choose, okay, which thoughts are healthy . . . which thoughts are not so healthy—those we can let go."

So far, then, Vipassana meditation looks pretty good in light of the modular model of the mind. And it looks good at two very different stages on the meditative path: that first time on a cushion, when focusing on your breath seems hopeless, thanks to the intrusion of thoughts; and much later on the path, when, like Goldstein, you've acquired the ability to watch thoughts bubble into consciousness, sit there inertly, and then evaporate without carrying your mind away. In the first case—while struggling to focus—you see thoughts capture you, and in the second case you see them fail to capture you, but in both cases you realize that the thoughts aren't coming from "you," from your conscious self. So both experiences make sense if thoughts are in fact propelled into consciousness by modules that are themselves beyond the reach of conscious awareness. In other words: if the modular model is correct, then the view of thoughts afforded us by meditation is truer than the everyday, unreflective view, the view that has thoughts emanating from a CEO self.

And this isn't the end of the validation that Vipassana meditation gets from the modular model. Just as the mindful view of thoughts makes sense in light of this model, so does the mindful view of feelings. As we've seen, in the modular model, feelings are the things that give a module temporary control of the show. You see someone who inspires feelings of attraction, and suddenly you're in mate-acquisition mode, seeking intimacy, being exquisitely considerate, maybe showing off, and in other ways becoming a different person. You see a bitter rival, and the ensuing feelings lead you to seek something different from intimacy (though showing off, depending on the circumstance, may still be in order). It stands to reason that if these *feelings*—of attraction and affection, of rivalrous dislike—didn't get purchase in the first place, the corresponding modules wouldn't seize control. So one of the ideas behind mindfulness meditation—that gaining a kind of critical distance from your feelings can give you more control over which you is you at any given moment—makes perfect sense in light of the modular model of the mind.

What Fuel Propels Thoughts?

There's a subtler, more fine-grained, and, I admit, more speculative connection between the mindful view of feelings and the modular model of the mind. The first step to seeing it is to pay really close attention while you're meditating. I'm tempted to change that last sentence to read "pay really close attention while you're *failing* to meditate," because the part of meditation I'm talking about is the part when you can't focus on your breath because thoughts keep intruding. But if you're paying close attention to this "failure" to meditate, then, of course, it isn't a failure to meditate—because paying attention to whatever is happening *is* mindfulness meditation.

Anyway, here's what I've noticed about thoughts that intrude when I'm trying to focus on my breath: they often seem to have feelings attached to them. What's more, their ability to hold my attention—in other words, to keep me enthralled, to keep me from *noticing* that they're holding my attention—seems to depend on the strength of those feelings. If you don't believe me, just sit down, close your eyes, focus on your breath, and then, once you start failing to focus on your breath (which shouldn't take long!), try to focus on the things that are keeping you from focusing on your breath. And I don't mean just focus on whatever thought is distracting you—I mean see if you can detect some feeling that is linked to the thought that is distracting you.

Sometimes this connection between thought and feeling is obvious because the feelings are so strong, even primordial. If you're thinking about sleeping with your neighbor's spouse, or worried that your spouse is sleeping with your neighbor, or fantasizing about giving that neighbor what he or she deserves for sleeping with a neighbor's spouse, then the associated feelings—lust, jealousy, vengeance—are too raw and powerful to overlook.

But even many of the less obviously animal, more "human" meanderings of mind have feelings pretty obviously associated with them. You reflect on a recent social triumph—maybe a well-received joke you told—and it feels *good*, so you keep reflecting for a while, and maybe you imagine how you could have followed it up with a witty coda and vow to throw in the coda next time. You're pondering an important deadline you seem likely to miss, and you feel worried—and the worry keeps you fixated on the impending debacle until you come up with a plan of action or convince yourself the deadline's not so important anyway, after which the worry fades and the thought fades with it.

Even that most cerebral of mind wanderings—wondering—seems to have feelings that accompany it. If I've sat down to meditate and I find myself indulging my curiosity about something—pondering some puzzle—and I pay close attention, I see that there's something pleasant about the pondering, a kind of continuously doled-out carrot that keeps me meandering along the path of the puzzle toward a solution; and if I find that solution, I'm given a culminating burst of satisfaction as a reward. As John Ruskin put it in the nineteenth century, "Curiosity is a gift, a capacity of pleasure in knowing."

At least, sometimes curiosity feels like that—like a pleasure so refined that you barely notice it. But Samuel Johnson, writing in the eighteenth century, put a different spin on it: "The gratification of curiosity rather frees us from uneasiness than confers pleasure; we are more pained by ignorance than delighted by instruction."

Sometimes that's true—sometimes the quest to know something feels more like an urgent drive, an unsettling thirst. If you're trying to find out whether the stock market, which contains your life savings, continued its recent plunge today, that's different from wondering why the stock market crashed in 1929. If you're trying to find out whether your spouse is sleeping with your neighbor, that's different from wondering whether your neighbor's spouse is sleeping with another neighbor, and more different still from wondering what makes spouses sleep with neighbors—or, for that matter, what makes birds sing or what makes stars shine or what makes anything do anything. Whether curiosity is more like a desperate hunger or a delightful lure seems to depend on how directly and urgently relevant it is to our interests as defined by natural selection; the less direct and urgent the connection, the more subtle and pleasant the feeling.

But the main point is just that all kinds of curiosity—ranging from a driving, headlong quest to a pleasant stroll along the byways of speculation—do seem to involve *feelings*. It's no surprise, then, that brain scans are showing that a curious state of mind involves activity in the dopamine system, the system involved in motivation and reward, in desire and pleasure.

So this is what I take away from many hours of failing to meditate (I mean, many hours of failing to meditate and occasionally succeeding at mindfully observing this failure): thoughts that grab my mind and carry it along with them have feelings attached, however subtle those feelings may be. I'm happy to report that this link between feeling and thought has been observed by people whose powers of meditative introspection are way better developed than mine. In June 2015, shortly after sending a rough draft of this book to my editor, I rewarded myself with a two-week meditation retreat at the Forest Refuge, an appendage of the Insight Meditation Society that is geared toward experienced meditators. The guiding teacher for those two weeks was a psychotherapist and former Buddhist monk named Akincano Marc Weber. One night during a dharma talk, he said, "Every thought has a propellant, and that propellant is emotional."

The word *propellant* suggests the answer to an important question: When your mind is wandering, when your default mode network is running the show, how does the network decide which module gets to propel its thought into consciousness at any given time? We've already heard references to some kind of competition among modules for dominance—references to a "dog-eat-dog world" that lies beyond the bounds of awareness. But what determines which dog wins? What makes one dog more powerful than another?

Feelings as Filing

So far as I can tell, the best candidate for that honor is feelings. Of all the thoughts engaged in subterranean competition at a given moment, maybe the thought that has the strongest level of feeling associated with it is the one that gains entry into consciousness.[†]

This is sheer conjecture and could well be wrong, but it would certainly make sense as a way for natural selection to organize the mind. After all, feelings are judgments about how various things relate to an animal's Darwinian interests. So, from natural selection's point of view, feelings would make great labels for thoughts, labels that say things like "high priority," "medium priority," "low priority." If you're a day away from some event that will markedly affect your social status—an important presentation, a big party you're hosting—preparation-related thoughts are high priority, hence high anxiety. But those thoughts are lower priority, and the anxiety less acute, if you're weeks from the event. If you and your best friend just had a huge argument, figuring out what to do and say about that is a matter of some importance—greater importance than thinking about a casual acquaintance you may have offended; hence the difference between feelings of inner turmoil and feelings of mild concern.

In all of these cases, the feelings associated with the thoughts will be commensurate in strength to the importance of the thoughts as natural selection defines importance. And when the default mode takes over—when your mind isn't focused on talking to someone or reading a book or playing a sport or some other immersive task—it is the most "important" thoughts, the ones labeled with the strongest feelings, that get priority.

There will be times, of course, when the most important thought competing for admission to consciousness isn't all that important; sometimes life is blessedly free of issues that need urgent attention. In that case, the feeling linked to the thought that enters consciousness via your default mode network may not be very strong. But I suspect that if you pay close enough attention—which is a lot easier if you're meditating—you'll pretty much always sense a feeling tone, one that is on balance positive or negative, associated with a thought that suddenly enters awareness. Because if the thought didn't have some such feeling, it wouldn't have gotten your attention in the first place. Feelings are, among other things, your brain's way of labeling the importance of thoughts, and importance (in natural selection's somewhat crude sense of the term) determines which thoughts enter consciousness.

Again, I don't want to suggest that this is a consensus view within psychology. In fact, even if we confine ourselves to psychologists who have embraced a modular model of the mind somewhat like the one I've described, there probably is no single view on what determines which modules carry the day. But this hypothesis strikes me as the most plausible one on offer. It makes Darwinian sense, and it meshes with the results of meditative introspection. And, though introspection isn't data, it's a legitimate aid in deciding which hypotheses merit further exploration.

This particular hypothesis may help explain something about the path of meditative progress. As I mentioned earlier, I find it easier to view my feelings with some measure of detachment than to view my thoughts that way. And I don't think I'm an aberration. Lots of meditators seem to have an easier time with feelings than with thoughts. That would make sense if, indeed, feelings are the glue that makes thoughts stick to your consciousness, that makes you unreflectively take ownership of them. After all, presumably you can't start dissolving that glue—and so can't get any distance from your thoughts—until you learn to see it clearly, learn to view feelings with some objectivity.

Indeed, in this scenario, you'd have to be good at viewing even very *subtle* feelings with objectivity before you could view a wide variety of thoughts that way. So it stands to reason that it's quite advanced meditators, like Joseph Goldstein, who would most clearly and vividly see thoughts fail to stick—see them arise and pass away without ever finding purchase in the mind.

This hypothesis—that feelings are, among other things, the mind's way of assigning priority labels to thoughts—is consistent with a broad trend in psychology over the past several decades: to quit talking about "affective" and "cognitive" processes as if they were in separate compartments of the mind and recognize how finely intertwined they are. And this trend is yet another case where modern psychology was anticipated by ancient Buddhism. In a famous sutra called *The Greater Discourse on the Destruction of Craving*, the Buddha says that a "mind object"—a category that includes thoughts—is just like a taste or a smell: whether a person is "tasting a flavor with the tongue" or "smelling an odor with the nose" or "cognizing a mind object with the mind," the person "lusts after it if it is pleasing" and "dislikes it if it is unpleasing."

As we'll see a few chapters from now, the fine entanglement of affect and cognition helps make sense of one of the crazier-sounding Buddhist propositions: that the things we perceive in the world out there—trees, airplanes, pebbles—don't exist, at least not in the sense that we naturally see them as existing. And as we'll see in the next chapter, this entanglement of affect and cognition can also help us wrestle with a conundrum I alluded to earlier: If the self doesn't exist, then what are the real dynamics of what is commonly called "self-control"? And what does Buddhism tell us about how to get some of this "self" control?

9

"Self"
Control

In the eighteenth century, the Scottish philosopher David Hume wrote that human reason is "the slave of the passions." If Hume had meant by "passions" what we mean by that word today, his observation wouldn't be worth noting. Obviously, when we're seized by intense feelings like lust or vengeance, our reasoning faculties are not running the show. But Hume meant "passions" in a different sense; he meant feelings, broadly speaking. He was saying that, though rational thought plays an important role in human motivation, it is in a certain sense never really calling the shots. When we decide to do something, we decide on the basis of a feeling.

Where did Hume get this idea? Apparently through introspection—carefully watching his mind at work. In a sense, Hume was being mindful before mindfulness was cool. Indeed, as Western philosophers go, Hume was pretty Eastern. A number of his views align almost uncannily with Buddhist thought, including an argument he mounted against the existence of the self. Some scholars have suggested that this may be no coincidence, that he may have somehow encountered Buddhist ideas even though they had barely begun to drift westward from Asia. Certainly the idea that feelings run more of the show than we realize is Buddhist in spirit.

Now, a quarter of a millennium after Hume caught up with Buddhism, science is catching up with Hume. It has developed tools to peer into our motivational machinery, to see which parts of the brain are active when we make decisions. And Hume's ideas about the relationship of reason to feeling, long considered radical, are looking pretty good.

Consider a decision as straightforward as whether to buy something. It's tempting to think of this as an exercise in rational deliberation. You look at the product and the price, and then you ask yourself a series of questions: How much would you use the product? Would the purchase take a big chunk of your cash? What else could you buy with that money? After answering such questions, you coolly weigh the factors for and against the purchase and decide.

But weighing factors may not be so cool after all, according to an experiment done by cognitive scientists at Stanford, Carnegie Mellon, and MIT. They gave people real money and offered them a series of things to buy: wireless headphones, an electric toothbrush, a *Star Wars* DVD, and so on. As these people were shown each product, and then its price, their brains were being scanned. It turned out researchers could do a good job of predicting whether someone would purchase something by watching which parts of the brain got more active and which got less active. And none of these were parts of the brain mainly associated with rational deliberation; rather, they were parts associated with feelings. Like, for example, the nucleus accumbens, which plays a role in doling out pleasure and gets more active when people anticipate rewards or see things they like. The more active the nucleus accumbens while subjects were looking at a product, the more likely they were to buy it. On the other hand, there's the insula, which gets especially active when people anticipate pain and other unpleasant things. The more active the insula got when people were shown the price, the less likely they were to buy the product.

Though weighing the pros and cons of a purchase sounds like a purely rational, even mechanical act, this experiment suggests that the way the brain actually does the weighing is through a contest of conflicting feelings. Even the factor of price—a purely quantitative index, the kind of thing that is easily fed into a computer's decision-making algorithm—ultimately enters the equation in the form of a feeling, a degree of aversion. And the stronger feeling—attraction or aversion—wins.

To be sure, these feelings may be *informed* by reason. If you remind yourself that the last electric toothbrush you bought went unused and infer that this is the likely fate of your next electric toothbrush, any feeling of attraction to the toothbrush may fade. If you remind yourself that the $20 they're asking for the toothbrush is less than you spent on dinner last Friday, your aversion to the price—and activity in your insula—may weaken.

Why Feeling Governs Thought

So reason does play a role in what a person finally does. Still, this experiment suggests that maybe reason can play that role only by influencing the ultimate motivator: feelings. As Hume put it, "Reason alone can never be a motive to any action of the will." Buying something ultimately comes down to feeling good about the purchase—or at least feeling better than walking away from the purchase feels. Of course, you may later regret walking away; "nonbuyer's remorse" is as real as "buyer's remorse." But either way, the key word is *remorse*. The Monday-morning quarterbacking comes in the form of a *feeling* because that's the form the Sunday quarterbacking assumed in the first place.

This all makes sense when you think about it in evolutionary terms. After all, feelings are the original motivators. Good and bad feelings are what natural selection used to goad animals into, respectively, approaching things or avoiding things, acquiring things or rejecting things; good feelings were assigned to things like eating and bad feelings to things like being eaten. Over time, bit by bit, animals got smarter, but the point of smarts, from natural selection's perspective, isn't to *replace* feelings but rather to make them better informed: intelligence helps animals do a more sophisticated job of figuring out what to approach or avoid, acquire or reject—that is, what to feel good about or bad about. So, over evolutionary time, though the calculations that inform our feelings get more and more elaborate, the feelings continue to be what ultimately steer us through life. We may buy a parka with a lining whose virtues we've confirmed through rigorous online research and extended contemplation, but the reason we finally buy the parka is because all that rational analysis gives us a good feeling about buying it.

For that matter, the reason we started the analysis in the first place is because being cold in the winter gives us a bad feeling. Feelings tell us what to think about, and then after all the thinking is done, they tell us what to do. Over the history of our evolutionary lineage, thinking has played a larger and larger role in action, but the thinking has always had both its beginning and its end in feelings.

Another thing that can happen over evolutionary time is that feelings are assigned to more and more things. As our species became more complexly social, getting food and sex came to depend on navigating a social landscape, which included goals like forging alliances and being held in high esteem. So making friends and earning respect came to feel good, and being rejected came to feel bad. This in turn opened up new avenues of thought: figuring out why a friend turned on you, imagining ways to impress people, and so on. Still, this growing web of feelings and thoughts was a straightforward extension of the basic value system evolution built into us to begin with—a system that prized surviving and getting our genes spread.

Natural selection being the thrifty thing it is, the biology behind those feelings and thoughts was a straightforward extension of the biology embodying those original values. Brain-scan studies have shown that the same parts of the brain that mediate physical pain also mediate the pain of social rejection. Which helps explain why opiates and other painkillers can take the sting out of social setbacks. Even extended doses of Tylenol, one study showed, can dull the pain of social rejection.

Reason and Chocolate

All of which brings us to the subject of chocolate. A bar of Godiva chocolate, as it happens, was one of the items on offer in that MRI shopping study. But even if it hadn't been, I'd probably be bringing up chocolate now, because I'm trying to steer us toward the subject of self-control, and when it comes to self-control, chocolate ranks pretty high on my list of challenges, right up there with powdered-sugar doughnuts and watching sports on TV rather than writing this book.

Self-control has often been described as a matter of reason prevailing over feelings. Plato invoked the metaphor of a charioteer (the rational self) keeping horses (the unruly passions) under control. This basic idea has survived more or less intact for about 2.5 millennia. In fact, some people say that brain science has located the charioteer. The prefrontal cortex, which sits right behind your forehead, is extolled in high school textbooks and museum exhibits as the thing that makes you human. It is said to be the "executive seat" of the brain, endowing us with a capacity for extended reasoning and planning and self-control. You can tell that our ancestors the australopithecines were lacking in these departments—just look at the embarrassingly sharp slope of their foreheads!

Certainly the prefrontal cortex is an important thing; I'm as proud of mine as the next guy. What's more, there is good reason to believe that this part of the brain plays *some* important role in what we think of as self-control. Studies show that the more formidable a temptation, the more activity there is in the prefrontal cortex of people who resist it.

Still, if Hume is right, this prefrontal activity shouldn't be framed as it's commonly framed, as reason "overcoming temptation" or successfully "opposing feeling." Reason has its effect not by directly pushing back against a feeling but by fortifying the feeling that *does* do the pushing back. Yes, that Hershey bar looks good, and the thought of eating it *feels* good, but reflecting on that article you read about the toll high blood sugar takes on your body makes the thought of eating the Hershey bar guilt-inducing. And it's the guilt, not the reflection, that does direct combat with the urge to eat the candy bar. "Reason alone," Hume argued, "can never oppose passion in the direction of the will." Nothing "can oppose or retard the impulse of passion but a contrary impulse."

In this view, the prefrontal cortex isn't a kind of command module that evolution invented when we got promoted from mere animals to human beings; it's not something that finally tamed our unruly feelings and put us under rational control. No, the powers of reason embedded in the prefrontal cortex are themselves under the control of feelings. The value system embedded in the feelings—natural selection's conception of what's good and what's bad, what we should pursue and what we should avoid—continues to be, more or less, the prevailing value system.

Natural selection has made us *want* foods with certain kinds of tastes, and has also made us *want* to live a long, healthy life. The struggle for self-control—in this particular case, at least—is a clash between these two values and between feelings associated with these two values. If reason is to play a role in the struggle, it is only as a proxy for these values. It's the *desire* to live a long, healthy life that focuses our reasoning on the link between sugar consumption and longevity, and it's *through* this desire that the results of the reasoning can overpower the desire for the chocolate itself. It's in this sense that reason remains a "slave" to the passions, as Hume put it—and thus a slave to natural selection's overarching value system.

The more we learn about the functioning of the brain, the more sense Hume's view makes. Joshua Greene, a neuroscientist at Harvard, has written of a particular region in the prefrontal cortex called the dorsolateral prefrontal cortex: "The DLPFC, the seat of abstract reasoning, is deeply interconnected with the dopamine system, which is responsible for placing values on objects and actions. From a neural and evolutionary perspective, our reasoning systems are not independent logic machines. They are outgrowths of more primitive mammalian systems for selecting rewarding behaviors—cognitive prostheses for enterprising mammals." In other words, as Greene himself notes, Hume seems to have gotten it right.

It isn't just the prefrontal cortex that's long been oversimplified. The part of the brain known as the limbic system is routinely identified as the "seat of emotion," but that description is turning out to be misleading. The neuroscientist Luiz Pessoa has written, " 'Affective' brain regions participate in cognition, on the one hand, and 'cognitive' brain regions participate in emotion." In his textbook *The Cognitive-Emotional Brain*, Pessoa, like many writers in the history of psychology, invokes Plato's chariot image—but, unlike most of them, he brings it up for the purpose of rejecting it.

Does Your Inner Judge Really Judge?

It's no surprise that Plato's view—the idea of a purely rational charioteer—has held sway for so long. After all, when you're deciding whether to indulge in, say, chocolate, doesn't it feel as if there's a rational you that's pondering the question—a kind of judge who hears the arguments for and against buying the chocolate? On the one hand, you're a few pounds overweight; plus, eating the chocolate this late in the day could make it harder to sleep. On the other hand, if you ate the chocolate, you'd feel energetic and could get some work done; plus, you deserve a treat, given how hard you worked yesterday (thanks in part, perhaps, to the chocolate you ate!).

Having considered the arguments on both sides, you—the judge—render a verdict. Being a stern judge, you decide that, no, you cannot have the chocolate today. Or maybe, on another day, being a lenient judge, you decide that you have indeed earned the chocolate bar. And court is adjourned. Or rather, court is recessed; after you buy the chocolate, you will begin adjudicating the question of whether to wait until you get home before eating it.

Either way, it does feel as if there's a moment where *you* decide. So what's wrong with describing it this way, as a rational "you" adjudicating the case? I once asked this question of Rob Kurzban. Since Kurzban is among the psychologists who have suggested that maybe the self doesn't exist, I was pretty sure he'd have a way of describing the chocolate decision that didn't involve some rational "you" being the judge.

And, indeed, when I asked him what's wrong with saying something like "I considered the pros and cons and decided not to eat the chocolate," he said that, strictly speaking, you should put it more like this: "There were certain systems in your head that were designed to be motivated to eat high-calorie foods, and those systems had certain kinds of motives or beliefs or representations, and there are other systems in your head that have motivations associated with long-term health, and those systems have certain beliefs about the chocolate." In the end, modules of the second kind, modules focused on the long term, "inhibited the behavior that was being facilitated by the short-term modules." In other words, neither kind of module was more "rational" than the other; they just had different goals, and on this particular day, one was stronger than the other.

You might ask, What exactly do we mean by "stronger"? Well, if Hume was right, and the drift of that shopping experiment was right, it comes down to a contest of feelings. A long-term module may generate a sense of guilt when you reach for that chocolate bar; it may also give you a feeling of pride when you resist the allure of chocolate. On the other side of the contest is the chocolate lust generated by the short-term module. But the short-term module may have subtler tactics as well. Is it, perhaps, the module that dredged up the memory of that article about the long-term benefits of antioxidants? It just thought the long-term module might find that article interesting?

All of this highlights a puzzle: Why does our conscious mind have to spend time witnessing the presentation of reasons—that is, participating in the "deliberation"? If it's just a show trial—if it all comes down to a contest of power between modules that have summoned whatever fortifying logic might support their cause—couldn't the whole thing happen subconsciously, freeing up the conscious mind to do something constructive, like ponder the mind-body problem? Well, recall that the conscious mind—being the part of your mind that communicates with the world   seems to be a kind of public relations agent. "My guess," said Kurzban, is that the reason your conscious mind observes the debate, including the winning rationale, is so that "if someone ever challenges you or asks you why you did x, y, or z," you'll be able to cite a plausible rationale.

So if you're walking out of a store jamming a 3.5-ounce chocolate bar into your mouth and a passerby looks at you quizzically, you can say, "This is so I can get more work done this afternoon." Presumably the passerby will then think more highly of you than if you'd said, "I'm out of control, okay?"

Sometimes the social stakes are higher than what a passing stranger thinks of you. If everyone you know finds out that you've been cheating on your spouse, you can't just say "I was driven by sexual urges that were designed by natural selection to maximize genetic legacy." Then people will go around saying you're the kind of person who cheats on a spouse. And of course, you're not that kind of person! So you need to be able to say something more like "But you have to understand: my spouse had grown emotionally distant and wasn't meeting my deep need for companionship and intimacy." Then people will say they can't really blame you. So it helps to have already heard that side of the argument, and watched it carry the day, before you decide to have the dalliance. Then you're ready.

This isn't to say that the *only* reason we're conscious of our reasoning process is so we can sell rationales for our behavior to a gullible public. Sometimes, while deliberating on a big decision, we consult with friends or family about what we should do; and this consultation will be more productive if we're already aware of some arguments for and against the decision. Of course, even here there may be a public relations agenda. "Consulting" may be a way of making sure, in advance, that we're not going to do something that will antagonize important people in our lives, or a way of getting commitments of support from these people in case our decision antagonizes other people. But—especially when we're talking to people who have our interests at heart—"consulting" may actually mean consulting: seeking guidance.

Either way, one virtue of your conscious mind being in touch with the reasons generated by competing modules is that you can share the reasons with others, and get their feedback, before making your decision. Strictly speaking, though, the way I should put it is this: You can share the reasons with others, and then their feedback will recalibrate how good or bad the two options *feel*.

You may have noticed a trend in this chapter: the more we ponder the connection between reason and feeling, the dimmer the prospects seem for keeping our behavior under truly rational control. First we learned that Hume seems to have been right: our "reasoning faculty" isn't ever really in charge; its agenda—what it reasons about—is set by feelings, and it can influence our behavior only by in turn influencing our feelings. Then we learned that, actually, even the term *reasoning faculty* suggests more in the way of orderly deliberation than is typical of the human mind. The view emerging here is that we don't so much have a reasoning faculty as reasoning *faculties*; modules seem to have the ability to recruit reasons on behalf of their goals.

This in turn suggests that "reasoning" is sometimes a euphemism for what these "reasoning faculties" do. Sure, one module may say something truly reasonable and well-documented, like "If you eat the chocolate, you'll have trouble sleeping." But another module may say something like "You'll do more work if you eat the chocolate"—even if history shows that what you'll actually do is peruse social media with unusual fervor. And it's hard to separate the valid reasons from the invalid reasons, because sometimes the least valid reasons *feel good*—and feelings tend to carry the day.

But cheer up! Just because feelings are critical players in this drama doesn't mean we're powerless to intervene. In fact, we have a tool—mindfulness meditation—that's well suited to intervening at the level of feelings and altering their influence. So maybe there's hope for dealing with the challenge classically associated with "self-control"—the overindulgence of various kinds of appetites.

In fact, it turns out there are specific meditative techniques being used to help people deal with such challenges as addiction to cigarettes. But before we get to those, it will help to understand how and why some appetites become dominant in the first place—what the evolutionary logic is behind the power they've amassed within your mind.

Is "Self-Discipline" Really the Problem?

If you smoke cigarettes—or for that matter if you have an addiction to anything, ranging from heroin to pornography to chocolate—there has probably been at least one occasion when you deliberated at length over whether to indulge in this form of gratification. Maybe it was back when, having tried it a few times, you recognized its allure and, at some level, realized that it might eventually become your master. In any event, the deliberations must have at some point gone in favor of short-term gratification. And as time wore on and opportunities for gratification kept arising, you spent less and less time deliberating. The drive for immediate gratification became so strong that resistance was futile. That's the way these things work.

High school football coaches have a way of describing this dynamic. They say that self-discipline is like a muscle. If you use it, it gets stronger, and if you don't, it gets weaker. This truism does seem to capture the broad pattern; if the part of you that's arguing against indulgence prevails a few times—if it gets successfully "exercised"— its chances of success will be better next time, whereas if it loses a few times in a row, it will be headed toward a very long losing streak.

In fact, this "muscle" metaphor is so apt that some psychologists who study these things have used it to describe the upshot of their findings. An interesting question these psychologists tend not to ask is *why* the muscle metaphor is apt. In other words, why is it that early successes at self-discipline lead to more successes, whereas early lapses lead to more lapses? If self-discipline is really good for the organism, you wouldn't expect natural selection to make it so easy for a few early lapses to destroy self-discipline. Yet there's no denying that a few injections of heroin can be the end of a productive life. Why?

One way to answer the question is to depart from the useful but limiting "self-discipline as muscle" metaphor. Let's translate the question into modular terms: after the module favoring indulgence wins a few debates, its strength grows to a point where countervailing modules don't even bother trying to muster counterarguments. Why would natural selection design things that way, such that the winning module gets stronger and stronger?

Imagine an ancestor of yours twenty thousand years ago—your great-great-great- (and so on) grandfather. Imagine him as a very young man. Imagine that one of his modules—roughly the one Freud called "libido"—is encouraging him to make sexual advances toward a woman. Another module is counseling caution, saying things like, "But maybe she'll reject your advances and you'll be humiliated, and maybe she'll tell people that she rejected your advances and you'll be further humiliated." Or, if she already has a mate, the cautious module may say, "What if she tells her brawny husband about your unwanted advances and he feeds you to a lion?"

Now let's say the first module wins, and your ancestor makes the advances. And let's say it turns out the libidinous module was right; the advances are not rebuffed, sex ensues, and the brawny husband is none the wiser. Well, next time there's a conflict between these two voices—one counseling sexual advance and the other counseling restraint—doesn't it make sense to give the benefit of the doubt to the first voice? After all, it was right last time. And the fact that it was right suggests two things: that it's not outlandish to think women would find this particular ancestor attractive, and that this ancestor's brain is good at picking up on cues of interest projected by women.

If, on the other hand, these advances had been rebuffed, and your ancestor had been humiliated and had become the laughingstock of the hunter-gatherer village—or, worse still, was roughed up by a brawny husband before becoming a laughingstock then things would be different. Then it would make sense to give the libidinous module less power next time around. And it would make sense to give the module counseling restraint more power. After all, it was right last time.

The point is just that it makes sense that natural selection would design a modular mind this way—that "winning" modules would amass more power when their judgment is vindicated. And note that the form vindication takes, in at least some cases, is sensual gratification. If the libidinous module counsels sexual assertion and this leads to an orgasm, then its counsel will carry more weight next time.

Of course, in a modern environment, this dynamic works differently. A module that counsels going to a porn site can lead to sexual gratification, so this counsel will carry more weight next time around—even though spending time at porn sites isn't doing anything to enhance your reproductive prospects, and may even have the opposite effect. Or a module counsels snorting cocaine and this gives you a self-esteem boost that, back in a hunter-gatherer environment, would have been the reward for impressing your peers—and would have strengthened not a module that urged you to snort cocaine but a module that urged you to repeat whatever behavior had impressed your peers. It's in this way that, in a modern environment, gratification can reinforce behaviors quite different from the kinds of behaviors it was designed to reinforce.

There are two virtues of describing the self-control problem this way—as a module getting stronger and stronger rather than as some all-purpose muscle called "self-discipline" getting weaker and weaker. First, this perspective helps explain why the problem would be so treacherous in the first place. It's hard to imagine why natural selection would design a "muscle" called "self-discipline" in such a way that a few early failures lead to enduring impotence. But it's easy to imagine why natural selection would design modules that get stronger with repeated success and why natural selection would use, as its working definition of success, gratification in one sense or another.

A New Approach

The second virtue of conceiving the problem of self-discipline in modular terms is that it can suggest new ways of addressing the problem. There's a difference between thinking of the goal as strengthening the self-discipline muscle and thinking of the goal as weakening a module that has grown dominant.

If you take the former approach, the tendency is to *fight* your temptations. You feel an urge to go buy cigarettes, and you try to push the thought out of your mind. After all, there's this thing called "self-discipline," and you have to exercise it—you have to get it out on the battlefield to vanquish the enemy!

But suppose you think of the problem as instead being this particular module that has formed a particular strong habit. How would you try to overcome the problem then? You might try something like mindfulness meditation. To see what I mean, let's take a look at the state-of-the-art mindfulness meditation approach to overcoming addictions.

This approach was explained to me by Judson Brewer, who did a study on it at Yale Medical School (and also did one of the main studies showing that meditation quiets the default mode network). Brewer said the basic idea is to *not* fight the urge to, say, smoke a cigarette. That doesn't mean you succumb to the urge and light up a cigarette. It just means you don't try to push the urge out of your mind. Rather, you follow the same mindfulness technique that you'd apply to other bothersome feelings—anxiety, resentment, melancholy, hatred. You just calmly (or as calmly as possible, under the circumstances) examine the feeling. What part of your body is the urge felt in? What is the texture of the urge? Is it sharp? Dull and heavy? The more you do that, the less the urge seems a part of you; you've exploited the basic irony of mindfulness meditation: getting close enough to feelings to take a good look at them winds up giving you a kind of critical distance from them. Their grip on you loosens; if it loosens enough, they're no longer a part of you.

There's an acronym used to describe this technique: RAIN. First you Recognize the feeling. Then you Accept the feeling (rather than try to drive it away). Then you Investigate the feeling and its relationship to your body. Finally, the N stands for Nonidentification, or, equivalently, Nonattachment. Which is a nice note to end on, since not being attached to things was the Buddha's all-purpose prescription for what ails us.

Brewer described this therapy as being about not "feeding" the urge to smoke. He said, "If you don't feed a stray cat, it quits coming to your door."

I like this metaphor, with its suggestion that, somewhere within you, there's an animal that needs taming. After all, the modular model of the mind holds that, in a sense, there are a number of animals in your mind—modules that have a certain amount of independence and sometimes struggle with one another for dominance. What's more, I've just suggested that, as with animals, the behavior of modules is shaped by positive reinforcement; if they keep getting rewarded for something, they'll do it more and more. That, apparently, is what addiction is. A rat learns that if it presses the bar, a food pellet comes out; one of your modules learns that, if it generates the urge to light up a cigarette, it will get some nicotine.

This comparison puts a finer point on the difference between fighting the urge to smoke and addressing the urge mindfully. Fighting the urge is like pushing the rat away every time it approaches the bar. This works in the short run; if the rat can't press the bar, no food pellet will come out, and maybe after a while the rat will even give up on approaching the bar. Still, whenever the rat *is* allowed to get near the bar, it will press it, because it has seen nothing to indicate that pressing the bar won't bring food.

Treating the urge mindfully, I'd say, is more like arranging it so that when the rat presses the bar, no food pellets come out. The urge—the thing that's analogous to pressing the bar—is allowed to fully form, yet it doesn't get reinforced, because your mindful inspection of it has deprived it of its force and so broken the connection between the impulse and the reward. Over time, after the urge has blossomed again and again without bringing gratification, the urge ceases and desists.

That is, if the technique works. And in the cigarette-smoking study Brewer conducted, this technique worked better than an alternative approach recommended by the American Lung Association.

Attention Deficit as Addiction

Most of our self-control problems aren't as dramatic and clear-cut as classic addictions like nicotine and cocaine. Some of them are so subtly interwoven into our lives that we don't think of them as self-control problems at all.

For example, when I was a child, I had a short attention span. Actually, I still have it—it's just that now they don't call it a short attention span. They call it attention-deficit disorder. What these two terms have in common is a particular way of characterizing the problem. They make it sound like there's a faculty people have—the faculty we call attention—and somehow my particular faculty of attention lacks something or other that would make it work better. Yet when I watch my attention-deficit disorder in action, when I pay really close attention to the dynamics of distraction, that characterization starts to seem wrong. The problem of losing focus starts to seem more like a problem of managing my feelings.

For example: right now I'm focused on writing this sentence, and writing this sentence feels fine; I like to succeed at things, and so long as this sentence keeps unfolding on my computer screen, I'm succeeding at something! But if I get to a point where I can't decide what sentence should go next, I'll start feeling a bit uncomfortable. And if it isn't just a question of how to word the next sentence—if it's a larger question about what the next sentence should say, and indeed where this whole stream of writing should head—I feel *really* uncomfortable. I like fiddling with sentences, but I hate pondering structural problems.

But wait—there's an alternative to the discomfort of confronting an unwritten and not obviously writable sentence. My browser is open, and it has occurred to me that I should do some shopping: I need a new smartphone. I mean, I don't *have* to have a new smartphone, but my old smartphone has developed this weird problem where it thinks the headphones are plugged in even when they're not. So if somebody calls me, I can't hear what they're saying unless I either plug in the headphones or switch the speakerphone on. Can you imagine trying to go through life with such a burden? Don't you think I should spend the next few minutes researching smartphones? Well, whether you do or not, I am a gadget freak, so the thought of doing that feels good—way, way better than the thought of figuring out what sentence should go next. Case closed. See you later.

I'm not sure which module injected this "Why don't you research smartphones?" thought into my mind—apparently a module that likes acquiring possessions. In any event, the module timed the thought masterfully, for just the moment when writing was starting to feel uncomfortable. Modules are crafty that way.

Anyway, the main point is that you can think of the problem of distraction as analogous to the problem of quitting smoking. And if you think of it that way—think of your goal as being to weaken the module that favors leading you away from your work—this might affect how you address the problem.

Ordinarily, if you were determined to stay focused on your work notwithstanding a strong desire not to stay focused on your work, you might respond to the thought of researching smartphones with a reprimand: No, *don't* think about smartphones—get back to writing! But if you take the mindful approach, you say: Go ahead, think about smartphones. Close your eyes and imagine how it would feel to search for the latest review of the latest smartphone. Examine the feeling of *wanting* a cool new smartphone and *wanting* to search online for one. Then examine it some more. Examine it until it loses its power. Now get back to writing!

Though we don't generally think of nicotine addiction and a short attention span as having much in common, both really are problems of impulse control. And in both cases, we can, in principle, weaken the impulse by *not* fighting it, by letting it form and observing it carefully.

This deprives the module that generated the impulse of the positive reinforcement that would give it more power next time around.

Hatred as Addiction

In principle, you can describe much of mindfulness meditation this way—as depriving modules of the positive reinforcement that has given them power. Because often when you mindfully observe feelings, you're keeping the module that generated them from getting some sort of reward. If you observe a feeling of hatred for someone, and just keep observing the feeling, then the feeling won't do what it might otherwise do—like, say, get you to imagine taking revenge for whatever this person has done to earn your hatred. If you *did* indulge in this revenge fantasy, it would feel good, right? What is more delightful than imagining a horrible fate befalling a mortal enemy? And the reason this is a good feeling, presumably, is that this is the kind of thing natural selection designed the module to get you to do: to imagine ways to undermine rivals and harm enemies. So, from natural selection's point of view, the module deserves a reward for accomplishing the mission of getting you to indulge in a revenge fantasy—and this reward will make the module stronger next time around.

This isn't the only mission hatred is designed to accomplish. It is also good at getting you to say hateful things about the people you hate (thus failing to exercise what Buddhists call "right speech," one of the eight factors in the Eightfold Path). Saying those hateful things feels good as well. But this positive reinforcement, like the positive reinforcement for having revenge fantasies, will never happen if, when you see the feeling of hatred coming, you view it mindfully rather than surrender to it.

In short, though we classically associate the term *self-control* with obvious self-indulgence—shooting heroin, scarfing down chocolate, and so on—it turns out that the lessons learned from these conspicuous cases go well beyond them. Hatred and a short attention span are problems of self-control and can be addressed through mindfulness.

Self-control is a slightly ambiguous term. Some people think of it as referring to control *of* the self, and some people think of it as referring to control *by* the self. Either way, it's an odd term to be using in a book informed by Buddhism—since, according to Buddhism, the self doesn't exist. And if the self doesn't exist, how can we talk about self-control? If there is no rational charioteer, how do we decide, say, to do mindfulness meditation?

For now I'll finesse that question by repeating what I said earlier: Don't get hung up on whether something called a "self" exists. Just use the parts of the not-self doctrine that are useful, in particular the idea that none of your feelings—the urge for cigarettes, the urge to research smartphones, the urge to hate—is intrinsically a part of you. You can observe these feelings for what they are: things that some module is trying to give force to. The more you observe them this way—observe them mindfully—the less force they will have, and the less a part of "you" they will be.

David Hume himself, though he argued against the existence of the self, certainly thought that what we call self-control is possible. He distinguished between the "violent" passions, such as revenge and hatred, and the "calm" passions, such as the love of beauty, and observed that, "generally speaking, the violent passions have a more powerful influence on the will; tho' 'tis often found, that the calm ones, when corroborated by reflection, and seconded by resolution, are able to control them in their most furious movements." It's even possible, he wrote, for the calm passions to have "absolute Command over the Mind."

Mindfulness meditation is, among other things, an attempt to give the calm passions more power and give the violent passions less power. Hume, notwithstanding speculations about his having encountered Buddhist philosophy, doesn't seem to have known about mindfulness meditation. However, when he described the benefits of empowering the calm passions, he sounded like a modern-day meditation teacher extolling the virtues of living in the present. He wrote that if we fail to empower the calm passions—if we let the violent passions carry the day—we will miss "the relish in the common occurrences of life."

Helping people with self-control problems is often thought of as a sheerly therapeutic exercise. And certainly helping people quit smoking or get off heroin qualifies as therapy in the common sense of the term. But when you see how seamlessly the discussion of self-control leads to discussion of overcoming hatred—and for that matter of seeing beauty in "the common occurrences of life"—you can see how blurry the line is between therapy and moral edification and between therapy and spiritual uplift.

This isn't surprising. According to Buddhist philosophy, both the problems we call therapeutic and the problems we call spiritual are a product of not seeing things clearly. What's more, in both cases this failure to see things clearly is in part a product of being misled by feelings. And the first step toward seeing through these feelings is seeing them in the first place—becoming aware of how pervasively and subtly feelings influence our thought and behavior.

Over the next few chapters, we're going to get to even subtler levels of this influence. And we're going to get further along the spectrum from therapy to spirituality.

10

Encounters with
the Formless

Here's a passage from the *Samadhiraja Sutra,* a Buddhist text that's about nineteen centuries old:

> *Know all things to be like this:*
> *A mirage, a cloud castle,*
> *A dream, an apparition,*
> *Without essence, but with qualities that can be seen.*

I first heard this at a meditation retreat where one of the teachers had been going on and on about "the formless." If you got to a point in your meditative practice where you apprehended the formless, I gathered, you were perceiving reality more truly than if you were still hung up on the world of "forms"—you know, tables, trucks, bowling balls.

"The formless" isn't a particularly well-known bit of Buddhist terminology. But there's a better-known word that means roughly what this teacher meant by the term: *emptiness.*†

Whichever term you use, the upshot is that, in the world out there, which seems so solid and so structured, so full of things with a distinct and tangible identity, there is less than meets the eye. This world of apparent forms is in some sense, as the *Samadhiraja Sutra* has it, a "mirage, a cloud castle, a dream, an apparition." Or, as the *Heart Sutra* famously and pithily puts it, "Form is emptiness."

Apparently some very accomplished meditators get to a point where they feel this truth deeply, and may even see the world as "empty" or "formless" on a regular basis. This is considered an important feat, especially if your goal is to attain enlightenment.

As you ponder these words—*formlessness* and *emptiness*—two other words may come to mind: *crazy* and *depressing*. It seems crazy to think that the world out there isn't real, that things that seem substantial are in some sense devoid of content. It also seems kind of depressing; I don't run into a lot of upbeat, fulfilled people who go around rejoicing in the emptiness of it all.

But I've slowly come to think that, actually, this idea isn't so crazy, and that in fact it makes more and more sense as psychology advances. And as for the depressingness: thinking of the perceived world as in some sense empty doesn't have to strip your life of meaning. In fact, it can allow you to build a new framework of meaning that's more valid—maybe even more conducive to happiness—than your old framework.

I hasten to add: my willingness to defend "formlessness" and "emptiness" depends on what exactly they're taken to mean, and different Buddhist thinkers have meant different things. I'm not here to defend the most extreme version of "mind-only" Buddhism, with its claim that the world out there doesn't really, ultimately exist. At the same time, I'm not just pulling a bait and switch; I'm not going to define formlessness and emptiness in some sense that's so narrow and technical that the "validity" I claim for the underlying idea turns out to be trivial. I think there's an important, if subtle, sense in which we attribute too much form and content to reality, and I think appreciating this can have—and should have—radical implications for our lives.

But let me start at the nonradical end of the argument. There is a pretty uncontroversial sense in which, when we apprehend the world out there, we're not really apprehending the world out there but rather are "constructing" it. After all, we don't have much direct contact with the world; the things we see and smell and hear are some distance from our bodies, so all the brain can do is make inferences about them based on indirect evidence: molecules that waft across the street from a bakery, sound waves emanating from a jet plane, particles of light that bounce off trees.

For example, the world is three-dimensional, yet we see it via two-dimensional fields of data: the points of light impinging on the surfaces of our eyes. In order for our minds to see a three-dimensional world in all its depth, we have to take these two depthless data fields and use them to build a kind of "theory" about that world.

And sometimes the theory is wrong. If you go to a 3-D movie and put on your 3-D glasses, your brain will be fooled into seeing superheroes leap off the movie screen toward your seat. Take off your glasses and you'll see that, no, actually, it's just you and popcorn in your immediate vicinity. Or look at a more old-fashioned optical illusion, such as the famous Müller-Lyer illusion, which makes you think one line is longer than another when in fact it's not.

These illusions take advantage of assumptions our mind makes about how the two-dimensional patterns on our eyeballs will reflect a three-dimensional world. The people who create the illusions have contrived situations where the assumptions don't hold.

Of course, in everyday life, the assumptions almost always *do* hold. Our minds do an impressive job of constructing a model of three-dimensional reality on the basis of two-dimensional data. More generally, our five senses are very good at what they do. By and large, the trees we see are trees, the jet planes we hear are jet planes, and so on. Still, the point is that, strictly speaking, this is a matter of *construction*. Perception is an active, not a passive, process, a process of constantly building models of the world. That's one reason different people see different things in the abstract ink blots used in Rorschach tests: our minds try to turn even the most ambiguous patterns into something that makes sense. We like to have a story about what things are and what they mean.

During meditation, our stories about things can fall away. For example, sometimes I meditate on sounds. I may do this rhythmically, focusing on my breath on the inhale and some sound in my environment on the exhale. Or I may go whole hog and just focus on the sounds, ignoring my breath entirely. In fact, sometimes at a meditation retreat, a teacher will devote a whole session to sound meditation. If you sink deeply enough into this practice, the structure you "impose" on sounds can start to dissolve.

For example, an airplane may fly overhead, and you hear an airplane-flying-overhead sound. Except you don't necessarily think, "Oh, an airplane." You're so immersed in the texture of the sound that you may not immediately think, "Oh, an anything." It's just pure sound, unattached to the idea of a particular, concrete object. I guess it's what an airplane would sound like to somebody from a culture that didn't have airplanes or to an alien from a civilization so advanced that its aircraft didn't make noise. It would just be sound—not the sound *of* anything.

A good question to ask me at this point would be: But what good does it do to forget that airplane noise is coming from an airplane? Glad you asked. The answer is: Not much good at all. But now consider another example, a case where this sort of forgetting *does* do some good.

Turning Noise into Music

Once I was at a meditation retreat, and a new dormitory was being built, so there was the sound of hammers and buzz saws. Now, you might think that construction noise isn't conducive to quiet contemplation, or for that matter to anything pleasant at all. (I've never seen "buzz saw" offered as a downloadable ring tone.) And in fact the meditation teacher who explained early on that we'd be hearing construction noises all week did so with an apologetic tone. But, as the teacher reminded us, a big part of mindfulness meditation is to accept the reality you face. Normally if you heard the abrasive, annoying sounds of construction, you might close your window or do something else to tune them out. But here the idea was to accept the sounds themselves while not buying into the idea that they're abrasive and annoying.

Doing this isn't easy, but it's straightforward in principle. The key is to meet the abrasiveness head-on—to, in a sense, examine the abrasions. You pay attention to the discomfort the noises create. Where in your body does annoyance or even revulsion reside? What is the texture of the feeling? The more fine-grained your examination, the more complete your acceptance of the feeling, the more its negative energy drains away.

In fact, not only did I manage to let go of the idea that these sounds were unpleasant; as I immersed myself in the sound waves emanating from hammers and buzz saws, the whole thing started sounding— pretty literally—like music. You may think of buzz-saw noise as abrupt and jarring, but I found a grace in the way the sound winds down, with its descending tone, and in the way it resumes with a more rapid tonal ascent.

The buzz-saw sound came to seem so beautiful that I found myself getting unsettled during long periods of silence, sitting there hoping that a construction worker would hurry the hell up and cut some plywood. Of course, this just shows how far from enlightenment I am;

according to Buddhist doctrine, I shouldn't become attached to things I find pleasant. But the point is that I had taken what is commonly called "noise" and found music in it.

It may be obvious where I'm headed: If we can turn literal noise into music, can't we turn figurative noise— all kinds of unwelcome perceptions and thoughts and feelings—into figurative music? Or at least take the harshness out of them? And it may be obvious how I'm going to answer that question: Yes, we can (with sufficiently diligent practice).

But before getting into these practical applications, let's get back to the original question: What exactly did my little buzz-saw symphony have to do with the formless, with emptiness? Well, for one thing, at this retreat I think I had managed to let go of what you might call "the buzz-saw form." The sound of a buzz-saw is part of a whole structure of connotations—central among them, of course, the idea of a buzz saw. And I think one reason we find buzz-saw sounds grating is because they're part of that structure—that is, because we know they're coming from buzz saws. Buzz saws, with their well-known capacity to sever bones as well as wood, are things many of us don't welcome contact with. Maybe the connotations of buzz saws—and the negative feelings those connotations evoke—help give us an aversion to the sound.

Of course, it may also be that humans by nature tend not to like the kind of sound a buzz saw makes. Certainly we're born with tendencies to like or dislike certain kinds of things—certain tastes, smells, sights, sounds. Still, there's no doubt that our reactions to perceptions are also to some extent a product of experience. At one point in my meditation, the buzz-saw sound, having escaped its usual buzz-saw form, started occupying another form; it started reminding me of a dentist's drill—and immediately, of course, it became *really* unpleasant. It was only when extracted from both of these "forms"—buzz-saw form and dentist-drill form—that the sound was pleasant.

Remember Ajahn Chah, the Thai monk who said that if you try to understand the idea of not-self by "intellectualizing" alone, your head will explode? He once recounted a time when he was trying to meditate and kept getting interrupted by sounds from a festival in a nearby village. Then, as he recalls it, he had a realization: "The sound is just the sound. It's me who is going out to annoy it. If I leave the sound alone, it won't annoy me. . . . If I don't go out and bother the sound, it's not going to bother me."

I wouldn't take that anecdote too literally; it's not as if sound bothers you in *retaliation* for your bothering it. The point is just that a sound by itself is a passive, not an active, thing, neither pleasant nor unpleasant. So to make it unpleasant, you have to go out and, in a sense, *do something* to it.

Look again at the final line of that passage from the *Samadhiraja Sutra*. It says that all things are "without essence, but with qualities that can be seen." This sutra isn't denying the reality of the buzz-saw sound waves that were hitting my ear, the "qualities" I was observing, but it seems to be saying that the "essence" I normally see beneath the qualities—essence of buzz saw—is a matter of interpretation; it's something I'm choosing to construct, or not, from the qualities. Essences don't exist independent of human perception.

This is the version of the emptiness doctrine that makes sense to me, and it's the version most widely accepted by Buddhist scholars: not the absence of everything, but the absence of essence. To perceive emptiness is to perceive raw sensory data without doing what we're naturally inclined to do: build a theory about what is at the heart of the data and then encapsulate that theory in a sense of essence.

An obvious rejoinder arises: But, um, *isn't* there, in fact, something at the heart of the buzz-saw sound? You know, something called a buzz saw? Something that's not empty and does, in fact, have form? It's wonderful that you were able to put that fact out of mind and thus turn noise into music, but if the buzz saw is really *there*, then your picture of reality wasn't getting clearer, but actually was in some sense getting less clear, right? And isn't the idea of Buddhism that you reduce your suffering by seeing the world *more* clearly?

The next few paragraphs do not contain a wholly satisfactory answer to these questions. Ideas as radical as emptiness can't be persuasively defended with one cute little buzz-saw anecdote. But I hope that within a couple of chapters this idea will sound, if not undeniably valid, at least much less crazy than it may have sounded at first. Meanwhile, let me just give a preliminary response to these questions about the alleged emptiness and formlessness of a buzz saw.

Yes, the buzz saw exists. It consists of things like a power cord, a blade, and a trigger. These, you might say, are among the buzz saw's "qualities." But when I talk about the "essence" of the buzz saw, I'm talking about something we perceive in a buzz saw that is more than the sum of such qualities, something that carries distinctive connotations and emotional resonance. And if I manage to divorce myself from some of those connotations and that resonance—enough that I can actually enjoy the sounds of a buzz saw—then that essence has started to erode.

To put it another way, before this particular meditation retreat I might have said, "It is part of the essence of buzz saws that they make unpleasant sounds." But it turns out that making unpleasant sounds isn't actually inherent in buzz saws. And if it isn't inherent in them, how can it be part of their essence?

In the next chapter I'll argue that the "essence" of *lots* of things— like, maybe, all of them—is not, in fact, inherent in them. For evidence, I'll draw on diverse findings from modern psychology. After that chapter I hope that this idea of formlessness or emptiness will seem more plausible—or, at the very least, that you'll have a clearer idea of exactly the sense in which I'm claiming it's plausible.

Meanwhile, one more retreat anecdote.

It's Stories All the Way Down

On the retreat at which I first heard about the formless, each yogi got one ten-minute meeting with one of the teachers, one-on-one, where we could raise any issues we were struggling with and get the teacher's guidance. My meeting was with a teacher named Narayan Liebenson. She is the one who read that passage from the *Samadhiraja Sutra*, but it was the retreat's other teacher, Rodney Smith, who had talked about the formless. This was my chance to get Narayan's take on exactly what he meant.

Narayan, by the way, is hard-core. Like most teachers at the Insight Meditation Society, she has done intensive contemplative practice, including months of solitude in the forests of Southeast Asia. She doesn't teach meditation just to reduce stress, though she is of course happy for that to be one of the benefits. She's here to help people achieve liberation.

For that reason, she didn't wholly approve of my writing this book. After all, writing a book about Buddhist meditative practice could impede the practice itself. If you're *trying* to achieve certain meditative states so you can describe them in a book, you may be less likely to achieve them—and less likely to make various breakthroughs that can come from approaching the practice in a different spirit. She once said to me, with a solemn look, "I think you may have to choose between writing this book and liberation."

But, I pointed out, the book might help other people follow the dharma—and if it helped enough of them, wouldn't that make up for my own failure to achieve liberation? She was unmoved. Her job is to teach liberation, and at that moment she was my teacher. Besides, she seemed to think that nothing does more good for the world than a truly liberated being—not even an unliberated author who steers others in the general direction of liberation.

Anyway, in this particular conversation, I asked Narayan whether

Rodney's perspective is widely shared among Vipassana teachers. Did she take the idea of the formless seriously? Yes, she said, she did. And, no, the things Rodney had said about the formless weren't considered radical in her circles. "Joseph would talk that way too," she said, referring to Joseph Goldstein.

So I pressed her on what precisely was meant by the term. She confirmed my suspicion that it didn't mean that the physical world doesn't exist or that it's devoid of structure. Tables exist, buzz saws exist. After a few minutes of conversation I felt I got her gist. I asked, "So the idea is that everything *meaningful* about the world is something we impose on it?" She answered, "Exactly."

I hasten to add that this doesn't mean we live in a meaningless universe. Deeply embedded in Buddhist thought is the intrinsic moral value of sentient life—not just the value of human beings but the value of all organisms that have subjective experience and so are capable of pain and pleasure, of suffering and not suffering. And this value in turn imparts value to other things, such as helping people, being kind to dogs, and so on. *Moral* meaning is, in that sense, inherent in life.

But the point Narayan was making is that, as we go about our day-to-day lives, we impart a kind of narrative meaning to things. Ultimately these narratives assume large form. We decide that something we've done was a huge mistake, and if we had done something else instead, everything would be wonderful. Or we decide that we must have some particular possession or achievement, and if we don't get it, everything will be horrible. Underlying these narratives, at their foundation, are elementary narrative judgments about the goodness or badness of things in themselves.

So, for example, if I start spinning a long narrative about how coming to this meditation retreat was a huge mistake, and I'm always making mistakes like this, and so on, there are a number of questionable premises on which this story rests. There's the premise that, had I not gone on this retreat, whatever I did instead would have gone swimmingly, whereas for all I know, I would have been run over by a bus. There's the premise that having a few painful experiences this week means the retreat was on balance bad for me, whereas in fact its long-term effects are unknowable. And at the base of this narrative lie the most basic kinds of premises: simple perceptual judgments such as "This buzz-saw sound I hear while trying to meditate is bad." And this kind of meaning, which seems so firmly embedded in the texture of things, isn't, in fact, an inherent feature of reality; it is something we impose on reality, a story we tell about reality.

We build stories on stories on stories, and the problem with the stories begins at their foundation. Mindfulness meditation is, among other things, a tool for examining our stories carefully, from the ground up, so that we can, if we choose, separate truth from fabrication.

11

The Upside of
Emptiness

One day, a fifty-nine-year-old man asked his wife where his wife was. "Fred"—the pseudonym given this man by the researchers who wrote up his case in the journal *Neurological Science*—wasn't kidding. "On her surprised answer that she was right there," the researchers wrote, "he firmly denied that she was his wife."

The problem wasn't that Fred didn't recognize his wife's face. Clearly this woman *looked* like his wife. But he insisted that she was a "double." His actual wife, he speculated, had gone out and would return later.

Fred suffered from Capgras delusion, which consists of being convinced that someone—usually a relative, sometimes a close friend—is an imposter. And a very good imposter, an exact replica—on the outside, at least. But not on the inside. This person may look exactly like, say, your mother, but she lacks what we might call essence-of-your-mother.

Essence, as we've seen, is central to the Buddhist concept of emptiness. At least its *absence* is central to the concept of emptiness. The idea of emptiness is that, while the things we perceive out there in the world do in some sense exist, they lack this thing called "essence." So when Fred looked at his wife and didn't see essence-of-wife, was he experiencing emptiness? Was he poised on the threshold of Buddhist enlightenment?

Um, no. The idea of enlightenment is to *lose* your delusions, whereas to start thinking that your wife isn't your wife is to *gain* a delusion. Hence the term Capgras *delusion*. Whatever was going on in Fred's brain, it wasn't what Buddhists mean by enlightenment.[†] At the same time, I think Fred's brain may have *something* in common with the brain of someone who, while in a deep meditative state, sees the world as wholly or partially "empty." And I think this prospect may shed important light on the experience of emptiness: what it is, why people experience it, and what we should make of it.

No one knows for sure what causes Capgras delusion. But a long-standing theory is that it results from a disruption of the connection between a part of the brain involved in visual processing (maybe the fusiform gyrus, which figures in facial recognition) and a part of the brain that processes emotions (such as the amygdala). What is clear is that there is some shortage of affect, of *feeling*; the feelings typically evoked by, say, your mother just aren't there. And if seeing somebody doesn't make you feel the way seeing your mother makes you feel, how could that person be your mother?

Identifying human beings is something we normally think of as a straightforward act of visual perception. It seems like the kind of thing a computer could do. In fact, computers do a good job of it, just by scanning faces. But apparently human beings have a more complicated way of identifying things: not just by how they look but by how they make you feel. At least—to judge by Capgras delusion—that seems to be the case when we're identifying friends and relatives.

Is it the case with lots of other things? Is our recognition of the house we live in and the car we drive, even the computer we use, dependent on our *feelings* about these things? Or, even if the absence of those feelings didn't impede recognition per se, would it overhaul our view of what these things are and what they mean? Does the meaning of the word *ocean*—not the dictionary meaning but the actual meaning of the word *to you*—depend on a mélange of feelings that you've come to associate with oceans? If you were suddenly cut off from those associations, would the ocean seem, well, empty?

I suspect so. And I suspect that this can help explain how the Buddhist doctrine of emptiness arose. Meditation can weaken the link between perceptions and thoughts, on the one hand, and the feelings, the affective resonances, that typically accompany them on the other. Well, if you do a really thorough job of that weakening, and perceptions become increasingly free of affective associations, this could change your view of the world. It could leave things looking the same on the outside but seeming as if they lack some inner something. In the words of the *Samadhiraja Sutra*, they would seem "without essence, but with qualities that can be seen." Maybe when the Buddhist idea of emptiness first took shape, it took shape in the minds of people who meditated very, very deeply—so deeply that the normal affective coloring of the world fell almost completely away; maybe as the feelings associated with various things faded, those things seemed transformed, deprived of a certain kind of substance.

One reason to doubt this possibility is that you may not think of yourself as having really strong feelings about, say, the ocean or your computer—at least, not so strong as to be integral to their very identities. But I want to make the case that feelings play a bigger role in perception than we normally appreciate.

The first piece of evidence is Capgras delusion itself—evidence that, notwithstanding the commonsensical division of the brain into "cognitive" and "affective" activities, the simple cognitive act of identifying someone can depend on affective response. After I trot out exhibits B and C, maybe it will seem more plausible that the doctrine of emptiness, before it was a doctrine, before Buddhist philosophers had articulated and defended it, was just an experiential apprehension had by people who meditated so long and so hard that they could see things and hear things without the overlay of feeling that had once clung to those things.

But that conjecture isn't the main point of this exercise. The main point is to explore more deeply the mechanics of this experiential apprehension—to get a clearer idea of what's going on in the brains of those committed contemplatives who see emptiness, as opposed to what goes on in the brains of the much larger number of people who see essences everywhere they look. This, in turn, will help us ask whether that second group of people—which is to say, pretty much all of us—is chronically deluded, and, if so, how grave the consequences of the delusion are. Plot spoiler: in some respects, I think, the consequences are pretty grave.

Exotic and Ordinary Essence

The psychologist Paul Bloom has written that "essentialism"—the tendency to attribute inner essences to things—is a "human universal." Some of his examples of essentialism are exotic: someone paid $48,875 for a tape measure that was owned by John F. Kennedy, apparently motivated by a sense that it was imbued with some sort of presidential "essence." Some of Bloom's examples are less exotic: a wedding ring typically evokes feelings—in the wearer, at least—that an identical-looking ring wouldn't evoke. But both the tape measure and the wedding ring are in some sense special, and the same is true of many things that project a particularly strong sense of essence.

Bloom writes in his book *How Pleasure Works* that such an object is special "because of its history, either through its relation to admired people or significant events or its connection to someone of personal significance. This history is invisible and intangible, and in most cases there is no test that can ever distinguish the special object from one that looks the same. But still, it gives us pleasure, and the duplicate would leave us cold."

Bloom thinks people are naturally "essentialists" in a broader sense than this, and I agree. In fact, that's part of the point of this chapter: that people infuse even things not "special" in Bloom's sense of the term with affectively charged essences.[1]

But there's some virtue in—temporarily, at least—confining the analysis to objects that are really, really special. This allows you to do a kind of informal experiment. You could, for example, say to the winning bidder at an auction, who is holding that presidential tape measure as if holding the crown jewels, "Oops, there was a mistake. That's actually the plumber's tape measure. We'll have to have the JFK tape measure sent to your house." Then you could watch the impact of this information. The bidder's altered facial expression would leave no doubt that there had been an alteration of feeling. A tape measure that moments ago inspired awe and adoration would now inspire nothing of the kind. A precious relic had turned into a mere object, emptied of the essence it possessed only moments earlier.

Such "experiments" occur in real life. Bloom relates the story of Nazi war criminal Hermann Goering learning that a painting he owned, which he'd thought was a genuine Vermeer, was in fact a forgery. At that moment, according to one observer, Goering looked "as if for the first time he [had] discovered there was evil in the world."

To watch Goering's face at that moment, or to watch the face of our hypothetical tape-measure owner, is to see a kind of correlation between perceived essence and affect. These "experiments" suggest that to see special items as having special essences is to have special *feelings* about them.

But what about the many less exotically special things in our environment, things that we don't think were owned by presidents or painted by Vermeer—the sight of a freight train or a pickup truck or a mountain stream; the sound of a foghorn or of crickets at night or birds in the morning? Here it's much harder to establish a link between essence and affect. For one thing, it's not so obvious that people *think* of these things as having essences. After all, people don't offer to pay exorbitant sums for them, and don't break into tears at the thought of parting with them on grounds that they're irreplaceable. And it's not so obvious that people have distinctive feelings upon seeing things as mundane as trains and trucks.

But there's long been a school of thought which holds that ordinary things *do* evoke affective reactions, if subtle ones. In 1980, the psychologist Robert Zajonc, expressing what was then a somewhat eccentric view, wrote, "There are probably very few perceptions and cognitions in everyday life that do not have a significant affective component, that aren't hot, or in the very least tepid. And perhaps all perceptions contain some affect. We do not just see 'a house': we see 'a handsome house,' 'an ugly house,' or 'a pretentious house.' We do not just read an article on attitude change, on cognitive dissonance, or on herbicides. We read an 'exciting' article on attitude change, an 'important' article on cognitive dissonance, or a 'trivial' article on herbicides."

Note, by the way, that Zajonc implicitly equates having *feelings* about things with making *judgments* about them. This equation is true to the Darwinian view (laid out in chapter 3) that, functionally speaking, feelings *are* judgments. It's also true to the meditative technique of relaxing judgment by critically inspecting our feelings. But I digress. Zajonc continues, "And the same goes for a sunset, a lightning flash, a flower, a dimple, a hangnail, a cockroach, the taste of quinine, Saumur, the color of earth in Umbria, the sound of traffic on 42nd

Street, and equally for the sound of a 1000-Hz tone and the sight of the letter Q."

The letter Q? That may be carrying it a bit too far, but not by much. I do think that, in addition to reacting affectively to particular things— that particularly handsome car, that particularly ugly car—we develop affective reactions to generic things, such as cars in general. Take tape measures: I really like them, even the nonpresidential kind. I like extending them and using them to get the answer to a question I have. (How long is the fluorescent light bulb that needs replacing?) And I like the feeling of letting them snap back into their coil. I don't generally pause in a hardware store to relish the sight of a tape measure, but I suspect that when I see one I have a subtly positive response, and this is part of my conception of a tape measure, part of what a tape measure means to me.

You can see why the "experiments" we can run with really special items, like JFK's tape measure or Goering's fake Vermeer, are hard to run when we're dealing with less special items. With special items, the affective connotation is a product of an explicit belief about the history of the item, so you can just tell the person that the belief is in fact false and then gauge the impact this news has on affect. But there's no comparable manipulation you can perform with much less special objects. You can't convince me that the many positive experiences I've had with tape measures didn't actually happen. And it probably wouldn't matter if you could, because my favorable disposition toward tape measures isn't the result of a conscious belief about my history with them anyway; it's the result of the emotional conditioning that happened unconsciously during that history.

The Infiltration of Perception by Feeling

Still, there's lots of evidence that people do tend to attach positive and negative associations to just about every kind of thing there is. There are two ways to show this, one subtle and cleverly revealing, and one not so subtle.

The not-so-subtle way is to just ask people what they think of things. In one study, people were shown pictures of things and asked to rate their goodness or badness on a scale of 4 to minus 4. Some of the pictures evoked stark and predictable judgments: swans were strongly positive; serpents' heads and bugs were strongly negative. Some of the pictures evoked more muted responses: chains and brooms and garbage cans were, on average, rated somewhat negatively, pumpkins and toothbrushes and envelopes somewhat positively.

The more subtle and cleverly revealing way to explore people's affective judgments goes beyond the question of whether people are natural evaluators and asks whether they're *automatic* evaluators. In other words, do they have affective reactions to things before they even have time to really think about them?

This question is explored through a process known as priming. Suppose you're shown two words in succession, and you're told that when you see the second word you should pronounce it out loud. It turns out that when the second word is *robin*, you'll utter it sooner— by a fraction of a second—if the first word is *bird* than if the first word is *street*. The word *bird* has "primed" your brain to respond to related words. This is called "semantic priming." There is also something you could call "affective priming." If you're shown the word *sunshine*, you'll more rapidly react to the word *glorious* than if you'd been shown the word *disease*. Likewise, you'll react to the word *horrible* more quickly if first shown the word *disease* than if shown the word *sunshine*.

These experiments aren't, of course, saying anything about what you feel when you reflect at length on disease. Things happen too fast for conscious reflection to matter. The presentation of the prime, the brief interval, and the presentation of the target word all happen in less than half a second. In fact, the effect holds up even if the prime is presented so briefly that the person isn't consciously aware of seeing it. So what these experiments show is that the word *disease*, before you call it consciously to mind, already has a negative tag.

That's not too surprising; disease is pretty horrible, and sunshine is pretty glorious. But we see the same dynamic with less obviously evocative things. In fact, the experimenters who surveyed people about their reactions to mundane things—to chains and brooms and garbage cans, to pumpkins and toothbrushes and envelopes—took those same pictures and, using a new group of people, did the priming experiments with them. And it turned out that, yes, pictures that had been judged negatively by the first group, the group asked to consciously evaluate them, tended to be judged negatively by the second group, the group that didn't even realize they *were* judging them but, by the speed of their reactions to subsequently displayed positive or negative words, rendered implicit judgments.

So Zajonc seems to have been right; human beings are automatic evaluators. We tend to assign adjectives to nouns, whether consciously or unconsciously, explicitly or implicitly.

When you think about it, Zajonc almost had to be right. From natural selection's point of view, the whole point of perception is to process information that has relevance to the organism's Darwinian interests that is, to its chances of getting its genes spread. And organisms register this relevance by assigning positive or negative values to the perceived information. We are designed to judge things and to encode those judgments in feelings.

With a species as complicated as ours, it may or may not always be obvious what relevance things have to Darwinian interests. Tape measures, for example, weren't part of the hunter-gatherer landscape in which we evolved. But we're designed by natural selection to get satisfaction out of finding the answers to questions, and over time, when I've asked how long something is, tape measures have given me the answer. Maybe that's why I've come to like them. Or maybe it has to do with how using a tape measure makes me feel about myself, a fact that may in turn be grounded in my watching various role models use them when I was a kid.

Anyway, to be clear: the claim isn't that everything I feel positively or negatively about will actually have an accordingly positive or negative impact on my chances of spreading my genes; the claim is just that the machinery in my mind that assigns feelings to things was originally designed to maximize genetic proliferation. That it no longer reliably does so is among the absurdities of being a human.

The Disturbing Invisibility of My Brother

One more clarification before we get back to emptiness: I'm not claiming that everyone has an affective reaction to everything. The studies I just described, like most studies, reported only aggregate statistics. Buried within that aggregation are particular subjects who reacted neutrally to particular words or pictures. And that's not surprising. After all, even back in our hunter-gatherer days, the landscape featured things that didn't affect our chances of spreading genes one way or the other. So there have always been things that didn't evoke much in the way of feelings.

Then again, things like that are things organisms don't pay much attention to in the first place—precisely because they're not important in Darwinian terms. The things organisms *do* pay attention to, on the other hand, *do* tend to be of Darwinian significance, and so will tend to evoke feelings. As a result, the *perceptual* landscape—the landscape of things that we're paying attention to, the things that dominate our consciousness—will tend to be infused, however subtly, with feeling. If there's something you don't have any feelings at all about, you probably won't much notice it in the first place. It may be only a slight exaggeration to say there's no such thing as an immaculate perception.

My older brother, after reaching the phase of middle age when women no longer paid much attention to him, said, "It isn't that they think I'm bad-looking. They just don't realize I exist." Exactly! As a heterosexual woman walks down a city block, there are tons of things she could focus on, so the first job of her perceptual apparatus is to filter out things that, with the most cursory, even unconscious appraisal, are seen to not merit extended, conscious appraisal. Sadly, that category of things includes my brother (who, also sadly, was younger than I am now when he attained this status).

But if things *do* merit further appraisal, the appraisal will ultimately be reflected in this woman's feeling. Attractive young male? Less attractive but kind-looking young male? Young male who is intriguingly attractive but looks like he may be insufferably egotistical? Male who is as old as my brother but, unlike my brother, drives a $70,000 car and wears a Rolex watch? All of these kinds of men elicit distinctive feelings. Anything that, by natural selection's lights, is worth paying much attention to at all should, in theory, trigger feelings.

And feelings infuse things with essence. At least, that's my hypothesis—that the dampened sense of essence some meditators feel has a lot to do with dampened feelings.

I once tried out this theory on the person I first heard talk about "the formless," Rodney Smith. Rodney is a tall, gangly, gray-haired man with an evangelical air that is unusual among meditation teachers. If you put him behind a Southern Baptist church pulpit, he wouldn't seem out of place—until, at least, he started talking about "the formless." In person, Rodney has a direct, no-nonsense style of speaking that can be a real time saver. I once asked him what the relationship was between this formlessness thing he kept talking about and the Mahayana idea of emptiness. With a bit of a shrug and a dismissive wave of his hand, he said, "Same thing."

It was some time after that exchange, during a longer conversation with him, that I decided to try out my theory that a dialing down of the affective reaction to things is what leads to the experience of emptiness.

Rodney had been trying to explain to me what the experience of emptiness is like. On the one hand, I gathered, there's a sense in which things in his perceptual field don't project their independent identities as strongly as they do for most of us. But, Rodney emphasized, you don't lose your ability to identify things. "You want to be able to pick up a pair of glasses and put it on, and not think that it's a pencil," he said. "You don't lose the shapes or colors of things. It's just that the space between them no longer divides."

I asked, "Do you have less strong emotional reactions to things than you might otherwise have? Do you invest them less with, kind of, emotional content?"

He replied, "That would make sense, wouldn't it—that if things weren't as substantial as you believed them to be, your reaction to things would also simmer? So that happens. You see, all the states of equanimity come through the realization that things aren't what we thought they were."

I felt vindicated, but not completely vindicated. In one sense, Rodney was corroborating my theory. He was saying that, yes, the perception of formlessness or emptiness is correlated with a dampened affective reaction to things. But his interpretation of this correlation seemed different from mine. Whereas I've been saying that the dampened affect leads to the perception of emptiness, he was saying that it's the other way around: the perception of emptiness dampens the affect; once you see that the thing you're accustomed to reacting strongly to isn't much of a "thing" in the first place, it only makes sense to react less strongly.

Which one of us is right? Maybe we both are. Or, at least, maybe the difference between what he's saying and what I'm saying isn't ultimately very meaningful.

Remember, for starters, that when I talk about our affect being dampened, our feelings being subdued, I'm not saying that's a *bad* thing. Indeed, I've tried to show why certain feelings are a poor guide to reality. And I've suggested, more broadly, that the entire infrastructure of feelings should be viewed with a certain suspicion, given that it was built by natural selection, whose ultimate aim isn't to foster clear perceptions and thoughts but rather to foster the kinds of perceptions and thoughts that have gotten genes spread in the past. So for me to characterize Rodney's experience as a dampening of feeling certainly isn't to say that it couldn't clarify his view of the world.

With this in mind, let's look at the two key claims Rodney is making: (1) The apprehension of formlessness or emptiness is a truer perception of things than our ordinary view, and (2) the feelings we normally experience in reaction to these things aren't appropriate in light of the truth about them. These claims are consistent with what I'm saying. Rodney and I are just disagreeing over the mechanics of insight. He says—and here he reflects the orthodox position within Buddhism—that the clarity of vision leads to the dampening of feelings. I say that the dampening of feelings leads to the clarity of vision. Indeed, I'd almost go so far as to say the dampening of feelings *is* the clarity of vision, so finely is affect intertwined with perception—in particular, with the perception of essence.[†]

Feelings and Stories

There's one other thing that essence seems to be intertwined with: stories. The stories we are told about things, and the stories we tell ourselves about things, influence how we feel about those things and, presumably, thus shape the essence that we sense in them. If the story behind a tape measure is that it belonged to JFK, that implies a different feeling—and a different essence—than the story that the tape measure belongs to a plumber. If we think of ourselves as having a successful marriage and wonderful, thriving children, then the sight of our home probably gives off more positive vibes than if we think of ourselves as trapped in an oppressive marriage that has bred ne'er-do-well kids. And so on.

This is a major theme of Bloom's: that the stories we tell about things, and thus the beliefs we have about their history and their nature, shape our experience of them, and thus our sense of their essence. One of his favorite examples is a study that involved wine connoisseurs. Forty of them deemed a Bordeaux with a premium label (*grand cru classé*) worth drinking, but only twelve bestowed that honor on a Bordeaux labeled as mere table wine (*vin de table*). You've probably guessed the punch line: the two kinds of bottles contained one kind of wine.

Wine is an especially clear example of how stories inform our pleasures ("That was a very good year"), but Bloom thinks that, if you look closely enough, every pleasure has a consequential story behind it. He once said to me, "There's no such thing as a simple pleasure. There's no such thing as a pleasure that's untainted by your beliefs about what you're being pleasured by." He used food as an example: "If you hand me something and I taste it, part of my knowledge is that it was given to me by someone I trusted, and I would taste it differently than if I found it on the floor, or if I paid a thousand dollars for it. Or take paintings. It's true that you can look at a painting and not know who painted it . . . and just appreciate it largely based on what it looks like. At the same time, you know it's a painting." In other words, he continued, "it's not a natural occurrence of paint splattered on a wall. . . . Somebody made it at some time for display, and that colors things." So too, he said, with "the simplest of sensations: an orgasm, drinking water when you're thirsty, stretching, anything. It's always under some sort of description. It's always viewed as an instance of some sort of category." There is always, in other words, an implied narrative.

The fact that pleasure is shaped by our sense of essence, and thus by the stories we tell and the beliefs we hold, suggests to Bloom that our pleasures are, in a sense, more profound than we may realize. "There is always a depth to pleasure," he has written.

But you could look at it the other way around. Given that our experience of a bottle of wine can be influenced by slapping a fake label on it, you might say that, actually, there is a *superficiality* to our pleasure, and that a deeper pleasure would come if we could somehow taste the wine itself, unencumbered by beliefs about it that may or may not be true. That is closer to the Buddhist view of the matter.

The Man without Stories

As Exhibit A, I give you the wine-tasting experience of Gary Weber. Weber is a compact, energetic, silver-haired man who has, over the decades, logged thousands and thousands of hours of meditative practice. By Weber's account, all this work has gotten him to a point where his day-to-day consciousness is very different than it used to be, and certainly different from, say, mine. He says his experience involves very little in the way of the self-referential thoughts that dominate the consciousness of most of us: Why did I say that stupid thing yesterday? How can I impress these people tomorrow? Can't wait to eat that chocolate bar! And so on. He calls these the "emotionally laden, I-me-my thoughts."

We'll have to take Weber's word for what it's like to be him, but his claim to have achieved some rare state of consciousness does have a kind of corroboration. He participated in a landmark brain-scan study at Yale Medical School that involved a number of highly accomplished, even renowned meditators. It's the study I alluded to in chapter 4, the one that found the default mode network quieting down during deep meditation. But in Weber's case, the study found something different: his default mode network was quiet—very, very quiet—from the get-go, before he even tried to meditate.

Though I'm using Weber to illustrate the Buddhist idea of emptiness, I should concede that he is in some ways not well suited to that purpose. He did study extensively in the Zen Buddhist tradition, but he has also studied in, and been influenced by, Hindu traditions. And there are parts of Buddhism he rejects—the most important of which, for our purposes, is the term *emptiness*. He considers the term, at best, misleading. He says he's never known anybody who reached great contemplative depths and reported, "Oh, it's a big void." His own experience of the world is too rich to just call it empty without qualification. "I've used words like *empty fullness* or *full emptiness*," he says.

But whatever you want to call Weber's experience of the world, it sounds very much like what Rodney Smith describes: a world in which things don't have distinctive essences that set them sharply apart from one another. Though Weber, like Smith, can of course tell the difference between a chair and a table and a lamp, and responds appropriately to each, these items don't project independent identities as forcefully as they used to; there's a continuity to things. "There's not that differentiation between them and their background," Weber says. "They're all one stuff." He sometimes describes this "stuff" they seem to be made of as a kind of energy, but "there's no differentiation in energy or how you feel about them."

I once tried to get Weber to elaborate on the nature of the enjoyment he gets from the world and how it differs from the enjoyment I get from the world. I said, "So you're saying, I gather, that there is a kind of pleasure that you can derive via your senses that does not constitute emotional involvement of a problematic kind."

"That's correct," he said. But he hastened to add, "You haven't lost your nerve endings. . . . Green tea still tastes like green tea, red wine still tastes like red wine. You don't lose that. What you lose is the carry-forward of that sensation: This is a *fantastic* glass of wine—this was a great year."

But, I pointed out, some people would say that if you don't at least consider it a *good* glass of wine—if you don't even get emotionally involved enough to *like* the wine—then there's not much point in living.

He answered, "But it's a much cleaner perception. If I'm tasting a glass of wine and I'm trying to impress some restaurant critics or some friend who's a great wine fancier, then I may have a story going, I may have an expectation for how this wine should be and how I should expect it to taste, and so it really blocks my clear, simple perception. . . . So by getting this thought out of the way, this emotional thought out of the way, I have a much higher likelihood of directly perceiving whatever the sensation is."

Oddly, I kind of know what he means. When I've been on meditation retreats, sitting in the dining hall, savoring food, I've at times gotten so immersed in the flavors and textures that I wasn't really conscious of *what* I was eating—what fruit, what vegetable, whatever. I don't recall any story, in even the most basic sense, accompanying the sensation. What I do recall is the sensation feeling very good.

Sometimes I think there are two different ways that "essence" can impede clear perception. In one case—the "fantastic glass of wine" case—the sense of essence is strong and evokes feelings that wouldn't be part of the "essenceless" version of the experience. But sometimes the sense of essence is weak—so weak it tends to steer you away from the experience altogether. When I'm on retreat and I get immersed in the texture of a tree's bark, maybe that's because I don't have my usual essence-of-tree feeling—a feeling so devoid of power that it says, basically, "It's just another tree, so you can walk right past it and move on to something more important." Through our sense of essence we give things labels, and one use of labels is to file things away so you don't have to spend time on them.

Maybe the reason babies get so immersed in shapes and textures is because they haven't yet developed their filing system, their sense of essence. In other words, they don't yet "know" what the "things" surrounding them are, so the world is a wonderland of exploration. And maybe this helps explain how Weber could say that "emptiness" is actually "full": sometimes not seeing essence lets you get drawn into the richness of things.

Another way to put it is to say that in some cases the story evoked by essence is a minimizing story: That's *just* a tree or *just* a piece of celery. But in other cases—the fantastic glass of wine, the tape measure that belonged to JFK—the story is an amplifying story, so loud that it overwhelms intrinsic experience. Maybe essences can be labels that discourage experience altogether, or labels that encourage experience but in some sense distort it.

At any rate, that Weber equates having a strong emotional reaction to something with having a "story" about it makes sense to me, and so does the idea that jettisoning both the story and the emotion would tend to leave things with a less distinctive essence than they'd otherwise project. But is this really possible—stripping away the story, the background knowledge, behind your sensory experience? And, if so, what is going on in the brain when that happens?

Stories and Brain Scans

A possible answer to the second question came from an experiment involving wine and a brain scanner. The experimenters gave people several different kinds of wine, labeled with several different prices. But two of the choices, the $90 bottle and the $10 bottle, were actually the same wine.

People liked the $90 version better. No surprise there. What was interesting was what their brains did as they made these evaluations. When they drank wine from the $90 bottle, there was more activity in the medial orbitofrontal cortex—the mOFC—than when they drank the same wine with a $10 label affixed. The mOFC is a part of the brain whose activity is correlated with pleasure of various kinds—not just tastes but aromas and music. This experiment suggests that it's also a part of the brain that's influenced by the story you've been told about the pleasure you're feeling and by the preconceptions this story gives you. The $90 story gets this part of the brain more excited than the $10 story.

But there are also parts of the brain that play a role in pleasure and *weren't* influenced by the wine's price tag. "Importantly," wrote the researchers, "we did not find evidence for an effect of prices on . . . the primary taste areas such as the insula cortex, the ventroposterior medial nucleus of the thalamus, or the parabrachial nuclei of the pons." A "natural interpretation," they continued, is that the mOFC—the part of the brain that changed in response to the price tag—is where "the top-down cognitive processes that encode the flavor expectancies are integrated with the bottom-up sensory components of the wine." In other words, the mOFC seems to be where story, and hence expectation, mixes in with raw sensory data to modulate what the researchers called "the hedonic experience of flavor."

You might ask if wine drinking is really worth all this study. What does it matter if, as Weber suggests, the story-free consumption of wine is a purer, even pleasanter experience than the more common kind of drinking? Most wine drinkers strike me as pretty happy with the way their wine tastes, however laden it may be with dubious narratives. It's not as if deficient wine drinking is a looming global crisis.

But the implications of all this go beyond wine. We're exploring the brain's capacity to create illusions. This particular experiment studied the specific illusion that the intrinsic taste of a beverage depends on the story that has been affixed to it. But that's just one example of a more general illusion: that the "essences" we sense in things really exist, that they inhabit the things we perceive, when in fact they are constructions of our minds, with no necessary correspondence to reality. Things come with stories, and the stories, whether true or false, shape how we feel about the things and thus shape the things themselves, giving them the full form we perceive.

In some contexts, this mental construction of essence can be way, way more consequential than whether wine tastes better with a $90 label than with a $10 label. One such context is when we're attributing essence not to tape measures or houses or any other inanimate object but to other human beings. That is the subject of the next chapter.

12

A Weedless
World

Several days into my first meditation retreat, I was taking a walk in the woods when I encountered an old enemy. Its name is *Plantago major*, and it is commonly known as the plantain weed. Years earlier, when I lived in Washington, DC, my lawn had been afflicted by this weed, and I spent many hours battling it—most of them just pulling it out of the ground, but sometimes I got so desperate that I'd use weed killer. I like to think that I'm not the kind of person who would devote much time to loathing forms of foliage, but I have to admit that my attitude toward this plant was in some sense one of hostility.

Yet now, on this meditation retreat, I was struck—for the first time ever—by the weed's beauty. Maybe I should be putting the word *weed* in quotes, because to see a weed as beautiful is to question whether it really should be called a weed. And that is the question I asked myself as I stood there looking at my former foe. Why was this green-leafed thing called a weed, whereas other nearby things that fit the same description weren't? I looked at those nearby things, and then at the weed, and found myself unable to answer the question. There seemed to be no objective visual criteria that distinguished weeds from nonweeds.

In retrospect, I guess I would call this my first close brush with the experience of emptiness. Maybe it wasn't as dramatic—and certainly it wasn't as pervasive and persistent—as the experiences described in the previous chapter by Rodney Smith and Gary Weber. But it had the key characteristic of their experience: the weed was projecting its identity less strongly than it traditionally had. Though as visually discernible as ever, it was in some sense less dramatically marked off from the surrounding vegetation than before. It now lacked the essence-of-weed that had previously made it stand out from the other plants and seem uglier than they seemed.

So essence matters! One minute you see a certain essence in something and you want to kill it, and the next minute the essence has vanished and you don't want to kill it.

Of course, the stakes aren't all that high here. So far as I know, weeds aren't capable of pleasure or pain, so yanking one out of the ground isn't a grave moral transgression. Still, with weeds—more than with lamps or pencils or eyeglasses—we are approaching the realm of moral psychology, the realm of judgments about good and bad that have consequences for the way we treat other beings. And when the beings in question are sentient—human beings, for example—the stakes can be high.

These moral stakes are the main reason I'm spending so much time on the doctrine of emptiness. At the root of the way we treat people, I think, is the essence we see them as having. So it matters whether these perceptions of essence are really true or whether, as the doctrine of emptiness suggests, they are in some sense illusions.

From a Darwinian standpoint, the reason people attribute essence to other people is the same reason they attribute essence to things in general. Fellow human beings, no less than food or tools or predators or shelter, were part of the environment in which we evolved. So natural selection designed us to react to them in particular ways, and it engineered those reactions by giving us feelings toward them, and those feelings give shape to the essence we sense in them. But fellow human beings were a more complicated part of our environment than, say, shelter or tools, and they were a very, very important part. So it stands to reason that we would possess specialized mental machinery for sizing people up and then assigning them an essence.

Our Essence-of-Person Machinery

Decades of social psychology experiments have shed light on how that machinery works. For starters, it works fast. We start sizing people up the moment we first encounter them, and in some cases we can do a good job on the basis of little evidence. For example, if you show people a short videotape of someone talking or engaging in social interaction and then ask them to assess something about the person—her professional competence, for example, or her status—the assessments match up pretty well with more objective measurements. That holds true even when there's no audio, so that all the cues are nonverbal. And a judgment rendered after thirty seconds is almost as likely to be accurate as a judgment rendered after five minutes.

Two Harvard psychologists conducted a meta-analysis of dozens of these "thin-slice" studies and concluded that, after a very brief observation, "some stable underlying essence is picked up by judges." By "judges," of course, they meant the people in the experiments who did the observing, but they might as well have been talking about all of us; judging is what we're designed to do.

Our judgments can rest on evidence that may seem laughably superficial. For example, people considered attractive are more likely to be rated as competent. But this makes a certain kind of sense; attractive people do seem to have an easier time getting their way socially, and being able to pull social levers can be a big part of competence.

When it comes to making *moral* judgments, we don't put so much stock in looks. Attractive people aren't much more likely to be judged as having integrity or being considerate than unattractive people. That too makes sense, since there's no reason to think they *are* more consid erate or conscientious.[†] However, one thing judgments about moral fiber have in common with judgments about competence and status is that we often make them on the basis of a single data point. Though various experiments show this, there's no point in trotting one out: just reflect on your own behavior. If you see a person stopping to help someone who is lying injured on the sidewalk, don't you think, "Oh, what a nice person"? If you see a person walking briskly past someone lying injured on the sidewalk, don't you think, "Oh, what a not-so-nice person"?

I know what you're thinking: But people who stop to help the needy *are* nice. And people who walk briskly past them *aren't* nice.

Actually, you're wrong! A famous study published in 1973 showed as much. The study was conducted by two Princeton University psy chologists, and it involved, for starters, setting up an opportunity for people to be Good Samaritans, to help a stranger in need. Here is how the psychologists described the scene they created: "When the subject passed through the alley, the victim was sitting slumped in a doorway, head down, eyes closed, not moving. As the subject went by, the victim coughed twice and groaned, keeping his head down."

Some of the experimental subjects stopped to help, and some didn't. If you had been watching all this, you probably would have seen essence-of-good-person in the former and essence-of-bad-person in the latter. But there's actually a different explanation for why some helped and some didn't.

The subjects of the experiment were students at Princeton Theo-logical Seminary. They had been told that they had to go give a short, impromptu talk in a nearby building. Some had been told they were late for the talk, while others were told they had time to spare. Of the former group, 10 percent stopped to help, and of the latter group, 63 percent stopped. So seeing essence-of-good-person in that 63 percent is misleading at best; it would be more accurate to see essence-of-not-being-in-a-hurry.

Aside from degree of hurriedness, there was only one other variable that the experimenters manipulated. Half of the subjects, before heading over to give their talk, were told to read the Bible story of the Good Samaritan and then give their talk on that. The other half read a passage unrelated to altruism. It turns out that even reflecting on the Good Samaritan didn't increase the chances of being a Good Samaritan.

This experiment fits into a large body of psychological literature about something called "the fundamental attribution error." The word *attribution* refers to the tendency to explain people's behavior in terms of either "dispositional" factors—in other words, the kind of person they are—or "situational" factors, like whether they happen to be late for a talk. The word *error* refers to the fact that these attributions are often wrong, that we tend to underestimate the role of situation and overestimate the role of disposition. In other words, we're biased in favor of essence.

The term *fundamental attribution error* was coined in 1977 by the psychologist Lee D. Ross, and its implications can be disorienting. For example, it's common to think of criminals and clergy as being two fundamentally different *kinds* of people. But Ross and fellow psychologist Richard Nisbett have suggested that we rethink this intuition. As they put it: "Clerics and criminals rarely face an identical or equivalent set of situational challenges. Rather, they place themselves, and are placed by others, in situations that differ precisely in ways that induce clergy to look, act, feel, and think rather consistently like clergy and that induce criminals to look, act, feel, and think like criminals."

The philosopher Gilbert Harman, after reviewing the literature on the fundamental attribution error, raised questions about the very existence of such character traits as honesty, benevolence, and friendliness. "Since it is possible to explain our ordinary belief in character traits as deriving from certain illusions," he wrote, "we must conclude that there is no empirical basis for the existence of character traits."

This may sound like an extreme view, and certainly many scholars interpret the literature on attribution error less dramatically. Most psychologists who study these things will tell you that some personality traits are, in the average person, fairly stable over time. Still, there is no doubt that our attribution of moral essence to people—seeing them as nice, mean, friendly, unfriendly—does run ahead of the actual evidence. I have more than once seen someone in public behaving so rudely or inconsiderately that I immediately saw him as—and *felt* him as—bad. And I have more than once, when under great stress, behaved just as rudely and inconsiderately. Yet I did not consider myself bad— at least, not *essentially* bad even on later reflection.

One reason I let myself off the hook is that I understand that the stress caused my bad behavior; it wasn't the "real me" who did the bad thing. But with other people, I'm less likely to ponder that possibility. That's what the fundamental attribution error is: I attribute their behavior to disposition, not situation; I locate the badness in them, not in environmental factors.

Why would the human mind be designed to ignore or downplay situational factors when sizing people up? Well, for starters, remember that natural selection didn't design human minds to size people up *accurately*. It designed human minds to size people up in a way that would lead to interactions that benefited the genes of the humans doing the sizing up.

Consider what, for my money, is one of the more ridiculous kinds of arguments people have. It typically starts with the assertion "She's a really nice person" or "He's a good guy." Then someone will beg to differ: "No, she's not so nice" or "No, he's actually a bad guy." These arguments can go on forever without either party saying, "Well, maybe she's nice to me but not nice to you" or "Maybe he's good in the context in which I tend to encounter him and bad in the context in which you encounter him."

From natural selection's point of view, there's no reason for people to give much weight to such a possibility—the possibility that niceness and goodness are largely situational, not dispositional, properties. After all, the essence model—the belief that each person has a generally good or a generally bad disposition—works pretty well. If someone is consistently nice to you, it makes sense to get into a relationship of reciprocal niceness—in other words, a friendship. And a belief that the person is essentially good does a fine job of drawing you into that friendship.

What's more, this belief will make it easy for you to go around *saying* that this person is good—which is handy, since speaking highly of a friend is part of the reciprocal altruism that constitutes friendship. Seeing essence-of-good in your friends lets you discharge this part of the deal effortlessly. It frees you from the nagging awareness that, for all you know, when you're not around, your friends spend their time bilking elderly people.

If, on the other hand, someone is consistently mean to you, then seeing essence-of-bad in him is what leads to optimally self-serving behavior on your part. Not only will you avoid doing favors that would probably go unreciprocated anyway; you'll go around saying, with conviction, that he is a bad person. And it makes sense to say that your enemies are bad people, since the more you can do to undermine their stature, the less they'll be in a position to hurt you.

Actually, in the modern world, this may not be such an effective strategy. But in the small hunter-gatherer societies in which humans evolved, persistently badmouthing people might indeed have had an appreciable effect on their social standing. It also would have served as a warning to others not to get on your bad side.

To summarize, there's one situational variable that always biases our evaluations of people: every time we see them doing something, they're doing it in our presence, and for all we know they behave differently around or toward other people. But it makes sense—in a self-serving way—for us to ignore this variable and attribute the behavior we see to their disposition. That way we'll see them as possessing the essence—good or bad—that it's most in our interest to see them possessing. Conveniently, our friends and allies will have essence-of-good, and our rivals and enemies will have essence-of-bad.

Our Essence-Preservation Machinery

But what if reality intrudes on this convenient illusion? What if we do happen to see or hear of an enemy doing something good? And what if we see or hear of a friend doing something bad? Doesn't this threaten to vaporize the essence we've come to see in them?

Yes, it does pose that threat. But our brains are very good at fending off threats! In fact, our brains seem to have a mechanism designed to deal with this particular threat. You might call it the essence-preservation mechanism.

It turns out that the fundamental attribution error—the tendency to overestimate the role of disposition and underestimate the role of situation—isn't quite as simple as psychologists originally thought. Sometimes we actually downplay the role of disposition and amplify the role of situation.

There are two kinds of cases in which we tend to do this: (1) if an enemy or rival does something good, we're inclined to attribute it to circumstance—he's just giving money to the beggar to impress a woman who happens to be standing there; (2) if a close friend or ally does something bad, then here too circumstance tends to loom large—she's yelling at a beggar who asks for money because she's been stressed out over her job.

This interpretive flexibility shapes not only our personal lives but international relations. The social scientist Herbert C. Kelman has noted how it keeps enemies on the enemies list: "Attribution mechanisms . . . promote confirmation of the original enemy image. Hostile actions by the enemy are attributed dispositionally, and thus provide further evidence of the enemy's inherently aggressive, implacable character. Conciliatory actions are explained away as reactions to situational forces—as tactical maneuvers, responses to external pressure, or temporary adjustments to a position of weakness—and therefore require no revision of the original image." This helps explain why, when wars approach, people who welcome them do their best to demonize the leader of the country they want to go to war with. In the run-up to one of America's two wars with Iraq, the (then) hawkish American magazine *The New Republic* put an image of Iraqi president Saddam Hussein on its cover with one embellishment: his mustache was cropped so that it looked like Hitler's. Not very subtle, but effective—because once someone is firmly placed in the enemy box, our attribution mechanisms make escaping the box very hard. If, for example, someone like Hussein lets international inspectors into his country to look for weapons of mass destruction—which he did shortly before the Iraq War of 2003—it must be a trick. He must be hiding those weapons of mass destruction somewhere. After all, Hussein has essence-of-bad, if not essence-of-evil!

And, to be sure, Hussein *had* done horrible things. But failing to think clearly about him led to more horrible things: the death of well over 100,000 innocent people in the Iraq War and its aftermath.

War offers a good example of how essence can spread from one level to another. You start out with the idea that a nation's leader is essentially bad. From this you move to the idea that an entire nation—the nation of Iraq or Germany or Japan—is your enemy. This then translates into the idea that all the soldiers of that country—or even all the *people* in that country—are essentially bad. And if people are bad, that means you can kill them without feeling the sting of conscience. The United States dropped atomic bombs on two Japanese cities—cities, not military bases—and drew virtually no protest from Americans.

Happily, most of us haven't been swept up in tribal psychology with such lethal consequence. But less weighty instances of this psychology altering our perception and moral calculus are common. A particularly telling example occurred in 1951, only a mile east of the Princeton Theological Seminary, site of that 1973 Good Samaritan experiment.

The Essence of Opposition

The place was Palmer Stadium, and the occasion was a football game between Princeton and Dartmouth. This was back in the days when Ivy League football was world-class football. The week before the game, Princeton's all-American tailback, Dick Kazmeier, had appeared on the cover of *Time* magazine.

The game was rough and, by some accounts, dirty. Kazmeier had his nose broken in the second quarter, and in the third quarter a Dartmouth player left the game with a broken leg. Two psychology professors, Hadley Cantril of Princeton and Albert Hastorf of Dartmouth, later wrote, "Tempers flared both during and after the game. . . . Accusations soon began to fly." Hastorf and Cantril turned the occasion into a study of tribal psychology. They showed films of the game to Princeton students and Dartmouth students and found sharp differences of perspective. For example, while Princeton students, on average, saw Dartmouth commit 9.8 infractions of the rules, Dartmouth students, on average, saw 4.3 Dartmouth infractions. These findings may not shock you; that tribal affiliation can skew perception is common knowledge. But this study took a real-world example of this bias and carried it from the realm of anecdote into the realm of data. That's how it became a classic.

What's less well-known than the study's famous quantification of bias is that the authors raised questions about whether *bias* was really the right word. When we think of a cognitive bias, we think of a distortion of what would otherwise be a clear view of the thing perceived. But that presupposes that there *is* a thing being perceived. Hastorf and Cantril wrote, "It is inaccurate and misleading to say that different people have different 'attitudes' concerning the same 'thing.' . . . The data here indicate that there is no such 'thing' as a 'game' existing 'out there' in its own right which people merely 'observe.' The 'game' 'exists' for a person and is experienced by him only in so far as certain happenings have significances in terms of his purpose. Out of all the occurrences going on in the environment, a person selects those that have some significance for him from his own egocentric position in the total matrix."

Hastorf and Cantril weren't talking about the movie *The Matrix*, of course. But, like the movie, they were raising doubts about how real "reality" is—about whether it makes sense to talk about "things" existing out there, independent of the minds that conceive them. They wrote, "For the 'thing' simply is not the same for different people whether the 'thing' is a football game, a presidential candidate, Communism, or spinach."

All this reminds me of a conversation I had with Leda Cosmides, whom we met in chapter 7 and who did much to develop the modular view of the mind. Actually, she no longer calls it the modular view. The term *modules*, she says, has come to be misunderstood, in part because some of the misconceptions about it that I tried to dispel in chapter 7 haven't been widely dispelled. She now uses other terminology, such as the more precise, if considerably less elegant, "domain-specific psychological mechanisms."

Leda and I were discussing the relationship between these modules and the various biases that afflict human apprehension of the world. Earlier in the conversation I had talked about how our view of the world can be colored by whichever module is dominating our consciousness at the moment. She questioned whether it made sense to talk about a process of "coloration"—as if there was some uncolored view that had existed before the color was applied. "There's always some psychological mechanism doing something," she said. "It's creating our world, it's creating our perception of the world. That's why I wouldn't say domain-specific mechanisms color our perceptions—I'd say they *create* our perceptions. There's no way of perceiving the world that doesn't involve carving it conceptually into pieces."

This sounds quite like the view from Buddhism: everything, from spinach to football games, is empty of inherent existence; things—forms—come into existence in our consciousness only after we have taken some combination of elements in our perceptual field and imposed a collective meaning on them. Hastorf and Cantril wrote, "An 'occurrence' on the football field or in any other social situation does not become an experiential 'event' unless and until some significance is given to it." And this significance, they said, comes from a kind of database of significances, a database that resides "in what we have called a person's assumptive form-world."

Until those significances are assigned, presumably, the world is in some sense formless. But once they are assigned, there is form; there is essence.

In fact, there are essences within essences. There is essence-of-football-game, essence-of-football-team, essence-of-football-player. And these different essences can inform one another. The specific essence that a particular football game has will depend on the essences of the two teams—for example, which team we like and how much we like it and the way in which we like it—and this will in turn inform the essences of the players.

Or maybe things will work the other way around, and the essence we see in a particular football player will determine which team we favor, which will in turn shape the form the game assumes in our memory. No doubt, somewhere in America in 1951, some kid who had never heard of Princeton read the *Time* magazine cover story about Dick Kazmeier and became a Princeton fan, and all subsequent news about Princeton football games was folded into the appropriate form.

I'm not saying—and I don't think Hastorf and Cantril were saying—that if you don't have a preferred football team, then the world of football is for you a world without form. If you're walking through an airport and look up and see a football game on TV, you perceive a kind of generic essence-of-football-game before you even know what teams are playing. But even though you don't have a team preference, you may notice, on close inspection, that this "generic" sense of essence does in fact involve a kind of preference. Though you're not a fan of either team, you may be a *football* fan, and thus be drawn into closer engagement with the game, curious to see who is playing or just eager to see some interesting plays. If, on the other hand, you're not a football fan, the essence you perceive will not be enthralling and may even be off-putting, however mildly.

This is a reminder that specifically *tribal* psychology is in one sense not all that different from psychology generally. We go through each day attaching positive and negative tags to things we see. Being affiliated with a tribe—a football team, a nation, an ethnic group—is a particular instance of that tendency, and sometimes a particularly intense instance of it: our tribe can be *very* good, and its enemies *very* bad.

At the same time, it would be misleading to act as if tribal psychology is just regular psychology with the volume turned up. Natural selection designed parts of the human mind specifically to steer us through conflicts—conflicts between individuals and conflicts between groups. Some of our mental machinery is exquisitely geared to that function, including the essence-preservation machinery that makes our enemies more readily blameworthy for bad behavior than our allies and makes it easy to witness the suffering of our enemies with indifference.

In fact, "satisfaction" is more like it than "indifference." One piece of moral equipment natural selection implanted in our brains is a sense of justice—the intuition that good deeds should be rewarded and bad deeds should be punished. So seeing evildoers suffer can give us the gratifying sense that justice has been done. And, conveniently, it's our enemies and rivals who typically are guilty of doing bad things; when our friends and allies do them, they are likely just victims of circumstance and so not deserving of harsh punishment. Unless, perhaps, they do bad things to *us*, which may be cause to start moving them out of the "friends and allies" category.

My Brief Flirtation with Loving an Enemy

All of which brings us back to the plantain weed. Though my long history of opposition to, even enmity toward, the plantain weed did have a kind of moral aura surrounding it, I wasn't deploying nearly all the moral weaponry I'm capable of deploying. The really heavy-duty weaponry is reserved for human beings. And yet the line across which the weaponry is deployed the line between "good" humans and "bad" humans—is often no less arbitrary than the line separating weeds from other plants.

There is a meditative technique specifically designed to blur this line. It is called loving-kindness meditation, or, to use the ancient Pali word for loving-kindness, *metta* meditation. Typically, the meditation starts with you making a point of feeling kindly toward yourself. Then you imagine someone you love and direct some loving-kindness toward him or her. Then you imagine someone you like and direct some loving-kindness toward that person. Then you think about someone you don't feel strongly about one way or the other. And so on—until you get to an actual enemy. If all goes according to plan, you manage to feel loving-kindness even for that enemy.

It seems only appropriate to say a few kind words about loving-kindness meditation, so here they are: It works for some people. But it doesn't work for me. I think the trouble starts at the beginning, when I'm supposed to direct loving-kindness toward myself. In any event, I'm happy to say that for me, non-*metta* meditation—plain-vanilla mindfulness meditation—has some of the effect that *metta* meditation is supposed to have: it tamps down my ill will and can even amp up my empathy.

In fact, once during a meditation retreat, after nearly a week of extensive mindfulness meditation, I thought about the person who is among my two or three most bitter enemies in the whole world, a former colleague of mine (let's call him Larry) whom I never found very collegial, to say the least. Normally if I see Larry or even think of him, I perceive a kind of bad-vibe aura—essence-of-Larry, you might call it. But on that retreat I started to think about him without that aura. I saw his most obnoxious behaviors (or at least the behaviors I find most obnoxious) as manifestations of insecurity. I vividly imagined him as the gangly, unathletic adolescent he likely was, imagined him not getting any respect on the playground, trying to find his identity, and finally settling on an identity that, as it happens, has rubbed me the wrong way. And for that moment I felt a kind of compassion for him. What I didn't feel was essence. At least, I didn't perceive the essence-of-Larry that I had always perceived before. And I think this was the key: breaking down the old essence-of-Larry allowed me to then conceive a new version of Larry that was closer to the truth.

The thirteenth-century Sufi poet Rumi is said to have written, "Your task is not to seek for love, but merely to seek and find all the barriers within yourself that you have built against it." It turns out there's some question as to whether Rumi *did* write that, but, anyway, if he did, I think he was on to something. To be sure, it would be an exaggeration to say that knocking down the barrier I faced—namely, the essence-of-Larry that my mind had painstakingly constructed over the years—led me to *love* Larry. Still, I did feel for a moment some measure of the kind of empathy a parent feels when viewing a young son or daughter trying and failing to fit in socially. Of course, that feeling passed. But I think there was a lasting impact: the next time I saw Larry, I shook hands with him and exchanged greetings and, for the first time in a long time, didn't feel like I was faking it. At least, I didn't feel like I was 100 percent faking it. It was somewhere in the 40 to 50 percent range.

On the same meditation retreat that led me to see a weed that lacked essence-of-weed, I also had an interesting encounter with a reptile. I was walking through the woods and, looking down, saw a lizard frozen in its tracks, presumably by the sight of me. As I watched it look around nervously and calculate its next move, my first thought was that this lizard's behavior was governed by a relatively simple algorithm: see large creature, freeze; if creature approaches, run. But then I realized that, though my own behavioral algorithms are much more complicated than that, there could well be a being so intelligent that, to it, I look as simple-minded as the lizard looks to me. The more I thought about it, the more that lizard and I seemed to have in common. We were both thrown into a world we didn't choose, under the guidance of behavioral algorithms we didn't choose, and were trying to make the best of the situation. I felt a kind of kinship with the lizard that I'd never felt with a lizard.

As with my burst of compassion for Larry, my sense of kinship with this lizard didn't require loving-kindness meditation. Mindfulness meditation itself, practiced diligently, tends to expand your understanding of other organisms. And I mean "understanding" not just in the mushy sense of peace, love, and understanding but also—in fact, mainly—in the sense of having a clearer comprehension of the organism. I was looking at that lizard the way a visitor from Mars might look at it: with interest and curiosity and fewer distorting preconceptions than I normally bring to such things. I think the reason I could look at that lizard with so little in the way of preconceptions is because I *didn't* see essence-of-lizard—or, at least, didn't see as much of it as I usually see.

In fact, you might say that not seeing essence and not having preconceptions are one and the same, because the essence we perceive in things *is* a preconception about them that has been programmed into our brain. These preconceptions typically get us to react to things in ways that are in some sense expedient, but not necessarily in ways that involve a true understanding of them.

Expediency has its virtues, of course. It can be expedient—in a good way—to know that your spouse is your spouse. So I wouldn't recommend relinquishing your sense of essence as thoroughly as Fred, the victim of Capgras delusion mentioned in the previous chapter. But that's not something you have to worry about anyway. I'm not aware of any meditators having taken things *that* far—not even those who seem to have gotten somewhere in the vicinity of enlightenment. Fred was useful in illustrating the link between essence and affect, but he's not useful in illustrating where the dharma leads.

Still, he does raise an interesting question about where the dharma can lead. Even if it isn't going to lead you to where Fred was—to a point where you see so little essence that you can't figure out who is who—is it possible that it could lead you too far? Suppose, for example, that, though you can still accurately identify your spouse as your spouse, you see less essence-of-spouse than you used to, and suppose your feelings change accordingly. Will that mean you love your spouse less deeply now? Or, to take another example, will parents who meditate intensively come to love their offspring less intensely? Indeed, doesn't the whole Buddhist idea that you should let go of your attachments encourage, in some sense, less parental love as we've always known parental love?

If you ask the average meditation teacher a question like this, you'll hear something to the effect that, no, meditative practice won't negate your love or even subdue it, but may change its nature. Maybe, for example, parental love will become less possessive. And, who knows, maybe that will produce a happier parent and a happier child than a more anxious, more controlling kind of love would produce.

For practical purposes, that's a fair answer. So far as I can tell, enhanced personal relationships—with kin and with nonkin—are a much more likely result of meditative practice than the opposite.

But suppose some meditation teacher, in response to this question about the prospect of diminished love, gave a less reassuring answer: "Yes, if you meditate a whole, whole lot, there's a chance that the actual *magnitude* of your love for your offspring will drop a bit." Would that scenario really be such a horrible one?

Imagine a world in which affluent American parents showered slightly less devotion and concern on their children. And imagine they spent the time saved thinking about children who don't have parents at all and asking what they could do to help them. Would that be so bad? It's great that natural selection gave us the capacity for love and compassion and altruism, but that doesn't mean we have to accept natural selection's guidance on how to allocate these precious resources.

I want to emphasize how hypothetical this is, this imagined trade-off between attention to the welfare of kin and of nonkin. The upshot of the standard, more reassuring answer to the question about diminished love is generally true: don't worry, your family relationships will on balance be enriched as you follow the dharma, even if—maybe especially if—you follow it a long way. Still, I don't want to gloss over this important point: from a *moral* perspective, the effect of your meditation practice on the people you already love isn't necessarily the only or even the central issue.

There's a second moral question lurking here: What if meditation didn't lead you to allocate your compassion differently, and perhaps more equitably, but somehow distanced you from feelings of compassion altogether, leaving you indifferent to the welfare of people broadly? After all, if meditation can drain things like hatred and resentment of motivating force, why couldn't it have a symmetrically subduing effect on the other side of the ledger?

It could, and the fact that it tends not to is in a way puzzling. But "tends not to" doesn't mean "never does," and this point is worth dwelling on: Taking some of the essence out of things is likely to make you a better person, but it's not *guaranteed* to make you a better person. Like the meditative path more generally, it can give you a perspective that is in some sense more detached, and can thus make self-control easier— but the world is full of horrible people who can summon detachment and self-control. Indeed, detachment and self-control have helped some of them become more adroitly horrible. There have been meditation teachers of great contemplative prowess who sexually exploited psychologically vulnerable students—including a famous teacher in Manhattan who became known as "the Zen Predator of the Upper East Side." It may even be that some of them, by viewing incipient pangs of guilt "mindfully," eased internal resistance to their misbehavior.

This two-edged nature of meditative mastery underscores the value of supplementing Buddhist meditation with moral instruction. That's not exactly an original insight on my part. When the Buddha laid out the path to liberation—the Eightfold Path that is unveiled in the last of the Four Noble Truths—moral precepts occupied a big place in it. The idea wasn't that intensive meditation would by itself bring enlightenment in all its dimensions.

Still, meditation is a crucial part of the program. One reason is that, as we'll explore more fully in chapter 15, the insights into the nature of being that it fosters—including the apprehension of emptiness—do tend to bring moral insight, even if the link between meditating and becoming a better person isn't fully automatic. Another reason is that meditation can be used to cultivate virtues that counter our less laudatory tendencies. Though I've already admitted to not having a natural facility for lovingkindness meditation, I haven't given up on it, and I encourage everyone to try it.

Party Time

Enough sermonizing. Let's have some fun! Or can we? Another commonly raised concern about the dharma is that it could take the joy out of life. This question came up in a discussion I had with Bhikkhu Bodhi, an American Buddhist monk who is well-known in scholarly circles for having translated reams of Buddhist texts into English. He is an exceedingly friendly man with a shaved head, one of the largest smiles I've ever seen, and a pronounced tendency to use it, often in the course of laughing. One of my daughters, after watching a video of my interview with him, said, "I want him to be my uncle."

During that interview I was, as is my wont, trying to get some firsthand corroboration for my pet theory that seeing "emptiness"—in other words, not seeing essence—consists largely of feeling less intensely toward things. I started by saying, "When we . . . bring interpretation to something and thereby attribute essence to it, some of that interpretation involves how we feel about it. So my enemy is a bad person, my home is a warm cozy place. Part of the essence I'm attributing to things is coming from my feelings, right?"

He said, "Exactly, exactly."

I then babbled a little about how, if you're seriously pursuing liberation, and trying to divorce yourself from the cravings and aversions that most of us have, then naturally things in the world wouldn't have "strong emotional connotations, and that might be part of your perception that they lack essence."

This time his assent didn't come so readily. After a long pause, he said, "If one takes that too literally, one might come away with the idea that the ultimate aim of Buddhism is to become a completely unemotional, emotionally flat, emotionally deprived automaton." At this point, one of his epic smiles erupted. He started laughing as he said, "As my mother used to say, as far as I'm concerned, between an enlightened Buddhist and a vegetable, there's no difference." He reared his head back and laughed for a full five seconds before continuing to quote his mother: "Is this why you become a Buddhist monk, to become a vegetable?"

Then he got serious again. "But I would say that in my opinion, my experience, as one continues to practice the Buddhist path, it enriches the emotional life, so that one becomes emotionally more sensitive, more happy and joyful. And I would say that one can respond to things in the world in a freer, more happy, more delightful way."

Makes sense to me. After all, one virtue of mindfulness meditation is that experiencing your feelings with care and clarity, rather than following them reflexively and uncritically, lets you choose which ones to follow—like, say, joy, delight, and love. And this selective engagement with feelings, this weakened obedience to them, can in principle include the feelings that shape the essence we see in things and people.

I pressed Bhikkhu Bodhi a bit further on this affect and essence business. I said, "Doesn't part of the freedom come from the fact that you are not attaching these judgmental, affective connotations to things? In other words, not attributing essence so strongly to things can be a source of freedom."

Nodding his head emphatically, he said, "Definitely."

13

Like, Wow, Everything Is
One (at Most)

Recounting experiences you've had while meditating is a delicate business. They're most worth recounting if they're unusual—but if they're *too* unusual, people look at you like you're crazy. I once had an experience that I hope falls in the sweet spot: weird enough to get people's attention, not so weird that they notify local authorities.

It was the fourth or fifth day of a meditation retreat. I was sitting on my cushion, legs crossed, eyes closed, as usual. I wasn't making a point of focusing on any one kind of thing—not particularly on sounds, not particularly on emotions, not particularly on physical sensations. My field of awareness seemed wide open; my attention moved easily from one part of it to another, resting lightly on each new perch, and meanwhile a sense of the whole remained.

At one point I felt a tingling in my foot. At roughly the same time, I heard a bird singing outside. And here's the odd thing: I felt that the tingling in my foot was no more a part of me than the singing of the bird.

You may ask: Was I feeling that the singing of the bird was actually a part of me? Or was I feeling that the tingling in my foot *wasn't* a part of me? To put a less fine point on it: Did I feel like I was at one with the world, or was I closer to feeling like I was nothing? If you are indeed asking these questions, you've hit on a fascinating philosophical issue that highlights a contrast among different strands of Buddhist thought and that, more fundamentally, divides mainstream Buddhist philosophy from mainstream Hindu philosophy. But you're probably not asking these questions. You're more likely to be asking whether I'm crazy. So I'll address that question first, and get to the deep philosophical questions later.

For starters, let me emphasize that if this experience makes me crazy, I'm in good company. I've had several chances to describe the experience to truly accomplished meditators—some of them monks, some of them famous meditation teachers—and invariably they've recognized the kind of experience I'm describing as one they've had.

What's more, it's a kind of experience that, they tend to believe, is very important. Indeed, I might go so far as to say that this is the central experience of Buddhism. Not central in the sense of most profound or most important, but, rather, central in the place it occupies in the landscape of Buddhist philosophy: the place where Buddhism's two fundamental, crazy-sounding but arguably valid concepts—not-self and emptiness—come together. It's a kind of grand unifying meditative experience.

Before explaining what I mean by that, I should try to put a little more flesh on the experience itself.

First, I should stress that any sense of continuity I felt between myself and the bird doing the singing wasn't really about the bird in particular. It wasn't like the feeling I had toward the lizard in the previous chapter, when I realized that the lizard and I had more in common than

I'd previously appreciated. It was less cognitive than that and more purely perceptual. It was a kind of dissolving of the perceived boundary between me and the rest of the world generally. In other words, this was an apprehension, not a conclusion. It's not like I had become convinced via some logical argument that a bird's song is no less a part of me than my foot's tingling.

Still, in the wake of this experience, I started to think that maybe there *is* an argument of this sort that you could make. It would start something like this: How much difference is there, really, between feeling my foot tingle and hearing a bird sing? In both cases, the perception seems to register somewhere inside my head, at some kind of center of consciousness—which means that in both cases, the perception requires that information be transmitted to my head from a remote location. My foot transmits information about a tingling; the bird transmits information about a song. What's the difference?

The obvious rejoinder is "But the tingling originates inside your skin; it's part of you!" Well, yes, it's inside my skin. But the whole question I'm raising is whether my skin is really as significant a boundary as we instinctively assume—whether it really makes sense to think of everything on the inside as *me* and everything on the outside as *other*. So you can't just reiterate that instinctive assumption and put my question to rest. If that tactic were considered fair, no assumptions would ever be overthrown.

Another rejoinder you could make is "But tinglings and other bodily sensations tend to come with deep, inherent affective qualities." A pain in your foot, for example, is inherently painful. A bird song, on the other hand, is a matter of taste—pleasant to some, annoying to others. The problem with this objection is that pain *isn't* inherently painful. I've already recounted the time that, via meditation, I converted an excruciating knot of anxiety into a mere object of interest; and the time meditation made waves of acute tooth pain kind of beautiful. And there was another time when, by changing my perspective toward modest lower back pain, I turned it into a mildly pleasant sensation. Granted, this transformation of lemons into lemonade isn't routine; it's the kind of thing that's easier to do on retreat, when I'm immersed in the meditative lifestyle, than when I'm back in the "real world," saying things like "It's such a pain that my back causes me pain." And to go even further than this in the reconceptualization of pain—to achieve the mind-set of that Vietnamese Buddhist monk who immolated himself without flinching—would take much deeper immersion.

But the point is that such immersion is possible, and it undermines the easy claim that "internally" originating sensations have fixed meanings, whereas "externally" originating ones don't. Besides, if the key criterion for whether something is part of my self is how close to "automatic" my interpretation of the signals it sends are, then what about the case of offspring? My daughters don't reside within my skin, yet when I see one of them in pain, it causes me to suffer as reliably as my own pain does.

The great American psychologist William James wrote, "Between what a man calls me and what he simply calls mine the line is difficult to draw." In that sense, he observed, "our immediate family is a part of ourselves. Our father and mother, our wife and babes, are bone of our bone and flesh of our flesh. When they die, a part of our very selves is gone."

Evolution and the Bounds of Self

If you ask why kin have this near-self property, the answer is that we were created by a particular process that embodies certain values. Actually, it seems to embody one value: the successful transmission of genetic material through the generations. Since close kin share many of our genes, taking care of them makes sense from natural selection's point of view. So genes for familial empathy and familial love—and for a host of related feelings, such as familial guilt—have flourished.

In other words, our instinctive definition of what is "us" and what is "ours" is a product of the particular rules by which a particular creative process known as natural selection works.

It's not impossible, by the way, that our species could have taken an evolutionary path that would have left us with feelings toward some birds that are reminiscent of our feelings toward kin. When two species have a form of symbiotic relationship known as mutualism—that is, they help each other—they can evolve warm feelings that sustain that relationship. Dogs seem to have coevolved with human beings, and that may help account for the fact that I've been accused by my children of loving our dogs as much as I love my children. I vigorously deny this allegation, but it's true that if my dogs are in pain, I in some sense feel that pain.

Symbiosis can also sponsor a different kind of relationship that calls into question the bounds of self. We have a symbiotic relationship with various kinds of bacteria that reside within us and that in various ways influence our moods and thoughts. Scientists have found that by replacing the gut bacteria in shy, anxious mice with bacteria from gregarious mice, they can make the shy mice gregarious. For ethical reasons, this kind of experiment isn't done on humans, but other evidence makes it clear that in our species, too, microbes influence the mind, in part by influencing neurotransmitters. In fact, maybe it's not too much of a stretch to say that the bacteria, kind of like that bird at the meditation retreat, send signals to my brain, even if the bacteria send their signals more subtly.

So if I routinely consider signals that are ultimately traceable to bacteria part of me, why can't I consider signals sent by a bird part of me? Especially given that, had evolution taken a different path, involving mutualistic symbiosis between humans and that species of bird, such signals might routinely seem more like part of me?[†]

The generic point I'm trying to make is this: Lots of information impinges on my brain, and my brain decides which information it will consider part of my self and which information it won't consider part of my self, and which information—say, the cry of an offspring—falls somewhere in between. And I take it for granted that those decisions comport with some deep metaphysical truth about what is *I* and what is *other*. But in fact my brain could have been wired in a different way, so that it interpreted this information differently, leaving me with a very different sense of the distinction between *I* and *other*.

For example, people with a condition known as mirror-touch synesthesia pretty literally share the feelings of people in their vicinity. If they see someone being touched, they *feel* the touch, and brain scans show much the same neuronal activity they would have if they *were* being touched. You can imagine a process for creating organic beings—either natural selection operating under quirky conditions or some process other than natural selection—that would make mirror-touch synesthesia the norm rather than an aberration, in which case the prevailing conception of what *self* means would be very different.

But we're getting ahead of the story. The question of how our view of the world might differ if the process that created us had taken a different turn here or there, or had been a different kind of process altogether, is one I'll explore more deeply in chapter 15. For now, the point is that what things we identify with and how closely we identify with them—things both inside our skin and outside our skin—is to no small extent the result of the path that human evolution did, as a matter of fact, take. Our intuitive conception of our self and its bounds is in that sense arbitrary.

I suppose I could go further in trying to defend the validity of the experience I had at that retreat, but there's not much point in persisting, because it's not as if I think I have some killer argument that would convince you that a bird's song is part of me. In fact, it's not as if I myself go around believing that bird songs are part of me. I'm mainly just trying to convince you that the perception I had isn't as crazy as it may have sounded. And that's about all I can do. Attempts to truly share the experience with you will ultimately fail; as with all mystical experiences, you had to be there.

Anyway, whatever you think of my little birdsong moment, one takeaway from it is that what I've been calling the not-self experience actually has two sides. Earlier in this book I talked about what you could call the interior version of the experience. This consists of looking "within"—at your thoughts, your feelings—and asking, "Wait a second, in what sense are these things really inherently a part of me?" This is the basic question that was asked by the Buddha in his famous discourse on not-self.

But there is also what you could call the exterior not-self experience. This consists of looking at the "outside" world—at things beyond your skin—and asking, "In what sense are these things *not* a part of me?" In other words, instead of asking whether the supposed contents of the self are really contents of the self, you're asking whether the supposed bounds of the self are really bounds of the self. In one case you're questioning your intuition that you should identify with pretty much everything "inside" you—such as feelings of pointless anxiety—and in the other case you're questioning your intuition that you shouldn't identify with much of anything "outside" you.

In my experience, the first question can lead to the second question. One reason it was hard to see a clear line between the tingling in my foot and the singing of the bird is that I wasn't identifying very closely with the tingling in the first place. The disaggregation of my "self" made its contents seem more like the contents of the world beyond me; the diffuseness of my "self" made its bounds less distinct.

In that sense, there's something like a logical progression connecting the interior and exterior versions of the not-self experience. But if there's a kind of logic here, there's also a kind of paradox. After all, the less sense it makes to talk about a "you" inside your skin, the less sense it would seem to make to talk about "your" continuity with the outside world. And if you take the orthodox Buddhist position that it ultimately makes *no* sense to talk about a "you" inside your skin, then the idea of "your" continuity with the outside world would seem to make no sense either.

Here we return to the question I sidestepped at the beginning of this chapter: When the boundary between foot and bird, between interior tingling and exterior singing, got fuzzy, did I feel like I was at one with the world, or did I feel like I was nothing—as if there was nothing "in here" to *be* at one with the stuff "out there"?

There are at least two reasons I'm reluctant to answer that question. One is that, to be honest, I'm not sure the experience I had aligns neatly with either option. The other reason for my reluctance is that the way you answer that question can land you in the middle of a big argument between Buddhist thinkers and Hindu thinkers—and, for that matter, a big argument between one kind of Buddhist thinker and another kind.

My Inadvertent Online Controversy

This was driven home to me shortly after I launched an online course called Buddhism and Modern Psychology, an adaptation of a course I had been teaching at Princeton University. One challenge in making the adaptation was that the on-campus version of the course had benefited from guest speakers, ranging from brain scientists to very serious meditators. I decided to create something like that experience for my online students with digital video. I had dialogues with brain scientists and serious meditators on a website I run called *Bloggingheads.tv*, and I wove excerpts of the videos into my online lectures. One excerpt started something of a controversy in the course's discussion forum.

The excerpt featured Gary Weber, whom we met in chapter 11. He's the one who participated in that Yale brain-scan study and whose default mode network, it turned out, was inordinately quiet even when he wasn't meditating. In my *Bloggingheads.tv* dialogue with Weber, I asked him about a line of his I recalled reading, something to the effect of: The bad news is that you don't exist; the good news is that you're everything. Elaborating on that passage, Weber said to me, "If you're nothing, if you disappear, you can then be everything. But you can't be everything unless you are nothing. It just logically follows that's the case."

Well, I'm not sure it *logically* follows, but apparently it seems like inexorable logic if you're in the state Weber is in. He continued, "If you are nothing, instead of just disappearing and becoming a void, you find out that in some strange way—you actually see this, you perceive it this way—that everything is all one thing. This is a cliché, mystical statement, but it really is perceptible: you can deeply sense that everything is all one thing. And somehow, strangely, it's inside of you."

It didn't take long for Weber's comments to get blowback in the discussion forum. Some of the blowback was the kind you'd expect: people finding the paradox at the heart of Weber's experience inscrutable, if not worse. One student wrote, "'I am nothing means I am everything' is pretentious twaddle which actually means 'I am on such a high spiritual plane that you can't possibly understand me.'"

Other students objected not to the paradox itself but to the second half of it, the "I am everything" part. One student, a meditation teacher herself, wrote, "Buddhist philosophy does not espouse oneness." And she was basically right. Though you can certainly find respected Buddhist thinkers who will put things roughly the way Weber did, you won't find this idea of the oneness of everything in the mainstream of Mahayana Buddhist philosophy, the philosophy that so emphasizes the idea of emptiness. After all, if the things we see in the world out there are in fact empty of essence, then in a sense they don't exist—at least, not as things per se. And of course the self, according to Buddhist philosophy, doesn't exist. So how could everything—a bunch of things "out there" that don't really, strictly speaking, exist, and a self "in here" that doesn't really, strictly speaking, exist—all be one? Nothing plus nothing adds up to nothing, not one, right?

That's a simplified, almost cartoonish version of the actual Buddhist argument. But it captures the spirit of the argument and helps explain why orthodox Buddhists would bridle at loose talk of "oneness." On the other hand, once you go beyond the caricature and look a bit more deeply at the mainstream argument, you start to wonder whether the bridling is really in order. In fact, pondering the students' reaction to Weber led me to believe that the line between the ideas of emptiness and oneness is pretty fuzzy.

Emptiness, Oneness—What's the Diff?

If you look at the logic marshaled by Buddhist philosophers on behalf of the doctrine of emptiness, you'll see that it has much to do with a Buddhist idea that's often rendered in English as "interdependent co-arising." This basically means that things which may seem to exist independently of other things are in fact dependent for their existence and their character on other things. Trees need sunlight and water, and indeed are continually being changed by these and other things they come into contact with. Streams and lakes and oceans need rain, and the rain needs the streams and lakes and oceans. People need air, and the air around them wouldn't have the composition it has if people weren't inhaling it and exhaling into it.

In other words: nothing possesses *inherent* existence; nothing contains all the ingredients of ongoing existence within itself; nothing is self-sufficient. Hence the idea of emptiness: all things are empty of inherent, independent existence.

This, according to Buddhist philosophy, is the fact about reality that you are intuitively apprehending if, through extended meditation, you come to feel that things lack essence. And if, at the same time, you feel the bounds of your self start to dissolve, then you're just experiencing a larger expanse of emptiness, an emptiness that pervades not just all supposed things out there but also the supposed self in here. (This helps explain why, especially in Mahayana Buddhism, the not-self doctrine is sometimes depicted as just a special case of the broader doctrine of emptiness.) By way of underscoring this pervasiveness of emptiness, Buddhist philosophers sometimes apply the term not-self to things "out there" as well as things "in here." Just as you lack self, trees also lack self, and so do rocks.† Or, if you want to switch the terminology: Just as trees and rocks lack essence, you lack essence. Either way, it's emptiness everywhere you look.

At least, that's the argument.

But it seems to me you could flip this Buddhist argument around to make the case that the ideas of pervasive emptiness and of oneness aren't really as different as they sound. The hinge for the flipping is the term at the center of the argument: *interdependent co-arising*.

Interdependence is a much-used term these days. You might, for example, track the stock markets in several countries, notice that they tend to be correlated, and say, "Wow, there's more interdependence among these economies than I had realized." And here the second part of that Buddhist term, *co-arising*, would also be apt. After all, none of these economies would have become what they are had they not been interacting with the other economies.

Now if, after noting this interdependence, you added, "There's more unity among these economies than I had realized," most people would consider that a reasonable thing to say: a bunch of highly interdependent systems is closer to unity than a bunch of noninterdependent systems. Indeed, one reason an organism is thought of as unified is that there is so much interdependence among its parts: kidneys, lungs, and so on.

So it seems kind of strange to object to someone describing an apprehension of unity or oneness by saying, "No, no, you're completely wrong; it's actually interdependence and interconnection, not unity or oneness." Don't interdependence and interconnection point to unity and oneness? I mean, they're not exactly the same thing, but isn't it fair to say that the more interdependence and interconnection there is, the closer you are to oneness? And aren't people who espouse the doctrine of emptiness basically saying that reality is pervaded by interdependence and interconnection?

It's almost enough to make you wonder why some people get upset when someone like Weber talks about oneness rather than pervasive emptiness. Why get indignant when somebody takes an arguably defensible position on a somewhat obscure semantic question? But the philosophical stakes are greater than you might think. And here we come to the aforementioned clash between Buddhist and Hindu philosophy.

In Hindu thought, specifically within a Hindu school of thought known as Advaita Vedanta, there is the idea that the individual self or soul is actually just a part of what you might call a universal soul. To put the proposition in Hindu terminology: *atman* (the self or soul) is *brahman* (the universal soul). Now, to say that *atman* is anything at all— *brahman*, whatever—is to say that *atman* exists in the first place. And the very birth of Buddhism, its distinct emergence within an otherwise Hindu milieu, is thought to lie largely in the *denial* that *atman* exists.

So you can see why bringing Gary Weber into a course on Buddhism might get me into trouble. To say that "everything is all one thing" is, by philosophical implication, to say that the self exists, which in turn is to suggest that, among Eastern philosophies, Buddhism isn't so special after all.

But here's the funny thing: Weber had actually *denied* that the self exists. He had explicitly tied his sense that "you are everything" to his sense that "you are nothing." Indeed, a later part of the video dialogue reinforced that link. In it, I said to Weber, "I have had a meditative experience where the bounds of my self in a certain sense suddenly seemed more permeable—that is, like the place where the bird's song enters my sensory apparatus no longer seemed like such a fine dividing line."

"Exactly," he replied.

I continued, "But that was like a one-time, brief experience. . . . You're saying that as you walk around every day, you in a way identify with everyone else as much as you identify with yourself?"

"Yeah, I'd say it's a little different from that, but not far different. I don't identify with anything. I mean, there's nobody here to identify with me or with anyone else. It's just an empty, still presence here [inside my body], which is there [beyond my body]."

I said, "So the problem with saying you identify with everyone is that first word, *you.*"

"Exactly, because there's no you there to do the identifying."

How can he talk this way—so paradoxically, and in a language that isn't fully Buddhist or fully Hindu? Well, as for the paradox part, as I suggested near the outset of this book, if you don't like paradox, maybe Eastern philosophy isn't for you. (And, as I also suggested, neither is quantum physics.) As for Weber's refusal to talk like a doctrinaire Buddhist or a doctrinaire Hindu, having studied for years in the Vedanta tradition and for years in Buddhist traditions, he's not wed to any particular philosophy. So when he has a meditative experience, he's not bound by allegiance to interpret it any one way. He just tells you how it feels.

And how it feels seems to put him right on the border between Buddhist philosophy and Hindu philosophy. He'll say one thing that tilts toward the Buddhist side and one that tilts toward the Hindu side. Which makes a kind of sense, if the claim I made earlier is right—if there's really not much difference between saying that things are so interconnected and interdependent as to lack individual identity and saying that things are so interconnected and interdependent as to be a single thing.

This suggests an interesting possibility: maybe the deepest meditative experiences had by Buddhists and the deepest meditative experiences had by Hindus in the Advaita Vedanta tradition are basically the same experience. There is a sense of dissolution of the bounds of self and an ensuing sense of continuity with the world out there. If you're Buddhist (at least, a Buddhist of the mainstream type), you're encouraged to think of that as a continuity of emptiness; and if you're a Hindu, you're encouraged to think of it as a continuity of soul or spirit. For that matter, maybe some Abrahamic mystics—Christians, Jews, Muslims—who during contemplative practice feel a union with the divine are having somewhat the same experience as the Hindus and Buddhists, and interpreting it in a way that is closer to the Hindu than the Buddhist perspective. The core experiences remain the same, but the doctrinal articulation varies.

And, actually, maybe the articulations aren't as different as they seem. Both the Hindus and the Buddhists—and, in a sense, even the Abrahamic mystics—are saying that our ordinary conception of the self as this distinct, sovereign thing is in some sense illusory: we feel a boundary that is not ultimately as real as we think, and moving toward the ultimate truth involves the dissolution of that boundary.

Anyway, my basic view of religious beliefs is that the ultimate question isn't their specific content, but rather: What kind of person do the beliefs make you? How do they lead you to behave? There is reason to think that this basic Buddhist-Hindu idea—that the bounds of self aren't really bounds—can lead to good behavior.

I once asked Judson Brewer, who conducted the Yale study that Weber participated in and is himself a very committed meditator, whether, if everyone in the world meditated intensively, there would be any wars. He answered with a question: "Why would someone want to harm themself? In that sense, I don't think there would be, because it's like, why would you cut off your right hand?" Weber himself put it this way: "If everything is one thing, then why should I do something—if there was an *I* there to do it—to perturb this? Why should I do something bad to you?"

I agree with Weber: he shouldn't do something bad to me. In fact,

I even agree, in principle, that I shouldn't do something bad to him or to other people. The problem is that, for me, this is just an abstract belief, not a deeply, experientially grounded intuition in the sense that I suspect it is for him. Which may help explain why I don't always abide by it. And, apparently, if I'm going to feel this intuition as strongly as he feels it, or as strongly as Brewer feels it, I'm going to have to log another, oh, ten thousand hours of meditation. And life is short!

Fortunately, there's a way that, without meditating three hours a day for ten years, I can get some idea of what kind of person that might make me. One great thing about meditation retreats is that, through total if temporary immersion, they give you a fleeting glimpse of what it might be like to live life as a really serious meditator. And I've gotten some sense on retreats of the connection between the not-self experience and being a better person.

The Time I Didn't Kill a Man Who Was Snoring

Consider my feelings toward a guy at a meditation retreat I went on in December 2013. He was sitting a few rows in front of me, falling asleep as I sat there meditating. You may ask: If I had my eyes closed, how did I know he was falling asleep? Because he was snoring!

When you're trying to meditate, snoring can get on your nerves— especially when you're not the one doing the snoring. Indeed, I noticed in my lower abdomen a feeling of wrath toward this man.

Actually, at first I didn't really *notice* it; I just felt it and reflexively obeyed it, thinking the kinds of thoughts such feelings are designed to make us think—such as, Who is this jerk? I felt a strong urge to open my eyes so that I could identify the culprit—the better, I suppose, to bring him to justice at some later date. But then, finally, I did what you're supposed to do in mindfulness meditation: observe whatever feelings you're having. And at that point I really *did* notice the wrath; I looked right at it. And after only a few seconds of clear observation, it completely dissolved. It was as if my attention was a killer laser beam and this feeling of wrath was an enemy spaceship. Zap! Gone.

So what exactly does my wrath-zapping experience have to do with the not-self experience? Two things, actually—one of them kind of obvious and having to do with the "interior" version of the not-self experience, and one of them subtler and having to do with the "exterior" version.

Here's the obvious, interior part: When I looked at my wrath mindfully, I was ceasing to identify with it, ceasing to own it. A feeling that had seemed a part of me, that had been so deeply ingrained in me that I was mindlessly obeying it, now seemed like something else, like an object to be observed. Once I trained my attention on it—even before it dissolved in the face of that attention—it effectively ceased to be part of me.

Granted, this wasn't a very thoroughgoing version of the interior not-self experience. I had only disowned a single feeling on a single occasion, slightly shrinking the scope of my self. Still, it was something. And it made me briefly a better person, a person no longer contemplating homicide.

As for the subtler sense in which this was a not-self experience, the sense in which it was an *exterior* not-self experience, well, this takes some explaining. Specifically, it takes explaining the work of Miri Albahari. Albahari is an Australian philosopher whose work on Buddhist philosophy is informed partly by the practice of meditation. But in keeping with her nearly compulsive humility, she emphasizes that she is "*not* a skilled meditator." During a long meditation retreat, she says, she can get to the point where she feels "less self," but not to the point where she feels "no self." And in between retreats she doesn't always manage to sustain a daily practice, though when she does, she says, her life "goes noticeably better."

In her book *Analytical Buddhism*, Albahari makes an argument that brings us back to the Buddha's first discourse after his enlightenment, the famous *Sermon at Deer Park*. Here the Buddha lays out the Four Noble Truths, which explain the cause of *dukkha*—of suffering, of unsatisfactoriness—and the cure. He says that the basic cause of *dukkha* is *tanha*, a word usually translated as "thirst" or "craving" and sometimes as "desire." To put a finer point on it, the problem is the unquenchability of *tanha*, the fact that attaining our desires always leaves us unsatisfied, thirsting for more of the same or thirsting for something new.

Albahari says that *tanha* is inextricably tied to the sensation of self, and that overcoming *tanha* is therefore tied to the experience of not-self. She's not just talking about the *interior* version of the not-self experience—she's not just saying that if you let go of a particular desire, then you have disowned it, so that part of your self disappears. She's saying that *tanha* is deeply involved in your sense that the self is *bounded*; *tanha* sustains and strengthens the sense of boundedness that, during the exterior not-self experience, weakens.

After all, she says, if you thirst for something—hot chocolate, say—then you are painfully aware of the gap between yourself and that chocolate, and that means you have a conception of the bounds of your self. Indeed, as I sit here thinking about that particular thirst being quenched, I do imagine some of those bounds—I imagine the surface of my hand making contact with the mug of chocolate and the surface of my tongue making contact with the chocolate itself.

To see the full breadth of the argument Albahari is making, you have to understand that, like many scholars, she considers *tanha* to include not just the desire for things you find pleasant—sex, chocolate, a new car, a newer car; it also includes the desire to be free of things you find unpleasant. In other words, *tanha* fuels not just attraction to alluring things but also aversion to off-putting things. In this view, my annoyance at the snoring in the meditation hall was *tanha*. It was a desire to be free of the snoring noise.

Well, Albahari says, if you desire to be *free* of something, then you have in mind the goal of creating more distance between yourself and that something (assuming you don't take the more straightforward approach of throwing a meditation cushion at the person generating the something). And wanting to create distance between yourself and something means having an idea of the place where your self ends. If you're trying to dodge a rattlesnake's lunge, you have a very precise conception of the space that you don't want the rattlesnake to reach: the space defined by your skin.

So either way, whether *tanha* is driving attraction or aversion, it entails defining the realm of self. As Albahari has written, emotions involving *tanha* "seem to point to, as a part of their content, an unspoken *boundary* between the identified-as self on one hand and the desired or undesired scenario on the other, as it is perceived or imagined by the witnessing subject." Thus, *tanha* "will not only *indicate* but also help *create and drive* the sense of self-other boundedness." And vice versa: the more clearly and deeply you feel that boundedness, the more *tanha* you'll be inclined to have. "For unless I identified fully as a self, then how could I care particularly about whether 'my' desires are fulfilled?"

So, you may be asking, what is the relevance of all this to the zapping of my wrath toward the snoring man? I might have asked the same question had I not gone back and reviewed the notes I took shortly after the zapping. It turns out that the version of the episode I just recounted is incomplete. It's the version I wrote from memory, before going back and reading those notes. It leaves out some important details.

For starters, right before this morning meditation session there had been a short talk by Narayan, one of the two retreat leaders. Her theme was acceptance—learning to accept conditions you're inclined to find unpleasant. So, after spending a little time finding the snoring unpleasant, I decided to practice what Narayan preached and try to overcome my aversion to the snoring. Which meant, of course, observing the aversion mindfully. As I put it in my notes later that day, I tried "feeling my aversion and anger (which I could definitely feel, and locate) in a neutral way." Then "basically the feeling just disappeared" as I accepted the snoring.

So, really, there were two intertwined feelings that I observed mindfully: the wrath toward the snorer and the aversion to his snoring. And when you overcome aversion, you are, by Albahari's logic, approaching the *exterior* version of the not-self experience more fully and directly than when you just overcome wrath.[†] You are diluting the *tanha* that reinforces the bounds of self.

This dynamic comes through clearly in the final passage from my notes: As I observed my aversion and my wrath, and these feelings lost their power, "there was a moment when I imagined that feeling in my gut and his snoring as a kind of single system or organism, unified by communication." In other words, I focused on the continuous stream of sound waves that had emanated from his nose, entered my brain, and elicited the aversion and wrath. For a moment, the annoyer and the annoyed weren't two rigidly distinct things—a *he* and an *I*. My boundaries became more porous as the power of *tanha*—of my aversion to the snoring—waned.

So Miri Albahari's view of the self, and of the self's connection to *tanha*, has one very welcome effect: it makes me seem like a more impressive meditator than I might otherwise seem like. Not only did my wrath-zapping involve a bit of the interior not-self experience, in the sense that I disowned the wrath as I zapped it; in overcoming the *tanha* that had fueled the wrath, I had also realized a bit of the more elusive exterior version of the not-self experience. And this exterior part of the experience, like the interior part, seems to have briefly made me a better person.

Two Sermons and Three Poisons

Albahari's view has one other virtue: it helps solve a puzzle posed by early Buddhist scripture. In the Buddha's first discourse after his enlightenment, the sermon at Deer Park, he says that the key to liberation from *dukkha* is overcoming *tanha*. But in his second discourse, the discourse on not-self, it seems that liberation lies in recognizing that the self doesn't exist; all the monks who hear this sermon are instantly liberated. So which is it? Does nirvana come by conquering *tanha* or by seeing that the self is an illusion?

Well, maybe the two are one and the same. We might have suspected as much even without Albahari's take on things. After all, the interior version of the not-self experience involves disowning feelings and disowning thoughts laden with feelings. And feelings tend to come in the two basic flavors of positive and negative, possessing an element, respectively, of attraction or of aversion; in other words, possessing *tanha.*[†] So the interior not-self experience inherently involves letting go of some *tanha.* (Indeed, the Buddha said much the same thing in emphasizing that the not-self experience involves ceasing to cling to— ceasing to "lust" after—thoughts and emotions and the like.) But Albahari adds a new dimension to this argument for a kind of equivalence between the Buddha's first two sermons by connecting the *exterior* not-self experience to the abandonment of *tanha.*

When you think about it, it makes sense that *tanha* would be tied to our outer limits no less than to our core. From a Darwinian perspective, *tanha* was engineered into us so that we would take care of ourselves—which is to say, so that each of us would take care of the vehicle that contains our genes. And that vehicle stops at the skin, at the bounds of the body. It's only natural, then, that *tanha* would reinforce a sense of the importance of those bounds, the bounds that define the zone of concern that natural selection assigned to it.

The connection between *tanha* and our sense of self nicely frames a refrain that appears over and over in Buddhist texts. The refrain warns people to avoid the "three poisons" of *raga, dvesha,* and *moha.* Those three words are typically translated as "greed, hatred, and delusion," a phrase that will be familiar to many meditators who have heard it roll off the tongues of meditation teachers, sometimes during dharma talks at retreats. But this translation is in some ways misleading. The word for *greed* refers not just to greed in the sense of thirst for material possessions but also to thirst in a more general sense: to any grasping attraction to things. And the word for *hatred* can mean not just negative feelings toward people but negative feelings toward anything—all feelings of aversion.

In other words, the first two poisons are the two sides of *tanha*: a craving for the pleasant, an aversion to the unpleasant. Well, if *tanha* is indeed tightly bound up with the sense of self, then it makes sense to see these two poisons as bound up with the third poison: delusion. After all, one of the most famous delusions in all of Buddhism is the illusion of self. So the first two poisons, you might say, are the ingredients of the third poison. *Raga* plus *dvesha* equals *moha*.[†]

This equation makes even more sense when you throw in that other famous delusion—the illusion of essence—and its corresponding grand insight: emptiness. Our intuition that things have essence, I argued in the previous chapter, is shaped by the feelings that infiltrate our perception of these things. On close inspection, these feelings would tend to be either positive or negative, involving either attraction to things, a kind of craving for them, or aversion to things. In other words, these feelings would tend to involve, in at least some measure, either *raga* or *dvesha*. So in this case—the case of the mistaken perception of essence—the third poison, delusion, does again seem to boil down to the other two poisons.

In light of all this, it's only logical that, in some ancient texts, liberation is said to involve eradicating the three poisons. After all, this eradication would mean both an end to *tanha*, the great cause of suffering identified in the Buddha's first sermon, and an end to the illusion of self, the great impediment to liberation laid out in the Buddha's second sermon—not to mention an end to the illusion of essence, an illusion that, especially in the Mahayana tradition, is also seen as an impediment to liberation.

Once Gary Weber, trying to describe his state of consciousness—a state apparently featuring little if any sense of self or of essence—said to me, "It's a space you can't imagine bringing anything in to improve it or taking anything away that would make it better." He was basically describing the opposite of *tanha*. *Tanha*'s premise, after all, is that things can always be made better by taking something away or adding something. Part of *tanha*'s job description is to never be satisfied.

Weber doesn't refer to the state he's in as nirvana or call himself enlightened. But the way he talks about his self—or his lack thereof—makes him sound like he's not far from meeting the criterion for enlightenment laid down in the Buddha's second discourse, the discourse on not-self. In any event, Weber's a lot closer to that than I am.

Still, at that moment when the bird's song seemed no less and no more a part of me than the tingling in my foot, I think I got a sense of what it would be like to be much farther down the meditative path than I am. And it felt very, very good. For that matter, abandoning the *tanha* that had been energizing my growing dislike of that snoring meditator also made me feel a lot better than I'd felt before. That it made me a better person, however briefly, is a nice bonus.

14

Nirvana in a
Nutshell

The rock group Nirvana, which became world famous in the early 1990s, wasn't always known as Nirvana. In its early years it went under a series of other names. One of them was Bliss.

Some people might ask: What's the difference? Aren't nirvana and bliss the same thing? As we've seen, the answer is no. Nirvana does *entail* bliss, but it entails a lot more than bliss—most notably enlightenment. Bhikkhu Bodhi, the prolific translator of Buddhist texts, including many that characterize nirvana, described it as "a state of perfect happiness, complete peace, complete inner freedom, and full awakening and understanding."

Another difference between bliss and nirvana is how easy they are to attain. If you're pursuing bliss, period, you can just take bliss-inducing drugs, an approach that is guaranteed to work for a while, though unlikely to work in the long run. Kurt Cobain, the lead singer of Nirvana, became a heroin addict and committed suicide.

If you pursue nirvana rather than mere bliss, the approach is less straightforward and more arduous. And even if you're diligent, you are, it is safe to say, less likely to attain nirvana than Cobain was to attain—however fleetingly—bliss. On the other hand, whatever measure of contentment you do attain will almost certainly be more enduring and stable than Cobain's bliss was.

The concept of nirvana occupies a unique place in Buddhist thought—not just because it represents the culmination of the Buddhist path, and not just because it represents the nicest imaginable place to be, but also because of the way it straddles the two sides of Buddhism. There is the side of Buddhism this book has been about: the "naturalistic" side, featuring ideas that would fit easily into a college psychology or philosophy course. And then there is the side of Buddhism featuring supernatural and exotic ideas that would be more at home in the religion department. Nirvana certainly has its exotic aspect: Buddhists who believe in reincarnation see nirvana as the thing that can free them from an otherwise endless cycle of rebirth. But this story about nirvana—the story about how exactly you find the escape hatch from endless rebirth—leads seamlessly to a more naturalistic story about nirvana, a claim about the mechanics of suffering and of contentment. And in the process of following one story to the other, you can see mindfulness meditation in a new light, a light that emphasizes what a radical undertaking it can be.

In ancient texts, nirvana is often described with a word that is commonly translated as "the unconditioned." For years I heard this strange-sounding term and wondered what it meant, but I figured that understanding it without actually reaching nirvana was probably hopeless and, for my purposes, not all that important. It turns out I was wrong on both counts. The question "What is the unconditioned?" has a pretty clear answer and a very important one, an answer that forms a kind of intersection between the exotically metaphysical and the naturalistic.

One obvious approach to deciphering "the unconditioned" is to drop the *un* and ask what *conditioned* means. "The conditioned," in Buddhist terminology, can be thought of as roughly synonymous with "the caused."[†] Which makes sense. After all, when we talk about the conditions that give rise to something—the conditions that lead water to boil or rain to fall or the crime rate to rise—we're basically saying these conditions are involved in the causal chain that led to that something. Things that are conditioned in the Buddhist sense are things that are subject to causes.

So if nirvana is "the unconditioned," then, you might think, it would involve some kind of escape from "the caused." And you would be right! But what does *that* mean?

The answer to that question involves one of the most important terms in Buddhism: *paticca-samuppada*. It is a term that has numerous applications and numerous translations.[*] For present purposes—when we're using it to illuminate the logic of nirvana—a good translation is "conditioned arising."

In its most generic sense, conditioned arising refers to the basic idea of causality: out of certain conditions some things arise; out of other conditions other things arise. But the term is also used to refer to a specific sequence of causal links—a series of twelve conditions, one giving rise to the next—that are said to enslave human beings in the cycle of endless rebirth.[†] It is this chain of causal links that nirvana is said to break.

---

*This is actually the same term that in chapter 13 was translated as "interdependent co-arising," another common rendering. However, these are more than just alternative translations for the same term. This term, like some other terms in Buddhism and other traditions, has come to be applied in different ways. When the term is applied to the concept of emptiness, one translation is more apt and illuminating, and when the term is applied to the concept of nirvana, another translation is more apt and illuminating.

I won't run through the exact sequence of twelve conditions, partly because some of them are, for my money, a little murky. But the part of the sequence that concerns us, the part that puts a finer point on nirvana in both the exotic and the naturalistic senses of the term, is reasonably clear. That part starts after a person's sensory faculties—eyes, ears, tongue, etc.—have taken shape. It is through these faculties that the person's consciousness makes contact with the material world. Or, as it is put more formally in ancient texts that spell out the twelve causal links: through the condition of the sensory faculties, contact arises. And here is the next link: Through the condition of contact, feelings arise—which makes sense, because, remember, in the Buddhist view (and in the view of many modern psychologists), the things we perceive through our sense organs tend to come with feelings attached, however subtle the feelings.

Then, in the next causal link, feelings give rise to *tanha*, to "craving": we crave the pleasant feelings and crave to escape the unpleasant feelings. Let's freeze frame right here, because this is where the action is. Here is how Bhikkhu Bodhi put it in a series of lectures he recorded in 1981: "It is here in this space between feeling and craving that the battle will be fought which will determine whether bondage will continue indefinitely into the future or whether it will be replaced by enlightenment and liberation. For if instead of yielding to craving, to the driving thirst for pleasure, if a person contemplates with mindfulness and awareness the nature of feelings and understands these feelings as they are, then that person can prevent craving from crystallizing and solidifying."

This is where we start to segue from the exotic to the naturalistic. The liberation that Bhikkhu Bodhi is talking about is, in the first instance, a liberation from perpetual rebirth, a liberation that will fully kick in at the end of this life cycle. But it is also liberation in the here and now, liberation from the suffering *tanha* brings—liberation from the craving to capture pleasant feelings and escape unpleasant feelings, liberation from the persistent desire for things to be different than they are.

These two senses of liberation are reflected in the Buddhist idea that there are two kinds of nirvana.† As soon as you are liberated in the here and now, you enter a nirvana you can enjoy for the rest of your life. Then, after death—which will be your final death, now that you're liberated from the cycle of rebirth—a second kind of nirvana will apply.

I'm sorry to say I can't describe the first kind of nirvana from personal experience, and I'm ambivalent about not being able to describe the second kind. But the main point is that whichever kind of nirvana you're focused on, the mechanics for getting there centrally involve mindfulness meditation: cultivating an awareness of your feelings that fundamentally changes your relationship to them. Regardless of how exotic or practical your aspirations—whether you believe in a cycle of rebirth and want to escape it, or just want to attain complete liberation in the here and now, or just hope to find *partial* liberation in the here and now—the essential tool for liberation is the same.

And, accordingly, some of the basic terminology is the same. Even if you're not trying to escape an eternal repetition of twelve successive conditions, even if you would just like your one and only life to be better, you are still seeking liberation from *conditions*—from chains of causation that otherwise shackle you. The things in your environment—the sights, the sounds, the smells, the people, the news, the videos—are pushing your buttons, activating feelings that, however subtly, set in motion trains of thought and reaction that govern your behavior, sometimes in ways that are unfortunate. And they will keep doing that unless you start paying attention to what's going on.

This has been the point of much of this book. The human brain is a machine designed by natural selection to respond in pretty reflexive fashion to the sensory input impinging on it. It is designed, in a certain sense, to be controlled by that input. And a key cog in the machinery of control is the feelings that arise in response to the input. If you interact with those feelings via *tanha*—via the natural, reflexive thirst for the pleasant feelings and the natural, reflexive aversion to the unpleasant feelings—you will continue to be controlled by the world around you. But if you observe those feelings mindfully rather than just reacting to them, you can in some measure escape the control; the causes that ordinarily shape your behavior can be defied, and you can get closer to the unconditioned.

How Weird Is the Unconditioned?

There are debates within Buddhism about how dramatically to conceive of nirvana and the unconditioned. Is there something like a transcendent metaphysical "space" that you in some sense occupy once fully liberated? Or is it a bit more mundane, just freedom from the mindless reactivity to causes, to conditions, that would otherwise control you? People who embrace a naturalistic Buddhism, and don't believe in rebirth, tend to go with the less dramatic interpretation. Indeed, some of them don't like the term *the unconditioned* because it *sounds* so dramatic. Stephen Batchelor, a longtime proponent of "secular Buddhism" and the author of the book *Buddhism Without Beliefs*, has written, "There is no such thing as the unconditioned, only the possibility of not being conditioned *by* something."

Personally, I wouldn't discourage even "secular" Buddhists from using the term *the unconditioned*. Thinking of complete liberation in the here and now as a kind of zone—a metaphorical if not a metaphysical zone—may be useful. And it may be useful regardless of whether you think the zone is realistically reachable or just think of it as something you can get closer and closer to.

I can testify that it's possible to get into something that *feels* like a zone. When I phoned my wife after my first meditation retreat, she said I sounded like a completely different person—before I had even said anything about the retreat, or said anything of substance at all. The very tenor of my voice sounded different, she said. And she liked the new tenor a lot.

Now, I grant you that this may have been more of a comment on the old tenor than on the new tenor. A few years earlier, trying to articulate what she liked about my brother, she had looked at me and said, "He's like a nice version of you." (She laughed when she said it, which I take as a good sign.) Anyway, the point is that there had been a real change of tenor.

Certainly the world as I saw it had a new tenor. I had shed so much of my usual self-absorption that I could take a new kind of delight in the people and things around me. I was more open, suddenly inclined to strike up conversations with strangers. The world seemed newly vibrant and resonant.

There's something ironic about the zone I was in. Science, in its displacement of traditionally religious worldviews, is sometimes said to have brought on the "disenchantment" of the world, draining it of magic. And you would think that a meditative discipline devoted, in some sense, to tamping down the influence of feelings on perception, to fostering a view of sober clarity, would only abet that tendency. But Batchelor says meditative practice can lead to the "re-enchantment" of the world, and I know what he means. After that first retreat, I felt like I was living in a zone of enchantment, a place of wonder and preternatural beauty.

No, that's not the same as entering a zone that is magically impervious to causation. I was still reacting at least somewhat reflexively to the causes impinging on me. Still, one source of the enchantment, I think, was that I was spending less time reacting, less time having my buttons pushed, and more time observing—which, as a bonus, allowed for more thoughtful responses to things. I assume living in the unconditioned would be great, but living in the less conditioned can be pretty great, too.

You could take many of the Buddhist ideas we've covered in this book and recast them in terms of the conditioned, the caused. Indeed, you could say that Buddhist philosophy consists largely of taking the idea of causality really, really seriously.

Consider the idea of not-self: what we call the "self" is in such constant causal interaction with its environment, is so pervasively influenced by the world out there, as to raise doubts about how firm the boundaries of the self—and, for that matter, the core of the self—really are. Remember how the Buddha emphasized, in that original not-self sermon, that the various things we think of as parts of our self are in fact not under our control? The reason they're not under our control is that—until we're liberated, at least—they're under the control of outside forces: they're conditioned. And remember the Buddha's emphasis on the impermanence of the things we think of as parts of the self? This too—the perennial arising and passing away of thoughts, emotions, attitudes—is a consequence of the ever-changing forces that act on us, forces that set off chain reactions inside us. The things inside us are subject to causes, to conditions—and it is the fate of all conditioned things to change when conditions change. And conditions change pretty much all the time.

You might say that the path of meditative progress consists largely of becoming aware of the causes impinging on you, aware of the way things manipulate you—and aware that a key link in that manipulation lies in the space where feelings can give rise to *tanha*, to a craving for pleasant feelings and an aversion to unpleasant feelings. This is the space where mindfulness can critically intervene.

Maybe I should have put an asterisk after the word *aware* in the previous paragraph. I'm not talking about an abstract understanding—an *academic* awareness—of these chains of causality. I'm talking about a carefully cultivated *experiential* understanding, a mindful awareness that brings the power to break, or at least loosen, the chains.

That said, undergirding this experiential understanding, and often accompanying it, is the more abstract understanding that is part of

Buddhist philosophy. Making real progress in mindfulness meditation almost inevitably means becoming more aware of the mechanics by which your feelings, if left to their own devices, shape your perceptions, thoughts, and behavior—and becoming more aware of the things in your environment that activate those feelings in the first place. You could say that enlightenment in the Buddhist sense has something in common with enlightenment in the Western scientific sense: it involves becoming more aware of what causes what.

All of this flies in the face of stereotype. Mindfulness meditation is often thought of as warm and fuzzy and, in a way, anti-rational. It is said to be about "getting in touch with your feelings" and "not making judgments." And, yes, it does involve those things. It can let you experience your feelings—anger, love, sorrow, joy—with new sensitivity, seeing their texture, even feeling their texture, as never before. And the reason this is possible is that you are, in a sense, not making judgments—that is, you are not mindlessly labeling your feelings as bad or good, not fleeing from them or rushing to embrace them. So you can stay close to them yet not be lost in them; you can pay attention to what they actually feel like.

Still, you do this not in order to abandon your rational faculties but rather to engage them: you can now subject your feelings to a kind of reasoned analysis that will let you judiciously decide which ones are good guiding lights. So what "not making judgments" ultimately means is not letting your feelings make judgments *for* you. And what "getting in touch with your feelings" ultimately means is not being so oblivious to them that you get pushed around by them. And all of this means informing your responses to the world with the clearest possible view of the world.

Underlying this whole endeavor is a highly mechanistic conception of how the mind works. The idea is to finely sense the workings of the machine and use that understanding to rewire it, to subvert its programming, to radically alter its response to the causes, the conditions, impinging on it. Doing this doesn't let you enter "the unconditioned" in the strict sense; it doesn't let you literally escape the realm of cause and effect. Then again, airplanes don't literally defy the law of gravity. But they still fly.

I don't want to overstate the parallels between the Buddhist and Western conceptions of enlightenment. Buddhist philosophy and modern science have different modes of inquiry, different standards of evidence. But lately the two traditions have started to interact in fruitful ways. There are brain scans of meditators, studies about the physiological and psychological effects of meditation, and so on.

Yet the most momentous interaction, I think, began in the mid-nineteenth century, with the theory of natural selection. For more than two millennia, Buddhism had been studying how the human mind is programmed to react to its environment, how exactly the "conditioning" works. Now, with Darwin's theory, we understood what had done the programming. And over the ensuing century and a half, as Darwinian theory matured and evidence accumulated, we got a clearer and clearer idea of the details of that programming. I think all of this puts us in a position to approach nirvana from a whole new angle, to mount a new kind of argument in defense of the basic validity of Buddhist enlightenment. That is the subject of the next chapter.

15

Is Enlightenment
Enlightening?

Over the ages, the equation of enlightenment and liberation has assumed many forms and found many audiences. The original headquarters of the CIA had Jesus's version of the equation etched in its wall: "And ye shall know the truth, and the truth shall make you free." And the movie *The Matrix,* as we saw at the outset of this book, offers a truth freedom linkage that echoes Buddhist philosophy: Life as ordinarily lived is a kind of illusion, and you can't be truly free until you pierce the illusion and look into the heart of things. Until you "see it for yourself," as Morpheus puts it to Neo, you will remain in "bondage."

But there are important differences between the *Matrix* scenario and the Buddhism scenario. For starters, the truth in *The Matrix* is easier to describe. Sure, Morpheus says you have to "see it for yourself," but the fact is that he could have given Neo a pretty clear verbal picture of it: robot overlords have put humans in gooey pods and are pumping dreams into their brains! There—how complicated was that? Certainly it's an easier claim to grasp than, say, that the self doesn't exist or that everything is empty.

There's another sense in which those robot overlords give Neo's predicament an appealing simplicity. Namely, they give him something to rebel against. And rebellions are energizing! An oppressive enemy focuses the mind and steels you for the struggle ahead. Which would come in handy with meditation, because it really *can* be a struggle— getting on the cushion every day, even when you don't feel like it, and then trying to carry mindfulness into everyday life. Too bad that in Buddhism there's no evil perpetrator of delusion to fight!

In *traditional* Buddhism, actually, there is: the Satan-like supernatural being named Mara, who unsuccessfully tempted the Buddha during the epic meditation session that led to his great awakening. Mara, though, has no place in the Western, more secular Buddhism that is the backdrop of this book. Kind of disappointing.

But there's good news on this front. If you would like to think of meditation practice as being a rebellion against an oppressive overlord, we can arrange that: just think of yourself as fighting your creator, natural selection. After all, natural selection, like the robot overlords, engineered the delusions that control us; it built them into our brains. If you're willing to personify natural selection, you can carry the comparison with robot overlords a bit further: natural selection perpetrated the delusion in order to get us to adhere slavishly to its agenda.

Its agenda being, of course, to get genes into the next generation. This is the core of natural selection's value system, the criterion that guided the engineering of our brains. And we have every right to decide, like Neo, that our values differ from those of the force that controls us and that we want liberation from it. Which means, first and foremost, liberating ourselves from the delusions through which that control is exercised. (This declaration of independence is of course in no way undermined by the irony that, in a modern environment, these delusions often fail to serve natural selection's agenda of genetic prolif- eration anyway.)

There's a second virtue of thinking of the Buddhist path as a re- bellion against natural selection. Looking at things that way helps us put a finer point on what we mean by liberation and by enlighten- ment. And it helps us answer the big question: Is enlightenment really enlightening? I mean, obviously enlightenment is enlightening— that's why they call it enlightenment. But is the *Buddhist* version of enlightenment—the end state, Enlightenment with a capital E— enlightening? Is it a radically truer view of things than our ordinary experience? Is it the *ultimate* truth? I've argued in this book that when you meditate you may, in various senses, see things a bit more clearly than you saw them before, and that this clarity can grow, increment by increment. But what about the sum of all increments? What if you made it to the end of the path? Would enlightenment be a pure, un- adulterated view of Truth?

This may seem like a moot point, since most of us have little real- istic hope of attaining full enlightenment. Still, to say that you'll never reach something isn't the same as saying you're not approaching it. Even if enlightenment is an idealized, hypothetical state we'll never experience—even if it's an idealized, hypothetical state that *no one* will experience and no one *has ever* experienced—it's what the meditative path is in theory headed toward. So if we want to know whether we're moving toward the truth—and whether we'll still be moving toward the truth no matter how far we go—it would help to know if this state is the truth itself.

The Enlightenment Checklist

We should start with a basic question: What *is* enlightenment? How would the world look if you were enlightened in the Buddhist sense of the term? Well, broadly speaking, the answer is that you would see the truth of the central ideas of Buddhist philosophy. And when I say "see the truth," I mean *see* the truth—actually apprehend the truth experientially. It's one thing to be led intellectually to the conclusion that, say, the self doesn't exist. As we've seen, there are psychologists and philosophers who have been led to suspect as much by some combination of data and logic and introspection. But most of them haven't had the kind of powerful *experience* of not-self that can impart deep conviction, a conviction that surpasses intellectual persuasion in its power to change lives.

So too with the idea of emptiness or formlessness. There are philosophical arguments for this idea, and some people find them persuasive. But attaining enlightenment would involve being experientially, not just intellectually, convinced: *seeing*, so to speak, the emptiness.

Okay, so not-self and emptiness—what other things would you have to see to qualify as enlightened? Well, there's no single, official definition of enlightenment that has been endorsed by Buddhists of all stripes. There's no list of prerequisites for an enlightenment certificate that you can check off. But if there were such a thing—an enlightenment checklist—it wouldn't, by mainstream Buddhist reckoning, end with these two experiences, fundamental though they are.

We've already seen a few additional bullet points on that list, some of which are more like insights (such as seeing the impermanence of everything) and some of which are more like feats[†] (such as overcoming *tanha*, or craving). It turns out there are various other feats, listed in one Buddhist text or another, that are linked to enlightenment. There is the overcoming of specific "fetters," such as lust and conceit and ill will. And there is compliance with the precepts laid out in the Eightfold Path: don't steal, harm other beings, indulge in malicious gossip, and so on.

So enlightenment in the fullest, most traditionally Buddhist sense isn't confined to the metaphysical dimension that has dominated this book—the idea that reality, both inside and outside of us, is very different than it seems. There are also explicitly moral dimensions.

On the other hand, as we've seen, in Buddhist thought the metaphysical and the moral are linked; meditatively apprehending Buddhism's central metaphysical claims is said to erode the psychological roots of bad behavior. Indeed, letting go of things like lust and conceit and ill will is an intrinsic part of the metaphysical apprehension known as not-self.

It's this metaphysical-moral linkage—the fact that certain moral values are *implied* by metaphysical enlightenment—that makes the clearer perception of reality tantamount to a rebellion against natural selection. The particular values implied by this clarity, the values you would fully embody if you reached full enlightenment, are in many ways directly at odds with the values implied by our ordinary view of reality, the values that natural selection embedded in that view.

Well, Aren't We Special?

Consider, for starters, what some would call the core experience of enlightenment: the not-self experience. More specifically, consider the subset of it that I've called the "exterior not-self experience." How does this experience imply a rejection of natural selection's values?

As we've seen, the experience involves a diminished sense of separation between you (or "you") and the other people and things in the world. In fact, there's such a sense of continuity between your "inside" and the world on the "outside" that you may start to see harming others as tantamount to harming yourself. In the fullest version of this experience, you start to doubt that there's any real difference between their interests and yours.

Well, from natural selection's point of view, this is heresy. If there's one idea that natural selection has built into me, it's that I have distinctive interests and should focus on them. On those occasions when some of my interests overlap with the interests of others, then fine, we can do business; but if there's no such overlap, my interests take priority.

This principle follows from the logic of natural selection. If inside me are genes that were selected because they've been good at getting copies of themselves into the next generation, then job one for these genes will be to take care of the vehicle that can carry them there—that is, my body. And that means these genes will build into my brain the idea that taking care of this body is much more important than taking care of other bodies (except, perhaps, when those other bodies belong to close kin). In other words, I'm special. My specialness lies very near the heart of natural selection's values system.

This premise is built into all animal life, and you see it in all kinds of ways. Animals kill each other, for example. That includes human animals, though often humans assert their specialness more subtly, as when they peacefully undermine rivals. Indeed, the premise of our specialness informs our most pedestrian behavior. If you're trying to hail a cab and you notice that someone next to you is also trying to hail a cab, you naturally reach your arm higher so that you'll get the cab and she won't—even though, for all you know, your rival is a physician who is on her way to save somebody's life.

So, this one element of enlightenment—the exterior version of the not-self experience, with its dissolution of the bounds between you and the world, hence a constant continuity of interest between you and all of life—involves abandoning one of the most basic precepts built into us by natural selection: that I am special by virtue of being me. Now *that's* rebellion.

But is it truth? Are the values of natural selection's that are being rejected in the course of enlightenment actually false? Yes, in some sense. Consider the absurdity of the current situation: this planet is full of people operating on the premise that their interests trump the interests of pretty much everyone else on the planet—yet it can't be the case that everybody is more important than everybody else. So a core tenet of natural selection's value system is internally contradictory. Rejecting it, then, would pretty much have to move you closer to the truth. In the case of the exterior not-self experience, rebellion against the values of our overlord does seem to amount to some measure of enlightenment in the everyday sense of the word: it moves us toward a truer view of the world.

And what about the flip side, the interior version of the not-self experience? This version, in which you cease to "own" your thoughts and feelings, also involves a rejection of natural selection's values. After all, the kinds of thoughts and feelings our brain is inclined to have were initially designed by natural selection to help take care of this vehicle containing our genes. So identifying with these thoughts and feelings—owning them, and thus letting them own us—is often just another way of asserting our specialness.

When I'm trying to hail that cab—and trying to keep the (less worthy!) person next to me from hailing it—I'm "owning" my desire to get in a cab ASAP and get to the next stop on my uniquely important itinerary. If I let go of that feeling and cease to identify with it—in other words, take a step toward the interior version of the not-self experience—I'm rejecting natural selection's insistence that I consider myself special. Take that, natural selection!

So too with the case of the snoring yogi in the previous chapter. As long as I identified with my dislike of him, I was obeying natural selection's instructions to consider myself special (certainly more special than a guy who wants to catch up on his sleep when I'm trying to meditate!). To the extent that I disowned those feelings, I experienced a bit of not-self and defied natural selection's values.

I don't know exactly what it would be like to have the full-on not-self experience, but I've got a feeling that my sense of specialness, of unique privilege, would approach the vanishing point. And if that sense of specialness is indeed false—an illusion implanted in us by natural selection—then, exactly to the extent that it *did* approach the vanishing point, I would be approaching the truth.

Emptiness as Truth

Aside from not-self, the most famously counterintuitive metaphysical truth claimed by Buddhism is emptiness. Like not-self, emptiness is both a philosophical doctrine and a meditative experience. If you ask Buddhist philosophers to defend the idea of emptiness, they will talk about how everything is too interconnected for anything to have independent, self-sufficient existence. If you ask *me* to defend the idea of emptiness, I would take a different tack: I'd focus on the experience of emptiness, not the philosophical doctrine, and argue that this experience is in a sense more valid, more truthful, than our ordinary experience of the world.

The argument for the truth of emptiness is basically the same as the argument I just made for the truth of not-self. The experience of emptiness, like the experience of not-self, defies and denies natural selection's nonsensical assertion that each of us is more important than the rest of us. But the logic of the argument is less obvious here than it was in the case of not-self. So let's take a closer look at it.

Emptiness, you may recall, is, roughly speaking, the idea that things don't have essence. And the perception of essence seems to revolve, however subtly, around feelings; the essence of anything is shaped by the feeling it evokes. It is when things don't evoke much in the way of feelings—when our normal affective reaction to things is subdued—that we see these things as "empty" or "formless." At least, that's my view, a view that draws support from psychology and from the testimony of some very adept meditators.

So if you want to know whether emptiness is closer to the truth than our ordinary apprehensions of the world, you might want to ask about the feelings that give us those ordinary apprehensions, the feelings that create the sense of essence. Should the feelings that come naturally to us be trusted as guides to the truth?

No one who has read this book up to this point will now be waiting in suspense for the answer to that question. We've touched on the question in various places, including earlier in this chapter, and, consistently, the answer has been that our feelings are in one sense or another dubious guides to reality. So in a way we've already established that, if our intuition that things have essence is indeed informed by subtle feelings we have toward them, this fact alone should inspire doubts about that intuition.

But there's a sense in which our feelings deserve even more mistrust than I've suggested so far. It's a pretty cosmic sense, and explaining it will require backing up and revisiting the question of what feelings are for in the first place. But if you can't get cosmic when you're pondering the meaning of enlightenment, when *can* you get cosmic? So let's back up and revisit.

Feelings in Cosmic Context

At the dawn of organic sentience, when feelings made their first appearance in the living world, their mission was to take care of the organism, specifically to get it to approach things that are good for it (like food) and avoid things that are bad for it (like toxins). As beings got more complex, the behaviors that feelings induced got more complex than just approaching or avoiding—like, for example, yelling at people who are doing things that are bad for you and flattering people who might do things that are good for you.

Another way to put this is that feelings, viewed in the context of their evolutionary purpose, are implicit judgments about things in the environment, about whether they are good for the organism or bad for the organism, and about what behaviors (approach, avoid, scream, flatter) will be useful for the organism, given these judgments.

This, as we saw in chapter 3, suggests one sense in which feelings could be called true or false: Are those judgments accurate or inaccurate? Sometimes, especially in the modern world, they're inaccurate. Witness road rage, rampant anxiety, and various other kinds of feelings that don't serve the interests of the typical twenty-first-century human being.

But note that phrase *serve the interests*. This whole evaluation, by accepting a particular organism's interests as the criterion for whether judgments are accurate, is accepting natural selection's basic frame of reference: that you, this particular organism, are special; your interests are the most important interests, and therefore your particular perspective—the perspective that judges everything in relation to those interests—is the appropriate perspective for evaluating the goodness or badness of things in the world. Is that the way feelings and the perceptions they foster should be evaluated—from your particular perspective, or, for that matter, from anyone's particular perspective?

Before we go further, I want to assure you that I'm not going to suggest that you start ignoring all your self-serving feelings. It makes sense for each of us to spend a certain amount of time taking care of ourselves and, for that matter, our loved ones. I don't recommend that you quit doing all the things you've traditionally done on the unspoken premise that you and yours are special. You should keep eating, for example. And brushing your teeth. (Imagine how awkward it would be for everyone to brush each other's teeth!) And you should drive close kin who are sick to the hospital. Although these kin are in fact not more important than your neighbor's kin, there's a certain social efficiency that results from people caring for other people who, conveniently, live in their house. It's feelings that motivate you to do these kinds of things, and, in these kinds of cases, I say it's fine to trust your feelings.

This will of course include feelings that inform the sense of essence. Even though, strictly speaking, it's a self-serving feeling that makes your home seem to possess essence-of-home, I don't see any reason to fight that feeling. It is fine to be drawn into your home, and it will lead to fewer uncomfortable encounters than being drawn into randomly selected homes. And once you're in your home, by all means feel essence of dog or cat or son or daughter or spouse or partner (unless, perhaps, domestic tensions have transformed one of those essences from warm and fuzzy to cold and harsh). Up to a point, seeing the world from your particular perspective has its virtues from a standpoint of social efficiency and even social harmony and, yes, simple pleasure—and is a pretty defensible way to approach the bulk of your daily business.

But what about when you're not going about your daily business but rather are asking basic metaphysical questions? What about when you're trying to figure out whether feelings, in informing our sense of essence, are fostering perceptions that are *true* in some objective sense? Should we ask *those* kinds of questions from your perspective, or from any particular person's perspective?

Einstein and Enlightenment

Einstein became famous by asking a similar question in the realm of physics. He acknowledged that our intuitions about the physical world—about how fast objects move, for example—work fine for the purpose of steering each of us through that world. After all, for practical purposes, what matters is how fast things are moving *in relation to us*. But, he said, if you want a deeper understanding of physics, you need to detach yourself from your particular perspective—from any particular perspective—and ask: Suppose I occupied no vantage point? Since I wouldn't be able to ask how fast things are moving relative to me, what exactly would it mean to ask how fast things are moving? Questions like this led him to the theory of relativity and the realization that E=mc^2.

Well, any path of inquiry that's good enough for Einstein is good enough for me! A type of question that leads humankind to understand the relationship between matter and energy as never before has a pretty good track record when it comes to enlightenment. So let's ask a question about essence that's analogous to the question Einstein asked: What happens to essence when we let go of our particular perspective—the perspective that the feelings that shape the perceived essences of things were designed to serve?

I think the answer is that essence disappears. After all, without a perspective to serve, there would be no feelings in the first place. As Robert Zajonc, the psychologist whose work figured centrally in chapter 11, explained, "Affective judgments are always about the self. They identify the state of the judge in relation to the object of judgment." In the absence of a particular point of view—yours or someone else's—the whole idea of an affective judgment, a feeling, makes no sense. If you truly and completely adopt the vantage point Einstein adopted—if you transcend the perspective of the self, any self, and view things from nowhere in particular—essence disappears, along with the feelings that created it in the first place.

When we do this, when we transcend the perspective of self, there's a sense in which we're also transcending the perspective of our whole species. After all, the basic thoughts and feelings that guide us through life—the ones designed to take care of us—are, broadly speaking, characteristic of our species. Though the feeling of "homeness" that my house exudes may be distinctive at a fine-grained level, in a rougher sense it's the same feeling lots of people have about their homes.

But other species, of course, have their own views of things. And if we're going to thoroughly follow Einstein's example, and assume that *no* single perspective has special access to the truth, then we need to transcend not only the perspective of individual people but also the perspective of our whole species. We need to drop the assumption that the way we look at things is inherently more valid than the way other animals look at things.

So, for example: The fear instilled in a human by a snake amounts to a judgment that the snake is bad—something to be avoided. But the lust inspired by that very same snake in a member of its own species means the snake is good—something to be copulated with. Rotting flesh fills us with revulsion because approaching it could bring contact with tiny parasites; but from the point of view of the tiny parasites, rotting flesh is the ideal culinary milieu. And so on: stagnant, fetid swamps are off-putting unless you're, say, a mosquito or an alligator, in which case they're sublime. Young pandas like a nice meal of mother panda dung; I think I'll pass, thanks.

This relativity of judgment is part of what Buddhists mean when they talk about the illusory nature of everyday perceptions. Chandrakirti, an Indian Buddhist scholar who lived in the seventh century CE, said that what a human would see as water might seem like nectar to a certain kind of god and like pus or blood to a hungry ghost—and would taste accordingly. (A hungry ghost is a type of being I won't bother to describe except to say that you definitely don't want to be reincarnated as one.)

If Chandrakirti had been writing after Darwin, he might have put the point this way: Our entire notion of good and bad, our whole landscape of feelings—fear, lust, love, and the many other feelings, salient and subtle, that inform our everyday thoughts and perceptions—are products of the particular evolutionary history of our species. If having sex with armadillos had been the only way our ancestors could get their genes into the next generation, you and I would think armadillos are attractive—not just cute in an offbeat way, but deeply enticing. You might have trouble controlling your urge to caress them. Alert drivers on country roads in Texas might screech to a halt every now and then for an impromptu armadillo liaison. And, needless to say, there would be no moral transgression more grave than killing an innocent armadillo.

It's tempting to dismiss such evolutionary hypotheticals as meaningless. Sure, if fruits were toxic to our species and dirt was packed with carbohydrates, then nobody would have a sweet tooth and the great dieting challenge would be to control your dirt tooth. But so what? We've always known that some things—what tastes good, what qualifies as sexy—are "subjective." So the question of what foods and mates are attractive isn't really a question of thinking something is true that isn't really true. Nobody thinks Coke is better than Pepsi in the sense that 4 is greater than 3.

Actually, I'm not so sure about that. I've seen people argue about what constitutes great wine, or great art, as if convinced they were really right and the other person was wrong. That's the thing about feelings, a thing that is particularly true when we talk about their role in shaping essence: they can render judgment so subtly that we don't realize that it's the feelings that are rendering the judgment; we think the judgment is objective.

When I see a Ferrari and feel "essence of exotic, pricey sports car," I don't think, "But this is just the opinion of one particular member of one particular species"—because the perception is too subtle to even register as a full-fledged opinion. More consequentially, when I see in the driver "essence of rich showoff," I probably won't discount that judgment either—because, again, I probably won't be reflective enough to realize it's a judgment; it feels more like a simple fact. That's the way the perception of essence works: it smuggles judgments into our mind by cloaking them in feelings that are themselves so subtle, or at least so routine, as to often escape conscious recognition. And these feelings, these elementary ingredients of perceived essence, are by their nature tied to a particular perspective—the perspective of a species, or (as in the Ferrari case) the perspective of an individual within that species. From the perspective that Einstein considered the truest perspective—the point of view from no particular point—feelings don't even exist, and so essence doesn't either.

Again, I'm not encouraging you to let go of the entire repertoire of feelings and thoughts that is the heritage of our evolutionary lineage. Your bias toward snake evasion is understandable if staying alive is high on your list of priorities, as I think it should be. Still, suppose—just as a thought experiment—that your goal wasn't living as long as possible but rather attaining the clearest vision possible. Suppose you wanted to view life on this planet, and reality in general, from some perspective less parochial than the perspective of any one species. Suppose you wanted to view it from some more objective, more transcendent, more universally "true" perspective.

Then you would want to look at a snake without the emotional biases of any species—without the fear and aversion and dislike that comes naturally to a human and without the lust that comes naturally to a snake's paramour. You'd want to look at a swamp from the standpoint of neither a human nor a mosquito. You'd want to view reality with *none* of the feelings that evolved in our species or any other species as a way to get genes into the next generation. You'd want, like Einstein, the view from nowhere in particular.

The Point of View of the Universe

The phrase *the view from nowhere* is famously associated with the philosopher Thomas Nagel, who made it the title of a book. The book wasn't about Buddhism; it was about the whole nature of knowing and about the mission of philosophy. And that includes moral philosophy. For example, is there such a thing as an objectivity so complete that you could address moral issues bearing on your own interests without any bias at all?

This degree of moral objectivity would be one important—some would say the most important—consequence of attaining enlightenment. And it may be that, given the nature of the human mind, the only way to fully realize this moral dimension of Buddhist enlightenment would be to realize the other dimensions, the metaphysical ones—to experientially apprehend the truth of, most notably, not-self and emptiness. Maybe to get the moral view from nowhere, you need the *complete* view from nowhere.

In any event, *the view from nowhere* may be the pithiest way of describing what Buddhist enlightenment would be like: the view that carries none of my selfish biases, or yours, and that in a certain sense isn't even a particularly human perspective, or the perspective of any other species. This, truly, would be a view that defied natural selection's authority, because natural selection is all about specific perspectives. It is about creating lots and lots of different perspectives, each of which is shaped fundamentally by the principle that it is truer than competing perspectives, and none of which is naturally imbued with awareness of that fact, much less awareness of its absurdity. Buddhist enlightenment is about transcending all these perspectives.

The view from nowhere, the view of impartiality, shouldn't be confused with a view of indifference. The view from nowhere can—and, I'd argue, should—involve concern for the well-being of all people (and, if we're going to be true to Buddhist teaching, and to fairly straightforward moral logic, concern for the well-being of all sentient beings †). The point is just that the concern would be evenly distributed; no one's welfare is more important than anyone else's.

If *the view from nowhere* sounds like an overly negative way of describing this sort of benevolent transcendence, you could use the phrase coined by the nineteenth-century moral philosopher Henry Sidgwick when he alluded to "the self-evident principle that the good of any one individual is of no more importance, from the point of view (if I may say so) of the Universe, than the good of any other."

Regardless of your preferred terminology—view from nowhere, point of view of the universe—the upshot is the same: our ordinary point of view, the one we're naturally endowed with, is seriously misleading.

So, yes, we can think of natural selection as somewhat like those robot overlords in *The Matrix*, perpetrating a pervasive and oppressive illusion on behalf of an agenda that we have every right to reject. If looking at things this way helps give you the determination it takes to sustain a serious meditation practice, by all means look at things this way.

At the same time, it is in the spirit of Buddhism to be skeptical of demonizing anyone or anything, so let me say a few kind words about natural selection: it did create sentient life, and sentient life can be a wonderful thing. Indeed, the bliss that is said to be part of true Enlightenment wouldn't be possible without sentience. Neither would the more modest growth of happiness that can be had with more modest progress along the meditative path. You might even say that sentience is what gives life meaning and makes it a matter of moral concern. Certainly Buddhism's moral emphasis on respect for sentient beings wouldn't make much sense if there weren't any sentient beings around.

In that sense, Buddhism and natural selection would seem to be on the same page: sentient life is a good thing. But if natural selection indeed holds sentient life in high esteem, it's got a funny way of showing it! After all, the creation of complex life has involved the premature death of lots of living things—things judged genetically inferior by natural selection—not to mention tons of violence and suffering. That is why the specialness of self is such a strong intuition. For our ancestors, it was often either them or the other guy, and genes that encouraged them to think the other guy was as important as they were wouldn't have gone anywhere. So the sense of specialness and the attendant baggage of "self," whatever you think of them, were unavoidable features of sentient life so long as life was created by natural selection.

And be honest: if you had to choose between a planet full of living things that consider themselves special and a planet as barren as Mars, you'd choose the former, right? I would. Yes, barrenness can be beautiful, but if there are no sentient beings, the beauty goes unappreciated and even, in a sense, unrealized.

But here's the unfortunate paradox: we've gotten to a point in human history when the sense of specialness could actually endanger the continued flourishing of sentient life. I said in chapter 2 that I'd spare you the full-length, high-volume version of my sermon about saving the planet—about how the psychology of tribalism threatens to break people apart along religious, national, ethnic, and ideological lines. And I'm a man of my word. Still, it's worth spending a few paragraphs conveying the cosmic context of this prospect, viewing the crossroads we stand at against the backdrop of the whole history of life.

A Brief History of Life

For four billion years, life on this planet has been ascending to higher and higher levels of organization. First there were just bare, self-replicating strands of information; then they encased themselves in cells; then some of these cells got together and formed multicellular organisms; then some of those organisms developed complex brains, and some species of brainy organisms became highly social. One species of social, brainy organism was so social and brainy that it launched a whole second kind of evolution: cultural evolution, the evolution of ideas and customs and technologies. And this second kind of evolution carried this species to higher and higher levels of social organization—from hunter-gatherer village to ancient state to empire and so on, until here we are, on the brink of establishing a cohesive global society. As if to underscore what a natural outgrowth of biological and cultural evolution this is, there is even a kind of emerging global brain—the internet, animated by the human brains that form its neurons.

If you saw all this from outer space and in time lapse, so that billions of years were compressed into minutes, it might seem like you were watching the growth and maturation of a single planetary organism. Indeed, this growth might seem driven by such powerful developmental logic that the continued congealing of that organism—that is, the emergence of a peaceful and orderly global civilization—was inevitable.

You'd be wrong about the inevitable part—that's the whole problem—but it's true that the logic behind the process has been powerful. For starters, natural selection is so wildly inventive that the advent of a species smart enough to launch cultural evolution was probably pretty likely all along. The subsequent expansion of our species' social organization, from hunter-gatherer village all the way to globalization, was also likely, because cultural evolution, like biological evolution, has a powerful creative engine behind it.

At least, that's the case I made in a book called *Nonzero*. I argued that, ever since the Stone Age, the expansion of human social organization has been impelled by a technologically driven growth in the range of interdependence. Over time, people at farther and farther distances from one another have come into contact and in many cases have come to trade or otherwise cooperate with each other. Today, more than ever, we depend on people halfway around the world for the goods and services that sustain us, as do those people. In other words, the fates of people around the world have become more and more correlated. That's what interdependence is.

And, oddly, this correlation is actually strengthened by such global problems as climate change, problems that are bad for people in diverse parts of the world and whose solution would therefore be good for people in diverse parts of the world. In various different senses, people on different continents are in the same boat. It is in our common interest to work together. What could go wrong?

Well, if you're viewing the whole thing up close, answers may spring to mind. Here's the answer that springs to my mind: groups of people fighting with each other. The lines of battle may be ethnic, religious, national, or ideological, but antagonism seems to have grown along many of these lines in recent years. What's more, there seem to be some dangerous positive feedback loops: antagonism on one side creates more antagonism on the other, which creates more antagonism on the first side, and so on. This is the kind of dynamic that can fuel a long downward spiral—which would be alarming even if we weren't living in an age of nuclear weapons and increasingly lethal and accessible biological weapons. But we *are* living in such an age.

What's more, we're living in an age when information technologies make it easy for relatively small numbers of people bound by a common enmity to find each other, no matter where on earth they are, and then coordinate to deploy violence. Hatred, even when diffuse and far-flung, has increasingly lethal potential.

What causes all the hatred? At some level, it's always the same thing: human beings operating under the influence of human brains whose design presupposed their specialness. That is, human beings operating under the influence of the reality-distortion fields that control us in many and subtle ways, convincing us that we and ours are in the right, that we are by nature good, and that, when we do the occasional bad thing, it's not a reflection of the "real us"; whereas they and theirs aren't in the right and aren't by nature good, and when they do the occasional good thing, it's not a reflection of the "real them." And it doesn't help matters that these reality-distortion fields often magnify, even out-and-out fabricate, the threat posed by them and theirs.

So, yes, we need to reject the core evolutionary value of the specialness of self. Indeed, there's probably never been a time in human history when this rejection was more vital. But we don't want to reject what is also in a sense a value of natural selection's: that the creation and sustenance of sentient life is good. Happily, mindfulness meditation is well suited to fighting that first value while serving the second one. As a bonus, it brings us closer to the truth.

You could even view mindfulness meditation itself as in some sense a part of the natural unfolding of life, part of the ongoing co-evolutionary process. Maybe, given the constraints under which this universe operates, the only way for complex consciousness to arise on this planet was for it to be warped in the process, distorted by the exaltation of self. And maybe, once social organization approaches the global level, the only way for complex consciousness to flourish on this planet—or even to survive—is for it to now be unwarped, or at least partly unwarped.

We can thank Buddhism for laying out a path to this unwarping. Buddhism isn't alone in deserving thanks. Thinkers in many religious and philosophical traditions, from ancient times onward, have in some sense seen the problem and have suggested ways of addressing it—which is good, because it means that many traditions have resources to draw on as humankind confronts its collective challenge. But Buddhism deserves credit for so early, so acutely, and so systematically diagnosing the problem and for offering such a comprehensive prescription. And now, finally, science has corroborated the diagnosis and revealed its roots: the problem was built into us by our creator, natural selection. Fortunately, natural selection also equipped us with the tools for addressing the problem—rational and reflective faculties that in principle can transcend the circumstances of their birth. And, who knows, maybe they will.

16

Meditation and
the Unseen Order

There were many wonderful things about that first meditation retreat I attended, back in the summer of 2003. And there was one not-so-wonderful thing: a song got stuck in my head. When you're on a silent meditation retreat, songs can stay in your head for a really long time, because there's not much input to displace them. And this song was one I don't especially like.

It's by Foreigner, a group that had a burst of prominence when I was in college, and it's called "Feels Like the First Time." The chorus begins, "And it feels like the first time, like it never did before / Feels like the first time, like we've opened up the door."

The song was haunting me from early in the retreat, and it proved oddly prophetic. By the end of the retreat, I did feel like a door had opened for the first time.

In fact, there was a distinct moment when it felt, almost literally, like a door had opened and I had walked into a strange new place. It happened during the overwhelmingly and vibrantly blissful experience I mentioned in chapter 4, the one I had while meditating at night amid loudly chanting insects. Though I had my eyes closed, the experience was very visual, and I remember a distinct moment when I felt I'd crossed some threshold and entered a kind of fuzzily defined cavernous room made of orange and purple light.

Before I explain what I saw in that room, I need to expand on something I've already mentioned: the fact that I had been kind of hard on myself during this retreat for not being a good meditator. This was actually part of a long-standing pattern. I've always been good at convincing myself I've made a mistake, at chastising myself for it, and sometimes at pretty literally hating myself for it. For decades people have told me I shouldn't be like this. They've said things like, "Don't beat yourself up about it." This has always annoyed me. My feeling has been that you *should* beat yourself up about things you do wrong. Otherwise you may keep doing them! And let's be honest, isn't one of the big problems with the world how many people do bad things and then don't feel any need for self-chastisement?

One thing about meditation teachers that bothered me from the get go was their frequent insistence that we yogis not be hard on ourselves. This is such a common refrain that I've encountered people who thought "Don't be hard on yourself" was a core Buddhist teaching, a message that pervades ancient scripture. It's not. Here's a passage from one of the Buddha's discourses: "Monks, true knowledge is the forerunner in the entry upon wholesome states, with a sense of shame and fear of wrongdoing following along." You will have to look a long time to find a mindfulness meditation teacher in modern America encouraging students to feel shame.

But I digress.

The experience I had that night wasn't a full-fledged hallucination. As I entered that weird visual space, I didn't lose contact with the real world. I was aware that I was sitting in a meditation hall and that intense concentration had put my mind in a place it had never been. But where was this place? Only after looking around a bit did I realize that the place my mind had entered was my mind—or, at least, my mind's representation of my mind.

The tipoff was that I "saw"—and, I guess, "heard"—a particular thought I've had many times after doing something arguably stupid or inept or wrong. The thought was "You screwed up." Actually, "screwed up" is a sanitized version of the phrase I tend to use and of the phrase that constituted the thought I observed that night. Anyway, the main thing is this: I now saw this thought assume a form I had never seen it assume before.

Come to think of it, I had never *seen* this thought assume any form at all. But it now looked as if—literally *looked* as if—one part of my mind was speaking the thought to another part. There was even a kind of line tracing the path of the message, like an arrow on a diagram indicating the direction of communication. I watched this intracranial conversation, watched the message travel from sender to recipient, as a kind of outside observer, even though I thought of the recipient as in some sense being me.

It's almost impossible to convey in words the power of this experience and its aura of significance. I felt as if I had been ushered into the inner sanctum, where deep truths are revealed. I don't know how much of this sense of revelation rested on the narcotic-caliber bliss that was enveloping me with growing warmth as the experience unfolded. But I assume bliss can be a potent revelation reinforcer. In any event, whatever neurochemicals impart conviction to our apprehensions, making us feel sure we've seen the truth, must have been in liberal supply that night.

And what was the truth I was seeing? What struck me at the time was that, for the first time ever, this standard thought of mine—"You screwed up"—didn't seem to be coming from me. It was just some guy in my head doing the talking. And it wasn't clear that he was worth paying attention to. Who the hell was he, anyway?

Now, more than a decade later, having thought about this stuff more and written this book, I might answer, "He was a module in my mind." But at the time I was thinking less academically, and the lesson seemed to be that in the future I could treat my inner critic with some critical distance, if not outright disdain. As much as I had resisted entreaties to quit beating myself up, as much as I had minimized the toll it took on me, the prospect of living without this self-torture now seemed powerfully appealing. I'm not much of a crier, but I started crying. I tried to do it quietly, but I did it fully.

It wasn't long before the bliss had given way to joyous excitement. I remember how frustrating it was, after the session ended, as people strolled silently out of the hall, not to be able to share my epic news with anyone. The news wasn't just about conquering self-loathing. I had a sense that many things that had come only with pain and struggle would now come more easily. I had reached a high spiritual plane, and I had found a technique—meditation—that could get me there again and again. It's hard to reconstruct this experience, but I think this sense of auspicious spiritual attainment had been implicit in my tears. What I know for sure is that the tears were in part tears of gratitude, and that the sense of liberation was massive.

And then I lived happily ever after.

Actually, no. Another line in that Foreigner song, right after "feels like the very first time," is "like it never will again." And, indeed, I haven't had a meditative experience that joltingly powerful since then. My belief that I would be able to access this plane again and again and use it to orchestrate my own personal spiritual renaissance was naïve. So was my belief that I would quit beating up on myself, though the frequency and severity of the beatings seem to have fallen off a bit.

I'm not saying I never again realized states of intense bliss when meditating. There have been times on retreat when I could precisely control the flow of bliss entering my being, opening up the spigot or, if I felt a need to pace myself, shutting it off for a minute or two before opening it back up.

And I'm certainly not saying that my experience on that summer night in Barre, Massachusetts, didn't in any sense change my life. I'm just saying that this book lacks a common feature of books like this: the author's claim of a single dramatic experience that is enduringly transformative.

Clarity Begins at Home

All of this raises a question: Why do I still meditate? Why do I devote somewhere between thirty and fifty minutes of each day to a practice that will not, apparently, get me very close to enlightenment anytime soon? There are several reasons. I'll start with the little ones.

1. *Moments of truth.* Imagine a refrigerator making that humming noise that refrigerators make. Sounds monotonous, right? Actually, it's not. When I'm meditating in the morning, if the tabletop refrigerator in my office starts humming, and I've cleared my mind enough to actually pay attention to it, I see that the hum consists of at least three different sounds, each of which varies in intensity and texture over time. This is a truth about the world that is ordinarily hidden from me but is revealed through an elementary exercise of mindfulness. And it is an *objective* truth. You could no doubt set up sound-sensing equipment that would depict these three sounds as distinct lines on a graph.

   This may seem like a trivial truth. In fact, it *is* a trivial truth. And I have to admit that, strictly speaking, it's not just the *truth* in this experience that helps keep me coming back to the cushion each day. There's also the pleasantness of the experience. If my mind is clear enough to sense the nuances of the refrigerator's hum, then it is free enough of everyday concerns to see this little three-instrument symphony, this infinitely rich unfolding of pattern, as beautiful. And to *feel* it as beautiful—sometimes really intensely beautiful.

But with all due respect for beauty, I don't want to downplay the truth angle here—the sheer clear perception of a refrigerator's hum. Because it's important to realize that, even if complete and utter enlightenment will remain remote for most of us, portions of enlightenment are available. Even if we can't apprehend the truth about all of reality and sustain that apprehension throughout our lives, we can apprehend the truth about little corners of reality and sustain that apprehension for a little while. And here's the key thing: seeing these little, almost trivial truths on a regular basis, in a disciplined way, can help us see bigger, less trivial truths. Which brings us to the second thing that keeps me meditating.

2. *Moments of more consequential truth.* If I'm feeling anxiety or dread or hatred, and, through meditation, I get to a point where I'm just *observing* the feeling rather than engaging with it, that is a moment of truth. Observing the feeling, after all, involves noting where in my body it resides and what form it assumes there. And that location and form—somewhat like the three separate sounds constituting the refrigerator's hum—is an objective fact. Presumably there will someday be body scans that give you a 3-D display of the physical manifestation of different kinds of feelings. I'm pretty sure the resulting graphs will have roughly the structure of what I'm sensing when I'm observing a given feeling.

What's fascinating is how much variation there is in the subjective experience that can accompany the objective fact of this feeling. The more you focus on the objective fact—on the feeling itself and its instantiation in your body—the less unpleasantness you may feel. This is not a trivially easy feat, but it's doable, and it counts in favor of the Buddha's claim that *dukkha* is in some sense optional, and that the way to reduce if not eliminate it is to see reality clearly, to see objective facts for what they are and for no more than what they are.

3. *The wisdom of clarity.* If, during my morning meditation, I'm tuned in to those three components of my refrigerator's hum, or for that matter if I'm observing my breath, or some feeling, with great clarity, it means my mind is calm—not just because if my mind weren't calm, I couldn't see these things so clearly, but also because getting absorbed in the clarity helps calm my mind. And here is an interesting feature of a calm mind: if some issue in my life bubbles up, I'm likely to conceive of it with uncharacteristic wisdom. Suddenly I see that an email in my outbox, the one with the subtle but discernible edge of annoyance that I made a point to add—since, after all, the email I'm responding to was itself annoying—might as well not include that edge of annoyance. No good will come of it, and some bad may come of it.

4. *Moments of moral truth.* Part of this revised perspective on sending that email may be a revised view of the person I'm sending it to. Indeed, the key to the whole revision may be that I view that person without the antagonism that, in a less calm state of mind, had accompanied every thought about him. Suddenly I'm willing to entertain the hypothesis that the annoying email I got from him isn't really proof that he's a jerk. Maybe there's some circumstantial reason he added an annoying edge to the email. Maybe I can guess the reason, maybe I can't, but in any event, who among us hasn't been in a circumstance that led us to do something annoying? In fact, didn't I just come very close to sending an annoying email?

5. *Timely interventions.* If at 5:00 or 6:00 p.m. I'm feeling unsettled or angry or resentful or despondent or anything else that I'd rather not feel, I can sit down on the meditation cushion and observe that feeling and, pretty reliably, make things better. If I wake up at night with anxiety, I can lie there and meditate on the anxiety

and, somewhat less reliably, but as often as not, make things better. And sometimes I even perform a feat previously thought (by me, at least) impossible: while sitting at the computer, staring at something I'm writing and feeling a painfully strong urge to do anything other than write, I close my eyes, observe the urge until it weakens, and then get back to writing. The reason I can do all these things— and, for that matter, the reason I even remember that doing them is an option—is that I'm spending some time on the cushion every morning. The same goes for not beating up on myself: the more time on the cushion, the fewer eruptions of self-chastisement.

The Slippery Slope toward Enlightenment

So there—that's five reasons I keep meditating even though I don't harbor serious hopes that this path will lead all the way to enlightenment. At least, that's one way you could put it. Another way you could put it is that I *am* pursuing enlightenment—it's just that, rather than think of enlightenment as a state, I think of it as a process. And I think of liberation—liberation from *dukkha*—in the same way. The object of the game isn't to reach Liberation and Enlightenment—with a capital L and E—on some distant day, but rather to become a bit more liberated and a bit more enlightened on a not-so-distant day. Like today! Or, failing that, tomorrow. Or the next day. Or whenever. The main thing is to make net progress over time, inevitable backsliding notwithstanding.

Thinking about enlightenment and liberation this way helps drive home how subtle the relationship between truth and freedom can be. One common and not-so-subtle conception of this relationship is that you see the truth in a flash of insight, and then you are free. Sounds great! And what a time-saver! But I don't think it happens very often that the truth sets you free, period. Sometimes it's the other way around: freedom lets you see the truth. Remember, part of what let me see the truth about that refrigerator hum, and about my email correspondent, is that my mind was calm—not in the grips of anxiety or rage or any other major source of *dukkha*.

Maybe the best way to put it is that enlightenment and liberation are mutually reinforcing: the more you do the things that bring liberation from suffering, the more clearly you see; and the more clearly you see, the easier it is to do the things that bring liberation from suffering. Which allows even more clarity of vision. And so on.

For example, suppose you start out with a modest meditative practice that's more about self-help than spiritual attainment: twenty minutes a day of mindfulness-based stress reduction. Suppose this does, as advertised, reduce stress. Being free—or freer—of stress is by definition liberating, even if you're not thinking of it that way. It's also enlightening. After all, if you're not stressed out, you're less likely to label someone a jerk just because he's at the checkout counter fumbling for his credit card and you're behind him and in a hurry. That little bit of progress—seeing a bit less essence-of-jerk in someone who is doing something you've done yourself—is a little bit of enlightenment.

What's more, this little bit of enlightenment can lead to more bits of liberation that then lead to more bits of enlightenment. If seeing less essence-of-jerk in people, and thus spending less time fulminating pointlessly, further reduces the amount of stress in your life, maybe this effect will be so gratifying—so liberating—that it encourages you to meditate for twenty-five minutes a day instead of twenty. And that leads to more liberation from stress, which further clarifies your view of other people. Now you're tolerant not just of people who fumble with credit cards but of people who fumble with them and then drop them on the floor. Congratulations!

Your meditation sessions don't have to be all that long before it becomes obvious that stress reduction can be more interesting than it sounds. It isn't just that you feel a little more relaxed by the end of a meditation session; it's that you observe your anxiety, or your fear, or your hatred, or whatever, so mindfully that for a moment you see it as not being part of you.

Note how profound—or at least incrementally profound—these experiences are. To see less essence-of-jerk in a credit-card fumbler is to experience, in very small measure, emptiness. And to see your anxiety or fear as not being part of you is to experience a tiny bit of not-self. These two ideas, emptiness and not-self, are two of the most arcane, most crazy-sounding, and most fundamental ideas in Buddhist philosophy. And here you are, meditating each day for the sake of stress reduction and apprehending both, at least in some measure.

I don't want to make this sound easy. Though incremental enlightenment and incremental liberation can gather momentum via mutual assistance, it's not as if they're automatically self-sustaining. There are obstacles, and they can be frustrating, and meditation can be a pain. The good news is that the pain can lead to gain if you hang in there, if you don't shrink from anxiety or sadness but instead observe them mindfully, if you don't give up on a morning's sitting in the face of restless boredom but instead observe it mindfully—which, oddly, can be harder than observing anxiety or sadness mindfully. I'll never forget something that Narayan said on my first meditation retreat: "Boredom can be interesting." It's true, but seeing its truth will involve first spending some time absorbing another truth—Boredom can be really boring!—and persisting in the face of it.

Maybe the biggest impediment to continued meditative progress is the unfortunate finiteness of time. If you have much in the way of responsibilities—a job, kids to rear, school to attend, whatever—you can't devote huge chunks of each day to meditation. And, in my own experience, the difference between thirty minutes a day and fifty minutes a day is big. And, in the experience of people I've talked to, the difference between thirty minutes a day and ninety is huge. But even if you're down near the twenty-minute end of the spectrum, your practice can have depth, and that's especially true if you keep in mind the basic take-home lesson of Buddhist meditative philosophy: those little moments of truth you're getting each day—at least, that you're getting on a good day—are pieces of a bigger truth, a truth about the nature of reality and about the distortions, even delusions, imposed by our default perception of it. Sure, it would be great if you attained enlightenment and spent all your life *feeling* that big truth. But even if you can't—even if you have to work to bring that truth intermittently to mind—it can be a guiding truth.

Saving the World through Clarity

Okay, so that's much of the argument I'd make if people who don't meditate asked me why they should meditate. I'd talk about lots of little moments of truth, and how cultivating those moments can turn someone into a happier, better person. But this doesn't really get at the heart of the reason I hope more people will meditate. What motivated me to write this book isn't just the prospect of sprinkling little moments of truth into the lives of receptive readers, or even to convey the larger "guiding truth" these moments point to. What motivated me to write this book is the idea of a *moment* of truth—in the singular.

Merriam-Webster's Collegiate Dictionary defines a moment of truth as "a moment of crisis on whose outcome much or everything depends." I don't think that's too strong a phrase for the planetary challenge I described in the previous chapter—the problem of ethnic, religious, national, and ideological conflict that can feed on itself, creating a spiral of growing hatred that leads to true catastrophe.

Suggesting that meditation can help save the world is a good way to get written off as hopelessly naïve. So let me stress that the idea here isn't to generate a worldwide wave of loving-kindness. I mean, that would be great, but I don't think it's going to happen anytime soon, and I don't think the salvation of the world requires it.

I think the salvation of the world can be secured via the cultivation of calm, clear minds and the wisdom they allow. Such minds can, for one thing, keep us from overreacting to threats and thus from feeding the vicious circles that intensify conflicts. Calm, clear minds can also help us soberly assess what animates the threats—and so figure out, for example, what kinds of things encourage people to join or support violent causes, and what kinds of things discourage them from doing that. We don't have to love our enemies, but seeing them clearly is essential. And one lesson from both Buddhist philosophy and modern psychology is that seeing them clearly involves dialing down the fear and loathing, but also more than that; it involves transcending much subtler distortions of perception and cognition, often distortions that are grounded in subtler feelings.

This clarity of vision doesn't have to suddenly envelop the world. Even isolated pockets of equanimity and wisdom can make a difference and can prepare the ground for their own expansion. As with individual progress toward enlightenment, global progress toward enlightenment can be incremental and yet, through commitment, can acquire a momentum of its own.

That said, I think there are going to have to be a whole lot of increments. In fact, I think there will have to be, in the long run, a revolution in human consciousness. I'm not sure what to call the revolution—maybe the Metacognitive Revolution, since it will involve stepping back and becoming more aware of how our minds work. But I think it's going to have to be something so dramatic that future historians will have an actual label for the transformation. Assuming there *are* future historians—and if there aren't, that will probably mean there was no successful transformation to label anyway!

Near the outset of this book I anointed myself a laboratory rat. I said that if I could get much in the way of benefits out of meditation, just about anybody could, because I am peculiarly ill-suited to calming down and focusing. Well, the results are in: just about anybody can benefit from meditation.

But those aren't all the results. The question I originally asked wasn't just whether I could get enough benefits from meditation to keep returning to the cushion every day, or even whether I could to some extent clarify my day-to-day moral vision. I also asked whether I could meet the particular moral challenge that centrally motivated the writing of this book: overcoming, or at least eroding, the psychology of tribalism. As I noted, along this dimension I am an especially valuable laboratory rat, because (with all due humility) I so powerfully exemplify the problem.

In a way, it's odd that I would be so tribalistic. I don't have a strong version of the most famously dangerous tribal allegiances: ethnic, religious, national. Maybe that's why I focus so much emotional energy on tribal boundaries defined by opinion—why I strongly identify with people who agree with me, and am capable of thinking somewhat unflattering things about people who disagree with me. Which goes double, or triple, when the disagreement is about ideology, about policies that should or shouldn't be adopted.

Here's an embarrassing irony: nothing so arouses tribalistic animosities in me as people who support policies that, in my view, tend to arouse tribalistic animosities. To take just one example, I think most American military interventions of the past couple of decades have been mistakes—examples of overreacting to threats and thereby exacerbating them—and the people who have most strongly supported these interventions drive me nuts. And I want them to keep driving me *kind of* nuts. I wouldn't want to travel so far down the path toward nirvana that I was drained of fighting spirit. If full-on enlightenment means you quit making value judgments of any kind and quit pushing for change, then count me out.[†] But believe me when I tell you that getting to that point in the path is not, for me at least, a looming peril. The question is whether I can get far enough down the path to conduct my ideological combat with these people wisely and truthfully, which in turn means viewing them more objectively and, in a sense, more generously than I'm naturally inclined to do. The answer is that I think meditation has, at a minimum, helped move me closer to this goal. But it's a struggle. When I exhort people to advance the Meta-cognitive Revolution by overcoming the cognitive biases that sustain tribalism, I can't hold myself up as one of the world's more compelling role models.

The other thing I don't claim is that I have a step-by-step plan for the revolution. My main point is more abstract: it would be tragic, to say the least, if, after billions of years of arduous effort on the part of organic life, effort that has gotten us to the verge of a global community of minds, we let the natural distortions in these minds blow the whole thing apart. It would be all the more tragic in light of the fact that these distortions are now a scientifically established fact and that we have ways of correcting them, including, though not confined to, meditative practice.

All I'm really saying is this: the means to the planet's salvation is at hand.

Speaking of Salvation

Speaking of salvation, in my conjectures as to why I cried at that meditation retreat, I left out one possibly relevant thing. I was brought up religiously, as a Southern Baptist. I started drifting away from the church as a teenager, after comparing the theory of natural selection with the Book of Genesis as accounts of how humans came to be. I've never felt a desperate yearning for something that would replace my Christian faith, but presumably the loss of it left a vacancy somewhere inside me, and that may account for my enduring interest in spiritual questions. On that summer night in Barre, maybe I didn't just feel like I'd gotten to the mountaintop—maybe I felt like I'd been climbing that mountain since I was a teenager and left my native spiritual tribe. In any event, I don't think it's overstating the case to say that on that night I had a feeling of salvation—a feeling that may have been as powerful as the feeling that impelled me, at age nine or ten, to walk to the front of the church during the minister's invitation and accept Jesus as my savior.

My departure from Christianity wasn't a bitter one, as some such departures are. I never felt that faith had damaged me. I guess, come to think of it, growing up with an ever-watchful and pretty strict God could help account for my acute and sometimes painful attention to my shortcomings. Indeed, maybe some residual sense of sinfulness is what drove me to embark on this whole exploration of Buddhist meditation, and maybe it's the reason the sense of salvation on that summer night was palpable. That would stand to reason: both Buddhism and Christianity say that at birth we inherit a kind of moral confusion, the dispelling of which is one object of the game.

In any event, I've never felt that my Christian years were some kind of brutal authoritarian brainwashing. I still love the Baptist hymns, notably "Just as I Am," a song often sung softly at the end of the service to accompany the invitation. The song's message is basically that, though you're far from perfect, you're worthy of salvation.

My most vivid memory of Sunday school is a good one, of singing "Jesus loves the little children, all the children of the world; red and yellow, black and white, they are precious in his sight, Jesus loves the little children of the world." Maybe I've selectively remembered the more enlightened parts of Christian ethics, but the Jesus-to-Buddha transition does seem in some ways a natural one.

The Insight Meditation Society, the place where my mind opened up before my very eyes on that summer night, happens to reinforce this continuity. Before being purchased by Goldstein, Salzberg, and Kornfield, the red brick building that houses the Society had been a novitiate, a place where Catholic priests trained. As you walk from the cloakroom toward the meditation hall, there are on either side of you stained-glass windows with images of Jesus—one of him at the Last Supper and one of him praying intently, presumably shortly before the Crucifixion. Every time I walk into that meditation hall—and I've now done so hundreds of times—I look at those images of Jesus. They pretty reliably give me some uplift. Which is apt, because Jesus said that our perception of the world is distorted and that we should work on correcting our blind spots rather than complain about the blind spots of others: "You hypocrite, first take the log out of your own eye, and then you will see clearly to take the speck out of your neighbor's eye." Amen to that.

I don't call myself a Buddhist, because traditional Buddhism has so many dimensions—of belief, of ritual—that I haven't adopted. I don't believe in reincarnation or related notions of karma, and I don't bow before the statue of the Buddha upon entering the meditation hall, much less pray to him or to any Buddhist deities. Calling myself a Buddhist, it seems to me, would almost be disrespectful to the many Buddhists, in Asia and elsewhere, who inherited and sustain a rich and beautiful religious tradition.

Still, it's fair to ask, especially given my personal history, whether my meditation practice, along with the philosophy that undergirds it, qualifies as a religion. Does it do the kinds of things Christianity did for my parents, even though I've jettisoned the supernatural parts of Buddhism—and, indeed, retained the naturalistic parts a bit selectively?

Is "Secular" Buddhism a Religion?

If you were hoping to make that case, one person to turn to would be William James, who, more than a century ago, in his book *Varieties of Religious Experience*, tried to find a framework that would encompass all the forms of experience, Eastern and Western, that we call religious. James said that, in the broadest sense, religion can be thought of as "the belief that there is an unseen order, and that our supreme good lies in harmoniously adjusting ourselves thereto."

Even naturalistic, "secular" Buddhism does, I'd argue, posit a kind of "unseen order." As enlightenment begins to dawn, reality, which had seemed all chopped up, turns out to possess an underlying continuity, a kind of infrastructure of interconnection. Some people call it emptiness, others call it unity, but all agree that it looks less sharply fragmented than it looked before they got the picture.

And what James called our "supreme good" does lie in harmoniously adjusting ourselves to this normally unseen order, regardless of whether you think of this supreme good as being our deepest happiness or our virtue. Of course, part of this adjustment of ourselves means thinking of our selves as being less substantial, or at least less distinctly substantial, than we might have previously thought our selves to be. Indeed, this diffuseness of the self, and this porousness of the bounds of self, are part of the "unseen order"—a newly perceived continuity between what's inside of us and what's outside of us.

There's also a second kind of unseen order posited by Buddhist teaching. Remember, a basic premise of Buddhism is that seeing the metaphysical truth—seeing the way things really are, both on the inside and the outside, and hence seeing the continuity between those two zones—in some sense amounts to seeing the moral truth, the moral equivalence between our welfare and the welfare of others. There is, in other words, a kind of structural alignment between metaphysical truth and moral truth. That's a kind of order, an order that can remain unseen if we don't practice the disciplines that make it manifest.

This unseen order is not something we should take for granted. You can imagine a universe in which there is no such alignment—a universe in which seeing the metaphysical truth has no effect on your conduct toward other beings, or even inclines you to treat other beings more unkindly. But according to Buddhism—even the Western, more secular version of Buddhism sometimes held to be insufficiently religious—we live in a universe in which seeing the metaphysical truth helps you see the moral truth. There is a natural unity of enlightenment.

Then there's the third leg of this alignment: our well-being. Happiness—the elimination or at least lessening of suffering, of unsatisfactoriness, of *dukkha*—tends to coincide with seeing the metaphysical truth and acting on the attendant moral truth. This too is a kind of alignment that, presumably, a universe doesn't *have* to have.

It's kind of amazing, when you think about it, that the world would be set up this way: that the path you embark on to relieve yourself of suffering would, if pursued assiduously, lead you to become not just a happier person but a person with a clearer view of both metaphysical and moral reality. Yet that is the Buddhist claim, and there is substantial evidence in favor of it.

This three-part alignment—the alignment of metaphysical truth and moral truth and happiness—is embodied in the richly ambiguous word that lies at the heart of Buddhist practice: *dharma*. This ancient word is most commonly defined as "the Buddha's teaching." That's accurate insofar as it goes, but the word also refers to the core truths that are being *conveyed* by the Buddha's teaching. *Dharma* thus denotes the reality that lies beyond our delusions and, for that matter, the reality about how those delusions give rise to suffering; and it denotes the implications of all this for our conduct. In other words, the dharma is at once the truth about the way things are and the truth about how it makes sense to behave in light of the way things are. It is both description and prescription. It is the truth and the way.

And because the Buddha's prescription is a prescription not just for liberation from suffering but for right conduct, the word *dharma*'s denotations include a specifically moral one. Indeed, dharma can be thought of as natural law both in the sense of the law that the physical universe complies with and the moral law that we strive to comply with.

The use of a single word to signify all this is itself testament to the order that, according to Buddhism, is normally hidden but can become more evident as we diligently, as James might say, try to adjust ourselves to it.

In case all this sounds too abstractly philosophical, let me try to put it in more practical form, as the answer to this oft-asked question: Will meditation make me happier? And, if so, how much happier?

Well, in my case—and, as you will recall, I'm a particularly hard case—the answer is yes, it's made me a little happier. That's good, because I'm in favor of happiness, especially my own. At the same time, the argument I'd make to people about why they should meditate is less about the quantity of happiness than about the quality of the happiness. The happiness I now have involves, on balance, a truer view of the world than the happiness I had before. And a boost in happiness that rests on truth, I would argue, is better than a boost in happiness that doesn't— not just because things that rest on truth have a more secure footing than things that don't, but because, as it happens, acting in accordance with this truth means behaving better toward your fellow beings.

So that's why I'd say that any increments of happiness that insight meditation may add to your life are especially worth working for: because these are increments of *valid* happiness. This is a happiness that is based on a multifaceted clarity—on a truer view of the world, a truer view of other people, a truer view of yourself, and, I believe, a closer approximation to moral truth. It is this fortunate convergence of happiness, truth, and goodness that is embedded in the word *dharma* and that, I think, makes even a naturalistic Buddhism comply with William James's conception of religion.

And if it turns out that the convergence has one more element—if widespread attention to the dharma could save the planet—well, that's a nice bonus.

Truth and Beauty

Late one day in mid-December 2012, I was at a meditation retreat and was outside doing some walking meditation. At some point I looked up at the horizon and saw that the sun had set. All that was left was its pink and purple residue, framed austerely by barren winter trees. I was already in a mildly morose state, having been mulling some personal issue or other, and now I felt a distinct wave of melancholy, as I sometimes do upon seeing a winter twilight. Then—this being a retreat and me having spent much of each day observing my feelings—I immediately, almost reflexively, examined the melancholy. And right away the feeling was drained of force. It didn't immediately disappear, but it now seemed like nothing more than physical waves, neither good nor bad, moving slowly through my body.

With the melancholy neutralized, the horizon took on a different aspect: it was stunningly beautiful. It had gone from being a reflection of sadness to being a source of delight, even awe.

This beauty—and all the other beauty I've appreciated more deeply as a result of meditative practice—is something I don't really understand. I mean, if meditation can give you a kind of distance from your feelings and lessen their hold on you, shouldn't it in principle do that equally for good and bad feelings? Shouldn't you wind up feeling more or less neutral—which is to say, feeling more or less nothing? Yet the way it seems to work is that some feelings actually get accentuated—first and foremost the sensation of beauty.

I sometimes think this heightened sense of beauty is what can give emptiness an Ironic moral power. Once you see less in the way of essence in people—once your perception of them is less imbued with judgments about their badness or goodness—there is, you might think, a greatly lessened reason to feel anything at all about them, including compassion. But if we're naturally inclined to think that things, including people, are beautiful, that inclination could translate into concern for their well-being. At least, that's one theory as to why meditation can make people more compassionate.

In any event, I remain flummoxed by what seems to be a natural tendency of contemplative practice to strengthen the sense of beauty. I guess one explanation is that, without really thinking about it, you're

using mindfulness to filter your feelings—working harder to get critical distance from the unpleasant feelings than from the pleasant feelings, such as aesthetic delight. But, for what it's worth, it doesn't *feel*
like that. The sense of beauty feels more like something the mind just
naturally relaxes into when the preoccupation with self subsides.

I'm tempted to invoke John Keats's famous verse, "Beauty is truth,
truth beauty." Maybe when you see the world more clearly, more
truthfully, you enjoy not only a measure of liberation but also a more
direct and continuous perception of the world's actual beauty. On the
other hand, the idea of the world having actual beauty, *inherent* beauty,
seems at odds with the Buddhist emphasis on our tendency to impose
meaning on the world. It's certainly at odds with the view from evolutionary psychology, which holds that our assignment of feelings to
perceptions is indeed that: an assignment, made by brains designed
to feel certain ways about certain kinds of things based only on the
relationship of those things to the organism's Darwinian interests.

Another possibility is that a certain affinity for the universe is a
kind of default state of consciousness, a state to which it returns when
it's not caught up in the inherently distorting enterprise of operating a
self. But here we're venturing beyond psychology, into the philosophical question of what consciousness is. And my general view on that
question is: beats me.

There's a lot to dislike about the world we're born into. It's a world
in which, as the Buddha noted, our natural way of seeing, and of being,
leads us to suffer and to inflict suffering on others. And it's a world
that, as we now know, was bound to be that way, given that life on this
planet was created by natural selection. Still, it may also be a world in
which metaphysical truth, moral truth, and happiness can align, and
a world that, as you start to realize that alignment, appears more and
more beautiful. If so, this hidden order—an order that seems to lie at
a level deeper than natural selection itself—is something to marvel at.
And it's something I'm increasingly thankful for.

Appendix
A List of Buddhist Truths

While I was writing this book, I didn't have in mind the title *Why Buddhism Is True*. But after I finished writing it I realized that the book did amount to an argument for the validity of what I consider the core ideas of Buddhism—or, at least, the core ideas of the "naturalistic" side of Buddhism, the side that "Western" Buddhism is mainly concerned with. So I went with the title, though—for reasons I assume are obvious—not without some trepidation.

In the course of reassuring myself that the title was indeed warranted, I started listing particular Buddhist ideas that the book defends. And I decided that maybe such a list would be useful to readers. So I offer the list below, a kind of skeletal summary of the argument made in the course of the book, along with pointers to relevant chapters.

Not all of the "truths" I list are Buddhist *doctrines*. Some are more like *takeaways*, clear implications of Buddhist thought. But all of them, I'm arguing, draw substantial corroboration from modern science, including modern neuroscience and psychology, with special emphasis on evolutionary psychology—that is, with special emphasis on the study of how natural selection shaped the human mind.

And speaking of substantial corroboration from modern science: it's important to understand that, strictly speaking, that's all science ever offers. There is no such thing as a scientific theory that has been *proven* to be true in the sense that mathematical theorems are proven true. To be sure, some theories now merit so much confidence that, for practical purposes, we can think of them as if they've been proven true. For example, I think the chances of the theory of natural selection being true are significantly greater than 99.99 percent—which is good enough for me. But some theories that merit much less confidence than that are nonetheless the leading theories in their field.

The point is just that when we speak casually of a scientific theory being "true," what we mean, strictly speaking, is that it has substantial corroborating evidence in its favor and has not yet encountered firm evidence that is incompatible with it. That's what the title of this book means in referring to core Buddhist ideas as "true." These ideas draw corroboration—in some cases overwhelming corroboration, in some cases substantial but less than overwhelming corroboration—from the available evidence. I've tried in this book to signal roughly how much confidence I think different Buddhist ideas warrant. But I certainly think the core of Buddhism's assessment of the human condition—its basic view of why people suffer and why they make other people suffer and, more broadly, its conception of certain basic aspects of how the mind works and of how we can change how our minds work—warrants enough confidence to get the label that the title of this book gives it.

Okay; without further ado, here are some Buddhist "truths":

1. Human beings often fail to see the world clearly, and this can lead them to suffer and to make others suffer. This costly misapprehension of the world can assume various forms, described in various ways in different Buddhist texts. For example:

2. Humans tend to anticipate more in the way of enduring satisfaction from the attainment of goals than will in fact transpire. This illusion, and the resulting mind-set of perpetual aspiration, makes sense as a product of natural selection (see chapter 1), but it's not exactly a recipe for lifelong happiness.

3. *Dukkha* is a relentlessly recurring part of life as life is ordinarily lived. This fact is less evident if you translate *dukkha* as it's conventionally translated—as "suffering" pure and simple—than if you translate it as involving a big component of "unsatisfactoriness." Organisms, including humans, are designed by natural selection to react to their environments in ways that will make things "better" (in natural selection's sense of the term). This means they are almost always, at some level, scanning the horizon for things to be unhappy about, uncomfortable with, unsatisfied with. And since being unsatisfied, by definition, involves at least a *little* suffering, thinking of *dukkha* as entailing unsatisfactoriness winds up lending credence to the idea that *dukkha* in the sense of suffering is a pervasive part of life. (See chapters 1 and 3.)

4. The source of *dukkha* identified in the Four Noble Truths— *tanha*, translated as "thirst" or "craving" or "desire"—makes sense against the backdrop of evolution. *Tanha*, you might say, is what natural selection instilled in animals so they wouldn't be satisfied with anything for long (see chapter 1). Seeing *tanha* as the source of suffering makes even more sense when it is construed broadly, as not only the desire to obtain and cling to pleasant things but also the desire to escape from unpleasant things (see chapter 13). Clearly, if you took the suffering associated with feelings of aversion out of the picture, that would take a lot of suffering out of the picture.

5. The two basic feelings that sponsor *dukkha*—the two sides of *tanha*, a clinging attraction to things and an aversion to things— needn't enslave us as they tend to do. Meditative disciplines such as mindfulness meditation can weaken the grip they exert. People disagree on whether complete and lasting liberation—nirvana in the classic sense of the term—is attainable, but there is no doubt that lives have been transformed by meditative practice. It's important to emphasize that becoming less enslaved by craving and

aversion doesn't mean becoming numb to feelings; it can mean developing a different relationship to them and becoming more selective about which feelings to most fully engage with. Indeed, this revised relationship can include the *accentuation* of certain feelings, including wonder, compassion, and the sense of beauty. (See chapters 2, 5, 8, 10, 13, and 16.)

6. Our intuitive conception of the "self" is misleading at best. We tend to uncritically embrace all kinds of thoughts and feelings as "ours," as part of us, when in fact that identification is optional. Recognizing that the identification is optional and learning, through meditation, how to make the identification less reflexive can reduce suffering. An understanding of why natural selection engineered various feelings into the human mind (see chapter 3) can help validate the idea that we shouldn't uncritically accept the guidance of our feelings and can help us choose which feelings to accept guidance from. To exercise this kind of discretion is to follow a strictly pragmatic rendering of Buddhism's famous "not-self" idea—a rendering that is a plausible interpretation of the foundational text on not-self, the second discourse the Buddha delivered after his enlightenment. (See chapter 5.)

7. The more expansive and more common interpretation of the Buddha's second discourse—as saying that the "self" simply doesn't exist—is rendered in various ways in various Buddhist texts. A common rendering—that there is no CEO self, no self that is the "doer of deeds," the "thinker of thoughts"—is substantially corroborated by modern psychology, which has shown the conscious self to be much less in charge of our behavior than it seems to be. A number of psychologists, including in particular evolutionary psychologists, subscribe to a "modular" model of the mind that is quite consistent with this view that there is no CEO self. This model can help explain a common apprehension of advanced

meditators: that "thoughts think themselves." All told, what I call the "interior" version of the not-self experience—an experience that calls into question your "ownership" of your thoughts and feelings and calls into question the existence of the chief executive "you" that you normally think of as owning these things—draws validation both from experimental psychology and from prevailing ideas about how natural selection shaped the mind. (See chapters 6, 7, and 8.)

8. What I call the "exterior" version of the not-self experience—a sense that the bounds surrounding the self have dissolved and were in some sense illusory to begin with—is not empirically and theoretically corroborated in the same sense that, I argue, the "interior" version of the not-self experience is corroborated. Indeed, I'd say the exterior version is not in principle *amenable* to corroboration in the same sense that the interior version can be corroborated, because it amounts to a claim that is less about psychology than about metaphysics (in the sense of the term *metaphysics* used in mainstream philosophy, not in any more exotic sense). At the same time, considerations from evolutionary biology suggest a distinct sense in which the bounds of the self can be thought of as arbitrary, which in turn suggests that sensing a kind of dissolution of the bounds of the self can be thought of as no less accurate an apprehension than our ordinary sense of the bounds of the self. (See chapters 13 and 15.)

9. Leaving aside the *metaphysical* validity of our ordinary sense of self, and of alternatives to that ordinary sense of self, there is the question of *moral* validity. In particular, when a sense of the dissolution of the bounds of self (perhaps paired with the "interior" version of the not-self experience in the form of reduced identification with selfish impulses) leads to a less pronounced prioritization of "my" interests over the interests of others, does that move

a person closer to moral truth? I argue that considerations from evolutionary biology support an affirmative answer to that question. (See chapter 15.)

10. The intuition that objects and beings we perceive have "essences" is, as the Buddhist doctrine of emptiness holds, an illusion. Specifically, it is an illusion engineered by natural selection to identify the significance of things with respect to the Darwinian interests of the organisms doing the perceiving. (See chapters 10 and 11. This Darwinian defense of the idea of emptiness is quite different from traditional Buddhist defenses of the idea, but it's compatible with them.) Seeing essences in things doesn't always lead us to suffer or to inflict suffering on others, but it can. In particular, an "essentialist" view of other people and groups of people can lead us to countenance or intentionally cause their suffering. (See chapter 12.) So awareness that essence is a perceptual construct, not a reality, can be valuable, especially if paired with meditative practice that dampens the sense of essence or permits selective engagement with it. Advanced meditators who report having lost a sense of essence fairly broadly—that is, who report apprehending emptiness or formlessness in a fairly thoroughgoing way—seem to be very happy and, in my (limited) experience, benevolent people. (See chapter 13.)

11. The preceding point about essence and essentialism is one illustration of the broader proposition that not seeing the world clearly can lead not just to our own suffering but to bad conduct in the sense of making others suffer needlessly. Or, to put a more positive spin on it: Seeing the world more clearly can make you not just happier but more moral. This isn't a *guaranteed* outcome. There have been very good meditators who were (apparently) very happy and (manifestly) very bad people. Still, there is a close enough association between the psychological dynamics that make us suffer and the psychological dynamics that make

us behave badly toward people that the Buddhist prescription for lessening or ending suffering will *tend* to make us not just happier but better people. That this moral progress isn't guaranteed is one reason meditative instruction has typically been paired with the sort of ethical instruction that is so prominent in Buddhism. (See chapter 16.)

12. Many Buddhist teachings, including several of those listed here, could be lumped under the rubric of "awareness of conditioning," where "conditioning" means, roughly speaking, causes. Mindfulness meditation involves increased attentiveness to the things that cause our behavior—attentiveness to how perceptions influence our internal states and how certain internal states lead to other internal states and to behaviors. This attentiveness includes an awareness of the critical role feelings seem to play in these chains of influence—a role shaped by natural selection, which seems to have calibrated feelings as part of its programming of our brains. Importantly, the meditative practices that bring awareness of these chains of influence also empower us to intervene and change the patterns of influence. To a large extent, that's what Buddhist liberation is: a fairly literal escape from chains of influence that had previously bound us and, often, to which we had previously been blind. (See chapter 14.)

So these are some of the main considerations that I hope justify the title *Why Buddhism Is True*. But if you want the shortest version of my answer to the question of why Buddhism is true, it's this: Because we are animals created by natural selection. Natural selection built into our brains the tendencies that early Buddhist thinkers did a pretty amazing job of sizing up, given the meager scientific resources at their disposal. Now, in light of the modern understanding of natural selection and the modern understanding of the human brain that natural selection produced, we can provide a new kind of defense of this sizing up.

A Note on Terminology

Writing a book on Buddhism confronts you with a number of choices about terminology.

For starters, there is the Sanskrit versus Pali question. In Western writing, Buddhist terms are usually rendered in one of these two ancient languages (though there are also ancient Buddhist texts in other Asian languages). Some authors of books about Buddhism pick one language or the other and stick with it. That's not the path I chose, and I thought I'd explain why.

The first big Buddhist concept this book engages with at length, "not-self," is emphasized more in Theravada Buddhism than in the other main branch, Mahayana Buddhism. The Theravada canon is in Pali, so it felt natural to render not-self as *anatta*, as opposed to the Sanskrit *anatman*. But the second big Buddhist concept the book tackles, "emptiness," gets more emphasis in the Mahayana tradition, and for that reason the term is usually rendered in Sanskrit: *sunyata*. And a few key terms that are prominent in both traditions have, as it happens, become well known in the West in their Sanskrit forms—in particular *nirvana* and *dharma* (as opposed to the Pali *nibbana* and *dhamma*). So here I went with Sanskrit.

Having made the decision to use both Sanskrit and Pali, I then had to face borderline cases, where there wasn't a particularly strong argument for either. I won't bore you with my reasons for making every choice I made. In some cases I more or less flipped a coin.

On the *sutra* (Sanskrit) vs. *sutta* (Pali) issue, I've played it both ways, depending mainly on whether the text in question is more closely associated with the Mahayana or Theravada tradition. But this issue comes into play more in the notes and bibliography than in the text of the book itself, because in the text I've tended to use the word *discourse* in preference to *sutra* (or *sutta*). One reason is that I think in some circles the word *sutra* has come to connote something more like a poem or a reflection than an argument. And by and large the Buddhist texts I'm focusing on make arguments. They may not make arguments in the modern sense of the word—all terms defined, each step in the argument clearly delineated—but they are advancing propositions about psychology or philosophy and giving reasons for them. And these propositions are at the heart of this book.

Finally: I use the word *enlightenment* a lot in the book. And, actually, *awakening* would be a more literally accurate translation of the ancient term that is commonly rendered as *enlightenment*. This is the term that is the basis both for "the Buddha" (awakened one) and for the name of the tree—the Bodhi tree—under which the Buddha is said to have had his great awakening. *Awakening* certainly has its appeal as a translation, given the Buddhist idea that we ordinarily live in such delusion as to be in a kind of dream world—and given that I begin the book by embracing that idea. At the same time, notwithstanding this metaphorical aptness, Buddhist awakening involves more than just waking up; there has to be actual enlightenment, in the sense of apprehending, often arduously, some elusive truths about the world. As it happens, the term *enlightenment* has another relevant dimension; it signifies the era when the West made a decisive turn toward rational analysis. This struck me as apt, given this book's argument that the Buddhist worldview, or at least the naturalistic part of it, makes great sense by the lights of the philosophy and science that emanated from that era.

Acknowledgments

The Meditation teacher Daniel Ingram wrote a book called *Mastering the Core Teachings of the Buddha*, and on the title page, right below the title, are the words "by the Interdependent Universe." Then, below that attribution of authorship, there is a more conventional attribution—Ingram's name. It's an inside joke, a nod to the fact that, according to Buddhist philosophy, the fruits of your labor are not best described as the fruits of your labor. They are best described as the product of all kinds of influences that have impinged on you over the years—so many influences that there is no practical hope of actually identifying them all.

But I'll do the best I can.

First, I owe a great debt to Princeton University. Shortly after I started writing this book, I began teaching a freshman seminar at Princeton called Science and Buddhism. Two years in a row I was gifted with a room full of curious, challenging students who, in addition to helping me clarify and organize my thinking on this subject, made me feel more optimistic about the future. Princeton further supported me in the development of an online version of the course—called Buddhism and Modern Psychology, available for free on the Coursera platform—that has allowed me to reach tens of thousands of additional students, whose energy and curiosity, even as apprehended remotely, has been a blessing. All of this was possible only with the sustained support of Clayton Marsh and the initial encouragement of Shirley Tilghman. Along the way I got vital help from others at Princeton, including Jeff Himpele, Laura Shaddock, Lisa Jackson, Jim Grassi, Mona Fixdal, and Shakuntala Sanyal. Rachel Connor and David Nowakowski, then graduate students in psychology and philosophy, respectively, served as excellent research assistants in the preparation of the online course, and in that role they provided feedback on parts of an inchoate draft of this book.

After teaching at Princeton I became Visiting Professor of Science and Religion at Union Theological Seminary in New York, where I was supported by a generous grant from the John Templeton Foundation. At Union—one of the most important and deeply ecumenical educational institutions in America's spiritual history, and one of the friendliest places on the planet—I found supportive colleagues who shared my interest in Eastern philosophy, notably John Thatamanil, Greg Snyder, Chung Hyuh Kyung, and Paul Knitter. I also profited from seminar discussions with students on whom I inflicted several draft chapters of this book: Andre Daughtry, Guthrie Graves-Fitzsimmons, Kate Newell, Duke Kwadwo Yeboah, Isabel Mares, Julio Torres, and Carole Wilkins. And all of this happened with the ongoing support of Union's president, Serene Jones (who, among other feats, has just launched a degree program in Buddhism at Union), and vice president, Fred Davie.

A number of people with relevant expertise generously agreed to read part or all of the manuscript and give me feedback. I'm very grateful to Miri Albahari, Stephen Asma, Paul Bloom, Bhikkhu Bodhi, Susan Gelman, Joseph Goldstein, and Scott Barry Kaufman. Particularly comprehensive feedback was provided by three people: Josh Summers, whom I met at my first meditation retreat; Jonathan Gold (whose excellent book on the Buddhist philosopher Vasubandhu, *Paving the Great Way*, was also useful); and Philip Menchaca, who also helped me greatly with various other endeavors at Union. (Bhikkhu Bodhi deserves a second shoutout for, by Skype and by email, patiently and cheerfully walking me through issues of translation and interpretation raised by some of the ancient texts this book draws on.) Reid Hoffman and Ben Casnocha graciously hosted gatherings that provided valuable feedback on ideas in this book.

Many scholars, meditation teachers, and monks had helpful conversations with me. I won't bother to thank the ones who are mentioned in the book. But, in addition to those, there are Shinzen Young, Jay Michaelson, Sharon Street, Kenneth Folk, Daniel Ingram, Buzzy Teiser, Erik Braun, Vincent Horn, Annabella Pitkin, Dale Wright, David Yaden, and Miguel Farias. Most of those conversations took place on meaningoflife.tv, a platform built and sustained through the work of Aryeh Cohen-Wade, Brian Degenhart, Nikita Petrov, Brenda Talbot, and the aforementioned Philip Menchaca.

I've spent a total of seven weeks at silent meditation retreats at the Insight Meditation Society, where the staff is always so helpful and supportive as to constitute a living advertisement for Buddhism. I'd like to be able to thank them all by name, but one thing about being at a silent meditation retreat is that you don't learn many personal details about the people you see. I do, however, know the names of Joseph Goldstein and Sharon Salzberg—two of IMS's three co-founders—and I'm grateful to both for illuminating conversations that go back some fifteen years.

At Simon & Schuster, I got early and undying support and guidance from my editor, Priscilla Painton. She's always been there when I needed her, and I've needed her a lot. Priscilla's assistant, Megan Hogan, has handled a variety of issues with great skill and, when necessary, diplomacy. The book's copyeditor, Judith Hoover, diligently pored over the text and did readers the favor of reducing the frequency of some of my more tiresome literary tics. As the book entered production, the burden of my propensity to keep fiddling fell largely on

Alex Su, who bore it with a cheerfulness that was more helpful than he knew. Among the others at Simon & Schuster who deserve thanks are Cary Goldstein, Nicole McArdle, Richard Rhorer, Alison Forner, Erin Reback, and, last but not least, Jon Karp. My agent, Rafe Sagalyn, has once again given me good guidance all the way from conception through publication.

Closer to home, I want to thank my dogs, Frazier and Milo, for appearing in the "office hours" videos that I made as part of the aforementioned online course, and also for comforting me in times of need. My two biking buddies, John McPhee and Steve Kruse, sometimes said useful things about the book when they weren't helping me take my mind off the book. My two daughters, Margaret and Eleanor, have been tolerant of me throughout my writing career and, as they've grown up, have become trusted sources of feedback on all kinds of book-related—and, for that matter, non-book-related—issues. Plus, they're great. (If being enlightened would mean not seeing essence-of-wonderful-daughter when I look at them, I'm glad I haven't attained enlightenment!) Finally, and above all, I want to thank my wife, Lisa, who read every word of this book more than once, and who is therefore responsible for all errors and omissions. Just kidding. Actually, she's responsible for this book being, in many places, much clearer and better than it would have been in the absence of her feedback. Over the past three decades, nothing has given me a more gratifying sense of relief than for Lisa to read something I've written and tell me it needs no further work—even though I know deep down that, characteristically, she's being too kind.

Notes

1: Taking the Red Pill

8 monkey dopamine study: See Schultz 2001; Schultz et al. 1992.

8 †*anticipating the pleasure . . . from the sweetness*: Though elevated dopamine often accompanies pleasure, many researchers now believe dopamine doesn't *cause* pleasure but, rather, tends to accompany it for other reasons, and is more directly involved in the anticipation of and longing for pleasure than in the experience of pleasure per se. For present purposes, the main thing is that, for whatever reason, the decline in dopamine presumably reflects a waning of pleasure as the monkeys get used to the sweet juice (a presumption consistent with the common human experience of pleasure waning as pleasurable stimuli are repeated). And the increase in dopamine triggered by the light presumably reflects a heightened anticipation of pleasure. Indeed, here, according to current thinking, the dopamine may well be causally, not just correlationally, linked to the subjective phenomenon.

10 *"discomfort of being ruled by them"*: Yongey Mingyur and Swanson 2007, p. 250.

2: Paradoxes of Meditation

22 *"wailing people around him"*: See "Thich Quang Duc" in Wikipedia: https://en.wikipedia.org.

3: When Are Feelings Illusions?

29 *"seek the one and shun the other"*: Romanes 1884, p. 108.

29 *kin share so many of our genes*: See Wright 1994, chapter 7. In general, see Wright 1994 and Pinker 1997 for an introduction to the logic of evolutionary psychology.

30 †*bad for the organism*: Some philosophers hold the view that, actually, feelings never cause organisms to do anything. The underlying idea here, called "epiphenomenalism," is that subjective experience is influenced by the physical workings of the organism but never influences those workings. If the epiphenomenalist view is correct, then the way I've described the primordial function of feelings—to get organisms to approach/avoid things that are good/bad for them—can't be, strictly speaking, right. (Indeed, in the epiphenomenalist view, the existence of feelings is something of a mystery, because they have no apparent function.) But even if so, it's fair to say that, for example, unpleasant feelings *accompany* behaviors that get organisms to avoid things that are bad for them, and thus *signify* that in natural selection's "view," aversion is appropriate. In that sense the *meaning* of feelings is essentially the same in the epiphenomenalist view of consciousness as in other views of consciousness. And, by the way, if the epiphenomenalist view is correct, then much of what behavioral scientists say about feelings—stating or implying, as it does, that feelings have functionality—is, strictly speaking, not accurate. So, strictly speaking, the behavioral sciences literature should be littered with disclaimers of the kind I'm making here. But, again, such disclaimers tend not to fundamentally undermine the accompanying analysis.

35 *averting their eyes from the scar*: Gazzaniga 2011.

38 *"fear of embarassment in assemblies"*: Thera 2007.

42 *"lifetime of discomfort"*: Beck and Emery 1985, p. 4.

4: Bliss, Ecstasy, and More Important Reasons to Meditate

46 default mode network studies: See Brewer, Worhunsky, et al. 2011; Andrews-Hanna et al. 2010; Farb et al. 2007; Holzel et al. 2011; Lutz et al. 2008; and Davidson and Irwin 1999.

47 *subdued default mode networks*: Brewer, Worhunsky, et al. 2011.

53　†*no term ... translated as "now"*: There is a term that can be translated as "in this world" or "in this very life" and is occasionally translated as "here and now," but in context it refers to the time when the rewards of a certain level of meditative attainment will come—that is, during this cycle of life, as opposed to after death—and isn't part of the instruction for how to realize mindfulness.

53　†*in the rest of the world*: Buddhist literature includes various depictions of what it would mean to be enlightened (or "awakened," to use a more literal translation of the term commonly translated as "enlightened"; see the Note on Terminology at the end of this book). But among the most commonly cited elements of enlightenment is the dispelling of these two illusions. As we'll see in chapter 13, another commonly cited element of enlightenment—overcoming *tanha*, or craving—is, arguably, so tightly intertwined with the dispelling of these two illusions as to be tantamount to it.

56　†*comprehension itself is a challenge*: In an ancient commentary on one Buddhist text is found this observation: "Impermanence is obvious, as when a saucer (say) falls and breaks; . . . pain is obvious, as when a boil (say) appears in the body; . . . the characteristic of not-self is not obvious." See Buddhaghosa 2010, p. 667.

5: The Alleged Nonexistence of Your Self

58　*"your head will explode"*: Kornfield and Breiter, eds. 1985, p. 173.

59　*"the evil in the world"*: Rahula (1959) 1974, p. 51.

62　*"form is not-self"*: Throughout this chapter, and in chapter 7, I'm using the translation of Mendis 2010.

62　†*even though we'd rather they didn't*: When the Buddha talks about our inability to control "feeling," he's not talking about our emotions. In Buddhist psychology, "feeling" refers to feeling *tone*—positive, negative, or neutral. To be sure, this feeling tone can *accompany* emotions (just as it can accompany perceptions and other mental phenomena), thus giving them their quality of pleasantness or unpleasantness. So when we are unable to dispel, say, anxiety, this *does* illustrate the point the Buddha is making here, because in failing to dispel the anxiety we are failing to dispel the predominately unpleasant feeling accompanying the anxiety. Still, as a technical matter, the anxiety itself would belong in the "mental formations" aggregate, not the feeling aggregate. So an inability to dispel anxiety would also illustrate the point the Buddha makes when he talks about mental formations defying our control.

62   †implicitly denying existence of CEO self: By the end of the discourse, after going through the five aggregates one by one, the Buddha has raised doubts about whether your whole system is under control—and if your system isn't under control, one might argue, then how could there be a CEO self? One could also argue that the two views of self I've contrasted here—self as something that's *in* control, like a CEO, and self as something that's *under* control—aren't so far apart, since anything that is *in* control would presumably be *under* control as well. In any event, as the anecdote that begins chapter 6 makes clear, in other texts the Buddha does invoke a "king" metaphor that calls to mind a self of the CEO sort.

64   *a few maverick scholars*: See, e.g., Harvey 1995, discussed in the text below, and Thanissaro 2013. For a reply to Thanissaro, see Bodhi 2015.

66   *"he personally attains nirvana"*: Samyutta Nikaya 22:53, Bodhi 2000, pp. 890–91.

67   †*But they're not*: For the sake of expository simplicity, I've omitted an important wrinkle that bears on the relationship between the "lust" and the "engagement." The commonsensical way to think about this might be that the consciousness aggregate lusts after the other aggregates—since, after all, a product of this lust is engagement between consciousness and the other aggregates. But according to Buddhist psychology, the lust for all the aggregates would originate in the "mental formations" aggregate (Bhikkhu Bodhi, personal communication). This includes a lust for consciousness and for specific contents of the mental formations aggregate itself. But the larger point still holds: it is lust for the contents of all the aggregates that sustains engagement between consciousness and the other aggregates.

67   †*any such simple scenario*: Among the problems with extracting this "simple scenario" from the discourse on engagement is the question of how to interpret the word *liberated*. One ancient commentary on Buddhist texts says that, in this discourse, consciousness is "liberated" in the sense that it will not generate rebirth after the person who has been liberated dies (see Bodhi 2000, p. 1060, note 72). The import of this interpretation will be easier to understand after you read chapter 14, but for now we can say that this interpretation complicates attempts to equate the liberation of

consciousness referred to here with the liberation of the person. (This interpretation, you might say, suggests that, while the person is liberated in the here and now, what is happening to consciousness at this moment of liberation is that it acquires properties that will grant it a somewhat different kind of liberation upon the death of the person.) That said, it should be emphasized that this interpretation is only an interpretation; the Pali version of the discourse doesn't *say* that this use of "liberated" refers only to the question of rebirth; it doesn't mention rebirth in this connection at all. And, moreover, ancient commentaries of this sort often had as one goal the elimination of seeming inconsistencies among discourses—so it's not surprising that this commentary would offer an interpretation that minimizes exactly the seeming inconsistency among discourses that I'm trying to highlight. Bhikkhu Bodhi says the interpretation in this commentary is plausible but not beyond dispute, and in any event wouldn't preclude simultaneously reading "liberated" in a broader sense (personal communication). Perhaps more important, he notes that, however this discourse is interpreted, there are various discourses in which the "mind" is said to be liberated upon enlightenment, and that in some discourses the word translated as "mind" is equated with the word translated as "consciousness." (In fact, Bodhi himself believes that the conspicuously puzzling line in the discourse on not-self that I've focused on in this chapter—the line that says that "he" is liberated—can be read as saying that the mind is liberated; the subject of the verb—as sometimes happens in Pali—isn't actually stated in the text, and most translators take it to be "he" on the basis of context, but Bodhi argues that "the mind" is on balance a more plausible reading.)

All told—given not only the reference to liberated consciousness in the discourse on engagement but also explicit descriptions in other discourses of liberated "mind"—it's far from crazy to suggest that the Buddha thought of consciousness as being liberated upon enlightenment. Still, any attempt to argue that the consciousness aggregate is where we find the "you" that is liberated must contend with the many discourses that, like the first discourse on not-self, depict liberation as involving the abandonment of all five aggregates, including consciousness. Indeed, even the discourse on engagement, when it encourages the abandonment of "lust" for the aggregates, includes the fifth aggregate, consciousness, and so remains true to that aspect of the discourse on not-self. Nonetheless, it is intriguing how the discourse on engagement suggests some kind of identification of the consciousness aggregate with the person—not only in the passage I've quoted in the text but also at the discourse's outset, where the Buddha declares, "One who is engaged is unliberated; one who is disengaged is liberated"—and then goes on to talk about engagement and disengagement as a relationship between consciousness and the other aggregates.

68   †*after liberation resides*: See Albahari 2006 for one such "dual mode" model of consciousness. I don't mean to suggest that everything I've said about such a model above would apply to Albahari's model. However, she does employ the phrase "witness consciousness" and in fact suggests that it's this witness consciousness that the Buddha is describing when he says in the *Bahuna Sutta* (see Thanissaro 1997) that, after a monk lets go of all five aggregates, "he dwells with unrestricted awareness."

69   *own the tooth in the first place*: Conze 1959, p. 18.

72   *"a baseless concept"*: Harvey 1995, p. 45.

72   *"as to be done"*: Ibid. Harvey writes that, even beyond the failure of the first discourse on the not-self to explicitly deny the existence of the self, "the early sources used by the Theravada are bereft of any such explicit denial" (p. 7).

72   *lead them toward liberation*: See in particular Thanissaro 2013; Thanissaro has translated many Buddhist texts into English, including the not-self discourse.

6: Your CEO Is MIA

75   *"consciousness is my self"*: I'm using the translation of Thanissaro 2012.

77   *"the prime minister"*: Kurzban 2010, p. 61.

79   *"'clean out the chicken shed'"*: Gazzaniga 2011, pp. 82–83.

81   *"subliminal and conscious movitation"*: Pessiglione et al. 2007.

81   †*doing the heavy lifting:* To be sure, the force of the hand grip tended to be higher when the image of the pound was consciously perceived than when the image of the pound was presented subliminally. But that could just be a product of how long the brain had been exposed to the image, rather than a product of conscious awareness per se. In other words, maybe the 100-millisecond exposure (the one that brought conscious awareness) would have led to greater grip strength even had it not triggered conscious awareness. In fact, there's evidence that this correlation between exposure time and grip strength is indeed independent of

conscious awareness. The experimenters used two exposure times in the subliminal range—17 milliseconds and 50 milliseconds—and the latter induced higher grip strength when the pound was presented than did the former. (In the case of the penny, logically enough, the opposite was the case.) By the way, 50 milliseconds wouldn't be in the subliminal range under all circumstances. But in this case the image of the coin was "masked" by being wedged between two presentations of a coin-sized pattern. The subjects saw that pattern at the beginning of each trial regardless of whether it masked an image of the coin.

81 Libet studies: See Libet 1985.

81 *questions of interpretation*: See Jarrett 2016 and Danquah et al. 2008.

83 beneffectance: Greenwald 1980.

83 driving skills study: Preston and Harris 1965.

83 moral self-evaluation study: Allison et al. 1989.

84 team member self-evaluation study: Greene 2013, p. 97. Regarding attribution bias more generally, see Mezulis et al. 2004.

84 susceptibility to bias study: Pronin et al. 2002.

84 "not being biased in thinking that we're better than average": Kurzban 2010, p. 105.

84 egocentric bias and memory study: D'Argembeau and Van der Linden 2008.

85 personality and self-perception study: Feldman Barrett 1997.

85 cultural variation in self-inflation: See Mezulis et al. 2004 and Sedikides et al. 2005.

86 *"as our folk psychology would have it"*: Barkow 1989, p. 104.

89 *"free-for-all, self-organizing system"*: Gazzaniga 2011, pp. 69–70.

89 *"the prize of conscious recognition"*: Ibid., p. 66.

90 *"anything else particularly special"*: Kurzban 2010, p. 56.

7: The Mental Modules That Run Your Life

92 †*doesn't explicitly say why*: The Buddha does emphasize in this discourse the linkage between impermanence and *dukkha*—suffering or unsatisfactoriness. And his wording suggests that both of these properties of the aggregates—impermanence and *dukkha* (in addition to the aggregates' resistance to control)—make it inappropriate to equate the five aggregates with self. One interpretation would be that it is *because* impermanence

leads to *dukkha* that impermanent things aren't self. This interpretation would make all the more sense in light of the fact that this discourse also links the aggregates' resistance to control to suffering (though here the word that connotes suffering isn't *dukkha*). In this reading, it isn't that resistance to control and impermanence in and of themselves disqualify the aggregates from "self" status; rather, it's because resistance to control and impermanence lead to suffering that they disqualify the aggregates from "self" status. But it's not clear why anyone would think that things conducive to suffering couldn't qualify as self, whereas it *does* make sense that things that aren't susceptible to control or that don't persist through time couldn't qualify as self. Thus I'm following the many interpreters who see the Buddha's argument as being largely about impermanence and resistance to control per se. That said, I would add that if we see the Buddha's argument as strictly pragmatic and therapeutic—as an argument that thinking of the aggregates as self leads to suffering, so you should consider them not-self just so you'll suffer less—then it *would* make sense that the Buddha is calling things that are impermanent and things that resist control not-self *only* because these properties are conducive to suffering. This reading would dovetail with the "heretical" interpretation of the Buddha's discourse discussed in chapter 5.

93   time discounting and mate acquisition mode study: Wilson and Daly 2004. See also Kim and Zauberman 2013.

93   study from *Journal of Marketing Research*: Griskevicius et al. 2009.

96   Tooby and Cosmides on sexual jealousy: Cosmides and Tooby 2000.

99   career aspiration and mate-acquisition mode study: Roney 2003.

100   †*career goals . . . become more materialistic*: Actually, the plural possessive pronoun *their* is misleading. In the case of the intertemporal utility function, the finding held for men but not for women; in the case of career goals, the experiment doesn't seem to have been done with women. In general, when it comes to mating psychology, there won't be complete symmetry between the genders, according to evolutionary psychology. At the same time, there's no reason to believe women's minds are any less transformed by courtship, or the prospect of courtship, than men's, even if the transformations may in some ways be different.

102   rating of facial expressions study: Maner et al. 2005.

103   *bad publicity we give rivals*: See Buss and Dedden 1990.

103   *"sorry, brainless fools"*: Burtt 1982, p. 37.

8: How Thoughts Think Themselves

108   default mode and "theory of mind" overlap: See Mars et al. 2012.

117   curiosity and dopamine brain scans: Sample 2014. See also Ikemoto and Panksepp 1999. The Ruskin and Johnson quotes come from Litman 2005. Litman posits that there are two different, sometimes overlapping kinds of brain processes that we call curiosity.

118   †*gains entry into consciousness*: This scenario raises the question of how thoughts could have *any* level of feeling associated with them *before* they reach consciousness. There are at least two possible answers: (1) As strange as it sounds, maybe there are realms in your mind that are sentient—that have subjective experience—but that your conscious mind doesn't normally have access to. Some people who have pondered the implications of the split-brain experiments discussed in chapter 6 take this possibility seriously. (2) Maybe "strength of feeling" is a latent property *until* the thought linked to the feeling is admitted to consciousness. During this latent phase, there would be some physical marker that signified the strength of the feeling, but this feeling would have no subjective manifestation until it was admitted to consciousness on the grounds of that signified strength.

120   *"dislikes it if it is unpleasing"*: Majjhima Nikaya 38: 30, Nanamoli and Bodhi 1995, p. 266.

9: "Self" Control

121   *"the slave of the passions"*: Hume 1984, p. 462.

122   Hume's exposure to Buddhism: See Gopnik 2009.

122   brain activity and purchasing behavior study: Knutson et al. 2007. The third brain region used by these researchers to predict purchasing behavior was the mesial prefrontal cortex, which responds to such things as the sight of a pleasing beverage.

123   *"any action of the will"*: Hume 1984, p. 460.

125   Tylenol and social pain study: Lieberman 2013, pp. 64–66.

125   prefrontal cortex and self control: See Sapolsky 2005.

126   *"direction of the will"*: Hume 1984, p. 461.

126   *"but a contrary impulse"*: Ibid., p. 462.

127   Greene on Hume: Greene 2013, chapter 5.

127   Pessoa on Plato's chariot: Pessoa 2013, pp. 2–3.

135 *RAIN*: The acronym is the creation of meditation teacher Michele McDonald (2015).

136 cigarette-smoking study: Brewer, Mallik, et al. 2011.

140 *"Command over the Mind"*: See Immerwahr 1992.

141 *"the common occurrences of life"*: Ibid.

10: Encounters with the Formless

143 †*the term:* emptiness: "Emptiness" is the translation of the Sanskrit word *sunyata* and the Pali word *sunnatta*. The term plays a bigger role in Mahayana Buddhism than in Theravada Buddhism, and when it is used in Theravada literature, it typically has a somewhat different technical meaning than it has in a Mahayana context. Perhaps the reason this meditation teacher used the term *formless* instead of *emptiness*—even though, as he later confirmed, he considered the two interchangeable—is that he teaches in the Theravada tradition.

143 *"Form is emptiness"*: Conze, trans., 1959, p. 162.

148 *"not going to bother me"*: Amaro 2002.

11: The Upside of Emptiness

153 The case of "Fred": Lucchelli and Spinnler 2007.

154 †*what Buddhists mean by enlightenment*: Interestingly, the scholar of religion Malcolm David Eckel, describing the perspective of people who take the Buddhist doctrine of emptiness seriously, once listed a series of questions that might occur to them, including these: "Mother, who's she? Brother, who is he? . . . That's all an illusion. It's empty." But even in this somewhat extreme description of the experience of emptiness, there's no suggestion that the person would actually think, as with Capgras delusion, that a mother or brother had been replaced by an imposter. See Eckel 2001.

157 *"duplicate would leave us cold"*: Bloom 2010, pp. 3–4.

157 †*affectively charged essences*: The meaning of *essence* as I'm using the term complies only partly with the definition of the term as it is typically used by psychologists. They typically mean a kind of invisible or hidden or non-obvious quality that something is thought to possess and without which it would not be what it is. This overlaps with what I mean by essence—*except* to the extent that "thought" is taken to imply explicit belief, as opposed to

a subtler, barely conscious conception. And often psychologists do mean to imply explicit belief—even to the point of talking about H_2O being seen as the essence of water. Their emphasis on explicit belief may be partly a product of their having studied essence by interrogating people about their beliefs about things (see, e.g., the very interesting work of Susan Gelman 2003). In any event, I'm focusing more on people's "sense" of essence—a sense that may be highly implicit—and I never mean *essence* to denote a thing's physical constituents. My use of *essence* also, by the way, doesn't align with uses of the word most common in Western philosophy.

157   *"there was evil in the world"*: Bloom 2010, p. 1.

158   *"sight of the letter Q"*: Zajonc 1980, p. 154.

159   judging pictures study: Giner-Sorolla et al. 1999. See also Jarudi et al. 2008.

160   affective priming studies: See Ferguson 2007.

161   implicit judgment of pictures: Giner-Sorolla et al. 1999.

165   †*perception of essence*: I want to emphasize the difference between my argument in defense of the idea of emptiness and the orthodox Buddhist argument in defense of the idea of emptiness. Emptiness is an "ontological" doctrine—a claim about the actual nature of reality. The orthodox Buddhist defense of this doctrine is, naturally enough, an ontological argument—an argument about the actual structure of reality, an argument that this structure, properly understood, doesn't support the claim that "things" have essence. (See chapter 13 for a slightly more detailed account of this standard Buddhist argument.) My defense of emptiness, though an argument made on behalf of an ontological doctrine, isn't itself fundamentally ontological, but rather is psychological. In other words, rather than argue that reality has a certain structure, and that this structure doesn't involve essence, I argue that the human mind is built to project onto reality a sense of essence, and that the Darwinian logic behind the projection gives us no reason to think that the projection corresponds to "objective" reality, and indeed gives us reason to doubt that the projection could correspond to "objective" reality. (See chapter 15 for elaboration on this logic.) Note that these two kinds of arguments on behalf of the doctrine of emptiness—the classic Buddhist ontological argument and my psychological argument—are logically compatible.

165   wine-tasting study: See Bloom 2010, p. 45.

166   *"a depth to pleasure"*: Ibid., p. 53.

171   *"hedonic experience of flavor"*: Plassmann et al. 2008.

12: A Weedless World

174   meta-analysis of "thin slice" studies: Ambady and Rosenthal 1992.

175   †*more considerate or conscientious*: See Eagly et al. 1991. Though attractiveness per se seems not to be an important cue in assessing moral fiber, other aspects of appearance may be. There is evidence, for example, that people are judged to be more trustworthy if they have high inner eyebrows and high cheekbones than if they don't. One brain-scan study that monitored parts of the brain known to correlate with evaluations of trustworthiness suggested that these evaluations are made even when facial images are presented subliminally—too briefly to be consciously perceived. See Freeman et al. 2014.

175   *"groaned, keeping his head down"*: Darley and Batson 1973, p. 104.

176   *"think like criminals"*: See Harman 1999, p. 320.

177   *"existence of character traits"*: Ibid., p. 316.

180   *"no revision of the original image"*: Kelman 2007, p. 97.

181   Hastorf and Cantril study: Hastorf and Cantril 1954, pp. 129, 131.

182   *"position in the total matrix"*: Ibid., p. 133.

182   *"candidate, Communism, or spinach"*: Ibid.

183   *"person's assumptive form-world"*: Ibid., p. 132.

186   *loving-kindness even for that enemy*: For an excellent exploration of *metta* meditation, see Salzberg 2002.

186   *whether Rumi did write that*: According to wikiquote.org, the quotation is misattributed to Rumi and should be attributed to Helen Schucman: https://en.wikiquote.org/wiki/Rumi.

190   *"the Zen Predator"*: See Oppenheimer 2013.

13: Like, Wow, Everything Is One (at Most)

196   *"a part of our very selves is gone"*: James 2007, pp. 291–92.

197   bacteria and the brain: See Wall et al. 2014 and Stein 2013.

197   †*seem more like part of me*: Our conventional sense of a unified self could itself be described as a product of mutualistic symbiosis. My various genes are in the same intergenerational boat (i.e., my genome) and so can profit (in the Darwinian sense of surviving and proliferating through the generations) by cooperating with one another. This, one could argue, is the reason my toes and my nose both feel like part of me: because the genes for

my toes and for my nose are playing a highly non-zero-sum game—and, perhaps more to the point, because they have a non-zero-sum relationship with the genes for the brain that is considering them part of me.

203 †*trees also lack self, and so do rocks*: The use of the term *not-self* to denote the absence of essence has one notable implication. Vipassana meditation, as we've seen, is intended to foster clear apprehension of the "three marks of existence"—to help us see that things in general are characterized by three properties, one of which is not-self. If, in keeping with this intention, we see the property of not-self in things "out there"—things out in the world we perceive, not just in ourselves or for that matter in other human beings—we are apprehending emptiness. The reason this is notable is that, in general, Theravada Buddhism is thought of as giving very little emphasis to emptiness compared to Mahayana Buddhism—yet Vipassana teaching, which took shape within the Theravada lineage, does turn out to give great emphasis to emptiness if you construe strictly its injunction to apprehend the three marks of existence.

210 tanha . . . *"the sense of self-other boundedness"*: Albahari 2006, p. 181.

211 †*than when you just overcome wrath*: One could ask whether the wrath and the aversion aren't so inherently linked that it's impossible to overcome "just" the wrath without overcoming the aversion. I don't know the answer to that question. But it's certainly true—in my experience, at least—that the aversion and the wrath are distinct feelings and that it's therefore possible to *focus* on the wrath alone, even if dissolving it by focusing on it does necessarily involve quelling the aversion itself.

212 †*in other words, possessing* tanha: In the Buddhist view, actually, feelings needn't be either positive or negative; rather, the "feeling tone" that is said to be such a pervasive part of our apprehension of the world can be positive, negative, or neutral. One could argue about whether a feeling tone that is truly neutral deserves to be called a feeling tone. But, in any event, it is fair to say that the general drift of Buddhist psychology is to emphasize how often positive or negative feelings, subtly or not so subtly, shape our perception of and reaction to the world.

213 †Raga *plus* dvesha *equals* moha: The logic of this "equation"—*raga* plus *dvesha* equals *moha*—is in a sense the reverse of Buddhist logic as it is commonly rendered. This "equation," broadly construed, says that craving and aversion give rise to delusion—to ignorance about the actual nature of the world. But a common Buddhist rendering of the relationship among these

things has it the other way around: ignorance and delusion (such as a failure to see the pervasiveness of impermanence, or to see the truth of notself or of emptiness) can give rise to craving and aversion. My own view is that the "equation" comes closer to capturing the actual direction of causality than the alternative rendering, even if both renderings, by themselves, are too simple. I also think that in at least some cases the dynamics of meditative progress imply the direction of causality suggested by the "equation." That is, mindfully observing and thereby to some extent overcoming craving and aversion is part of the process by which one overcomes ignorance and delusion in the sense of achieving an experiential apprehension of such ideas as impermanence, not-self, and emptiness.

14: Nirvana in a Nutshell

215 *"full awakening and understanding"*: Bodhi 1981, lecture 6.

217 †*"The conditioned"* . . . *"the caused"*: Buddhist thinkers sometimes take pains to distinguish the Buddhist notion of conditioning from the Western notion of causality. But the attempts to emphasize the distinction that I've come across have left me unpersuaded that the difference is deeply significant. These attempts sometimes depict Western notions of causality in simplistic terms, as if Western science can't accommodate the idea of the complex interaction of multiple influences.

217 †*twelve conditions . . . cycle of endless rebirth*: My rendering of the generic sense of conditioned arising is technically incomplete. The classic formulation in the ancient texts goes on to add that if the condition for the arising of something is absent, then the something will not arise, and if the condition for the arising of something ceases, then the something will cease (all of which, of course, is consistent with Western notions of causality). As for the less generic sense of conditioned arising, not all early Buddhist texts have the number of links as twelve, but the twelve-link sequence has become by far the most widely accepted rendering. I've relied particularly on the account of the twelve links in Bodhi 1981, lecture 4. See also, for concise accounts, Gethin 1998, pp. 149–59, and Harvey 2013, pp. 65–73.

218 *"prevent craving from crystallizing and solidifying"*: Bodhi 1981, lecture 4.

219 †*two kinds of nirvana*: These two kinds of nirvana are sometimes depicted as two stages in the realization of nirvana, with the nirvana reached upon

death—parinirvana—being *complete* nirvana. The nirvana experienced before death is referred to in some ancient texts as "nirvana with remainder"; enlightenment has been attained, and the suffering caused by *tanha* has been overcome, but existence continues to involve physical embodiment and to involve unavoidable pain upon, say, physical injury—pain that will be endured mindfully and with equanimity and that will not bring the kind of suffering it would have brought before enlightenment but will nonetheless keep one's experience from being unalloyed bliss twenty-four hours a day. See Kasulis 1987 and Bodhi 1981, lecture 6.

220 *"not being conditioned* by *something"*: Batchelor 2015, p. 145.

221 *"re-enchantment" of the world*: Ibid., p. 17.

15: Is Enlightenment Enlightening?

228 †*insights ... feats*: Of course, there is overlap and interaction among different "bullet points." For example, the insight into impermanence facilitates the feat of overcoming *tanha*. And, as we've seen, another commonly cited element of enlightenment, the eradication of the "three poisons," is tantamount to overcoming *tanha*, and, for that matter, entails insight into impermanence just by virtue of the fact that the third poison is delusion. And the insight into impermanence—specifically the impermanence of the five aggregates, discussed in chapter 5—facilitates the insight of not-self. And so on.

236 *"in relation to the object of judgment"*: Zajonc 1980, p. 157.

240 †*the well-being of all sentient beings*: As a logical matter, there's a fairly straightforward path from "the view from nowhere"—the view that no person's welfare is more important than any other person's—to the view that concern for everyone's welfare is in order. After all, the only premise you need to add is that human well-being is better than human suffering—a pretty uncontroversial proposition. For that matter, it's not hard to go further and bring all sentient beings under this umbrella of moral concern, since there's not much disagreement over the premise that, all other things being equal, the well-being of a sentient being is preferable to the suffering of that sentient being.

240 *"point of view ... of the Universe"*: Sidgwick 1884, p. 381.

16: Meditation and the Unseen Order

247 *"fear of wrongdoing following along"*: Samyutta Nikaya 45:1, Bodhi 2000, p. 1523.

258 †*quit making value judgments ... count me out*: The prospect I'm raising here is far from original. Scholars of Buddhism have long pondered the question of whether a likely, and perhaps logical, culmination of Buddhist practice is an extreme form of nihilism, a refusal to attribute value to anything.

After all, a common refrain in meditation instruction is that you shouldn't be judgmental: you shouldn't judge feelings as good or bad, sounds as good or bad, sights as good or bad. Well, if you get better and better at not making judgments, don't you wind up making no judgments of any kind? No judgments about what's right and wrong? And wouldn't you then be devoid of any desire to do anything to right what are commonly considered wrongs?

Another way to look at the problem is via the Buddhist emphasis on equanimity. One aim of Buddhist practice is to allow you to preserve a stable sense of well-being regardless of the objective circumstances of your situation—to remain an island of calm amid even the most violent storms. Wouldn't this involve maintaining a certain indifference to everything that's going on beyond your island, including really bad things that, if you were less calm, you might get agitated by and want to do something about?

Just to zoom in on this logic a bit: the Buddhist approach to maintaining equanimity, to preserving a sense of calm and well-being, involves transcending both your natural aversion to unpleasant things and your natural desire for pleasant things. Well, if you succeed completely in this mission, then don't you, in a sense, have no preferences?

And aren't preferences an essential part of having a value system at all? If you don't prefer a just world to an unjust world, you won't work to make the world more just; indeed, you won't recognize a meaningful difference between what other people call just and what they call unjust. And, for that matter, why would you have feelings of compassion and love—aren't they just a form of preference, a way of preferring that certain things happen to the people for whom you feel compassion or love?

These may sound like hypothetical and extreme extrapolations from Buddhist thought, but they aren't far from the views associated with some venerated Buddhist thinkers. Consider a poem attributed to a sixth-century Chinese monk known as the Third Patriarch of Zen (sometimes called the

Third Patriarch of Chan, Chan being the Chinese school of Buddhism that was the precursor of Zen). The poem begins:

> *The Great Way is not difficult*
> *for those who have no preferences.*
> *When not attached to love or hate,*
> *all is clear and undisguised.*
> *Separate by the smallest amount, however,*
> *and you are as far from it as heaven is from earth.*
> *If you wish to know the truth,*
> *then hold to no opinions for or against anything.*

Granted, some qualifiers could be added to this poem. There is, as usual, the question of translation (an alternative translation to "When not attached to love or hate" is "If you cut off all likes or dislikes"). Moreover, this poem is a declaration made in a particular social and intellectual context, an argument for a certain interpretation of Buddhism and against other interpretations that were then prevalent. Still, this passage rests on a fairly straightforward extrapolation from core Buddhist ideas. That is the reason the "problem of nihilism" has long been considered a serious problem for Buddhism.

I have nothing radically new to say about the problem, but I do want to try to be clear on what the problem *is*.

The problem of nihilism, as I see it, is *not* the problem I mentioned in chapter 12—the problem of people using the equanimity and clarity afforded by meditation to more effectively exploit other people. After all, to want to exploit people is to have a preference, to place value on the things that can be had via exploitation. The "Zen Predator of the Upper East Side," whom I mentioned in that chapter, preferred having sex with lots of women, and he attached great value to sexual gratification. That isn't nihilism in the most sweeping sense of the term—the idea that nothing matters, that the world is so lacking in meaning that no goals are worth pursuing. The Zen Predator definitely believed there were goals worth pursuing.

In other words, the Zen Predator had not traveled as far down the path as the Third Patriarch of Zen would have advised him to travel. He had not attained enlightenment. And I don't say that just because abandoning such "fetters" as lust is sometimes listed as a prerequisite for enlightenment. I say it also because enlightenment, in the strictest sense, involves the complete abandonment of craving in general, and lust is a form of craving. If you get to the place that the Third Patriarch of Zen seems to be talking about—a place with "no preferences"—you have so thoroughly overcome craving as to not behave as the Zen Predator behaved.

To be sure, the Zen Predator seems to be a nihilist in one common sense of that term: he seems to lack the kind of values that most of us would consider moral, and he is therefore unconstrained by scruple as he pursues the things he personally values. My point is just that this is not the "nihilism problem" that, in my view, is legitimately raised by the actual logic of Buddhist philosophy. The nihilism problem legitimately raised by Buddhist philosophy is the problem of not having values at all; it's the problem of just sitting there not having any particular desire for things to change—not having a desire to bring about social justice or the desire to bring about sex.

As a practical matter, people who are led by Buddhist thought and practice into this kind of nihilism aren't much worth worrying about. One reason is that, though they aren't part of the solution, they at least aren't part of the problem. They may have no particular moral values, but they have by definition lost all selfish desires, so it's not as if they'll go around exploiting people and wreaking havoc.

The other reason people like this aren't much worth worrying about is that there aren't many of them. Do you know any people who have actually attained enlightenment? I just spent years seeking out and talking to highly adept meditators, and I'm not sure I know any. At least, I'm not sure I know any who have attained enlightenment in such a strict sense of the term—in the sense of overcoming all craving and all aversion—that they embody the problem of nihilism in the most sweeping sense of the term.

Besides, when we talk about the problem of nihilism, we're talking about people who have attained enlightenment not just in a strict sense of the term but also in what you might call a narrow sense of the term. Following the dharma in a full-bodied way involves absorbing Buddhist moral values and, accordingly, cultivating compassion. Indeed, in much of the Buddhist world the ideal of enlightenment is embodied in the *bodhisattva*, someone who is devoted above all to helping others.

All that said, there are two kinds of people I do think are worth worrying about.

First, of course, are the Zen Predators of the world—people who use meditative prowess to gain such detachment that they can more effectively manipulate other people to their selfish ends. But this isn't a problem of following the Buddhist path too far; it's a problem of not following the path far enough, a problem of not being a good Buddhist.

Second, there are people who follow the Buddhist path pretty far, and become happier people, with more equanimity than they had before—and this equanimity does indeed diminish their passion for making the world a better place. These people aren't generally part of the problem, because, as a rule, their selfishness has diminished more or less to the extent that their passion to realize good in the world has diminished. And in a certain sense they're part of the solution, because in their personal interactions they tend to be kinder and gentler than they would be if they hadn't followed the Buddhist path. Still, they're not as big a part of the solution as they could be.

And I wish they were a bigger part of the solution. I hope in the future we'll see more people who earnestly follow the Buddhist path and are deeply activist. Still, there are worse things than not being a bigger part of the solution. If the most searing indictment you could make of anyone in this world was that they weren't a bigger part of the solution, we would have much less in the way of problems.

All told, I'd say that the problem of nihilism is, in an abstractly logical and hypothetical sense, a serious problem for Buddhism and, in a real and practical sense, not much of a problem at all.

261 *"harmoniously adjusting ourselves thereto"*: James 1982, p. 53.

Bibliography

Albahari, Miri. 2006. *Analytical Buddhism: The Two-Tiered Illusion of Self*. Palgrave Macmillan.

Alicke, Mark, M. L. Klotz, David Breitenbecher, Tricia Yurak, and Debbie Vrendenburg. 1995. "Personal Contact, Individuation, and the Better-Than-Average Effect." *Journal of Personality and Social Psychology* 68(5): 804–25.

Allison, Scott, David Messick, and George Goethals. 1989. "On Being Better but not Smarter Than Others." *Social Cognition* 7(3): 275–96.

Amaro Bhikkhu. 2002. *Small Boat, Great Mountain*. Abhayagiri Monastery.

Ambady, Nalini, and Robert Rosenthal. 1992. "Thin Slices of Expressive Behavior as Predictors of Interpersonal Consequences: A Meta-analysis." *Psychological Bulletin* 111(2): 256–74.

Andrews-Hanna, Jessica, Jay Reidler, Jorge Sepulcre, Renee Poulin, and Randy Buckner. 2010. "Functional-Anatomic Fractionation of the Brain's Default Network." *Neuron* 65: 550–62.

Asma, Stephen. 2014. "Monsters on the Brain: An Evolutionary Epistemology of Horror." *Social Research* 81(4): 941–68.

Barash, David. 2013. *Buddhist Biology*. W. W. Norton.

Bargh, John. 2011. "Unconscious Thought Theory and Its Discontents: A Critique of the Critiques." *Social Cognition* 29(6): 629–47.

Barkow, Jerome. 1989. *Darwin, Sex, and Status*. University of Toronto Press.

Batchelor, Stephen. 2015. *After Buddhism: Rethinking the Dharma for a Secular Age*. Yale University Press.

Beck, Aaron, and Gary Emery. 1985. *Anxiety Disorders and Phobias: A Cognitive Perspective*. Basic Books.

Bloom, Paul. 2010. *How Pleasure Works: The New Science of Why We Like What We Like.* W. W. Norton.

Bodhi, Bhikkhu. 1981. "The Buddha's Teaching as It Is." Ten-part lecture series. http://www.buddhanet.net/audio-lectures.htm.

Bodhi, Bhikkhu, trans. 2000. *The Connected Discourses of the Buddha: A Translation of the Samyutta Nikaya.* Wisdom Publications.

Bodhi, Bhikkhu. 2015. "Anatta as Strategy and Ontology" in *Investigating the Dhamma: A Collection of Papers by Bhikkhu Bodhi.* Buddhist Publication Society.

Brewer, Judson, Jake Davis, and Joseph Goldstein. 2013. "Why Is It So Hard to Pay Attention, or Is It? Mindfulness, the Factors of Awakening and Reward-Based Learning." *Mindfulness* 4(1): 75–80.

Brewer, Judson, Sarah Mallik, Theresa Babuscio, Charla Nich, Hayley Johnson, Cameron Deleone, Candace Minnix-Cotton, et al. 2011. "Mindfulness Training for Smoking Cessation: Results from a Randomized Controlled Trial." *Drug and Alcohol Dependence* 119(1/2): 72–80.

Brewer, Judson, Patrick Worhunsky, Jeremy Gray, Yi-Yuan Tang, Jochen Weber, and Hedy Kober. 2011. "Meditation Experience Is Associated with Differences in Default Mode Network Activity and Connectivity." *Proceedings of the National Academy of Sciences* 108(50): 20254–59.

Buddhaghosa, Bhadantacariya. 2010. *The Path of Purification.* Trans. Bhikkhu Nanamoli. Buddhist Publication Society.

Burtt, E. A., ed. 1982. *The Teachings of the Compassionate Buddha.* New American Library.

Buss, David, and Lisa Dedden. 1990. "Derogation of Competitors." *Journal of Social and Personal Relationships* 7: 395–422.

Conze, Edward. 1959. *Buddhism: Its Essence and Development.* Harper Torchbook.

Conze, Edward, trans. 1959. *Buddhist Scriptures.* Penguin.

Cosmides, Leda, and John Tooby. 2000. "Evolutionary Psychology and the Emotions." In Michael Lewis and Jeannette M. Haviland-Jones, eds., *Handbook of Emotions.* 2nd ed. Guilford Press.

———. 2002. "Unraveling the Enigma of Human Intelligence: Evolutionary Psychology and the Multimodular Mind." In Robert Sternberg and James Kaufman, eds., *The Evolution of Intelligence.* Lawrence Erlbaum Associates.

D'Argembeau, Arnaud, and Martial Van der Linden. 2008. "Remembering Pride and Shame: Self-Enhancement and the Phenomenology of Autobiographical Memory." *Memory* 16(5): 538–47.

Danquah, Adam N., Martin Farrell, and Donald O'Boyle. 2008. "Biases in the Subjective Timing of Perceptual Events: Libet et al. (1983) Revisited." *Consciousness and Cognition* 17(3): 616–27.

Darley, John M., and C. Daniel Batson. 1973. "From Jerusalem to Jericho: A Study of Situational and Dispositional Factors in Helping Behavior." *Journal of Personality and Social Psychology* 27(1): 100–108.

Davidson, Richard J., and William Irwin. 1999. "The Functional Neuroanatomy of Emotion and Affective Style." *Trends in Cognitive Sciences* 3(1): 11–22.

de Silva, Padmasiri. 2000. *An Introduction to Buddhist Psychology.* 4th ed. Palgrave Macmillan.

Eagly, Alice, Richard Ashmore, Mona Makhijani, and Laura Longo. 1991. "What Is Beautiful Is Good, But . . . : A Meta-analytic Review of Research on the Physical Attractiveness Stereotype." *Psychological Bulletin* 110(1): 109–28.

Eckel, Malcolm David. 2001. "Buddhism." *The Great Courses.* Audio lecture.

Ekman, Paul, Richard Davidson, Matthieu Ricard, and B. Alan Wallace. 2005. "Buddhist and Psychological Perspectives on Emotions and Well-Being." *Current Directions in Psychological Science* 14(2): 59–63.

Farb, Norman, Zindel Segal, Helen Mayberg, Jim Bean, Deborah McKeon, Zainab Fatima, and Adam Anderson. 2007. "Attending to the Present: Mindfulness Meditation Reveals Distinct Neural Modes of Self-Reference." *Scan* 2: 313–22.

Farias, Miguel, and Catherine Wikholm. 2015. *The Buddha Pill: Can Meditation Change You?* Watkins.

Feldman Barrett, Lisa. 1997. "The Relationships among Momentary Emotion Experiences, Personality Descriptions, and Retrospective Ratings of Emotion." *Personality & Social Psychology Bulletin* 23(10): 1100–1110.

Ferguson, M. J. 2007. "The Automaticity of Evaluation." In J. Bargh, ed., *Social Psychology and the Unconscious: The Automaticity of Higher Mental Processes.* Psychology Press.

Freeman, Jonathan, Ryan Stolier, Zachary Ingbretsen, and Eric Hehman. 2014. "Amygdala Responsivity to High-Level Social Information." *Journal of Neuroscience* 34(32): 10573–81.

Gazzaniga, Michael. 2011. *Who's in Charge? Free Will and the Science of the Brain.* Ecco.

Gelman, Susan. 2003. *The Essential Child: Origins of Essentialism in Everyday Thought*. Oxford University Press.

Gethin, Rupert. 1998. *The Foundations of Buddhism*. Oxford University Press.

Giner-Sorolla, Roger, Magda T. Garcia, and John A. Bargh. 1999. "The Automatic Evaluation of Pictures." *Social Cognition* 17(1): 76–96.

Gold, Jonathan. 2014. *Paving the Great Way: Vasubandhu's Unifying Buddhist Philosophy*. Columbia University Press.

Goldstein, Joseph. 1987. *The Experience of Insight: A Simple and Direct Guide to Buddhist Meditation*. Shambhala Dragon Editions.

———. 2002. *One Dharma: The Emerging Western Buddhism*. HarperSanFrancisco.

———. 2016. *Mindfulness: A Practical Guide to Awakening*. Sounds True.

Goleman, Daniel. 1998. *The Meditative Mind: The Varieties of Meditative Experience*. G. P. Putnam's Sons.

Gopnik, Allison. 2009. "Could David Hume Have Known about Buddhism? Charles Francois Dolu, the Royal College of La Flèche, and the Global Jesuit Intellectual Network." *Hume Studies* 35(1/2): 5–28.

Greene, Joshua. 2013. *Moral Tribes: Emotion, Reason, and the Gap between Us and Them*. Penguin Press.

Greenwald, Anthony. 1980. "The Totalitarian Ego: Fabrication and Revision of Personal History." *American Psychologist* 357: 603–18.

Griskevicius, Vladas, Noah Goldstein, Chad Mortensen, Jill Sundie, Robert Cialdini, and Douglas Kenrick. 2009. "Fear and Loving in Las Vegas: Evolution, Emotion, and Persuasion." *Journal of Marketing Research* 46(3): 384–95.

Gunaratan, Henepola. 1991. *Mindfulness in Plain English*. Wisdom.

Hanson, Rick, and Richard Mendius. 2009. *Buddha's Brain: The Practical Neuroscience of Happiness, Love, and Wisdom*. New Harbinger Publications.

Harman, Gilbert. 1999. "Moral Philosophy Meets Social Psychology: Virtue Ethics and the Fundamental Attribution Error." *Proceedings of the Aristotelian Society* 99: 315–31, new series.

Harris, Dan. 2014. *10% Happier: How I Tamed the Voice in My Head, Reduced Stress without Losing My Edge, and Found Self-Help That Actually Works—A True Story*. Dey Street Books.

Harris, Sam. 2014. *Waking Up: A Guide to Spirituality Without Religion*. Simon & Schuster.

Harvey, Peter. 1995. *The Selfless Mind: Personality, Consciousness and Nirvana in Early Buddhism*. Routledge.

————. 2013. *An Introduction to Buddhism: Teachings, History and Practices*. 2nd ed. Cambridge University Press.

Hastorf, Albert H., and Hadley Cantril. 1954. "They Saw a Game: A Case Study." *Journal of Abnormal and Social Psychology* 49(1): 129–34.

Holzel, Britta, Sara Lazar, Tim Gard, Zev Schuman-Olivier, David Vago, and Ulrich Ott. 2011. "How Does Mindfulness Meditation Work? Proposing Mechanisms of Action from a Conceptual and Neural Perspective." *Perspectives on Psychological Science* 6(6): 537–59.

Hume, David. 1984. *A Treatise of Human Nature*. Penguin.

Ikemoto, Satoshi, and Jaak Panksepp. 1999. "The Role of Nucleus Accumbens Dopamine in Motivated Behavior: A Unifying Interpretation with Special Reference to Reward-Seeking." *Brain Research Reviews* 31: 6–41.

Immerwahr, John. 1992. "Hume on Tranquilizing the Passions." *Hume Studies* 18(2): 293–314.

Ingram, Daniel. 2008. *Mastering the Core Teachings of the Buddha: An Unusually Hardcore Dharma Book*. Aeon Books.

James, William. 1982. *The Varieties of Religious Experience*. Penguin.

————. 2007. *The Principles of Psychology*, vol. 1. Cosimo Books.

Jarudi, Izzat, Tamar Kreps, and Paul Bloom. 2008. "Is a Refrigerator Good or Evil? The Moral Evaluation of Everyday Objects." *Social Justice Research* 21(4): 457–69.

Jarrett, Christian. 2016. "Neuroscience and Free Will Are Rethinking Their Divorce." *New York Magazine*, February 3.

Jones, Edward, and Richard Nisbett. 1971. "The Actor and the Observer: Divergent Perceptions of the Causes of Behavior." In Edward Jones, David Kanhouse, Harold Kelley, Richard Nisbett, Stuart Valins, and Bernard Weiner, eds., *Attribution: Perceiving the Causes of Behavior*. General Learning Press.

Kasulis, Thomas P. 1987. "Nirvana." In Mircea Eliade, ed., *The Encyclopedia of Religion*, vol. 10. MacMillan.

Kelman, Herbert C. 2007. "Social-Psychological Dimensions of International Conflict." In William Zartman, ed., *Peacemaking in International Conflict*. US Institute of Peace.

Killingsworth, Matthew, and Daniel Gilbert. 2010. "A Wandering Mind Is an Unhappy Mind." *Science* 330: 932.

Kim, B. Kyu, and Gal Zauberman. 2013. "Can Victoria's Secret Change the Future? A Subjective Time Perception Account of Sexual-Cue Effects on Impatience." *Journal of Experimental Psychology: General* 142(2): 328–35.

Knitter, Paul. 2009. *Without Buddha I Could Not Be a Christian*. Oneworld.

Knutson, Brian, Scott Rick, G. Elliott Wimmer, Drazen Prelac, and George Loewenstein. 2007. "Neural Predictors of Purchases." *Neuron* 53: 147–56.

Kornfield, Jack. 1993. *A Path with Heart: A Guide through the Perils and Promises of Spiritual Life*. Bantam Books.

Kornfield, Jack, and Paul Breiter, eds. 1985. *A Still Forest Pool: The Insight Meditation of Achaan Chah*. Quest Books.

Kuhn, Simone, and Marcel Brass. 2009. "Retrospective Construction of the Judgement of Free Choice." *Consciousness and Cognition* 18: 12–21.

Kurzban, Robert. 2010. *Why Everyone (Else) Is a Hypocrite: Evolution and the Modular Mind*. Princeton University Press.

Libet, Benjamin. 1985. "Unconscious Cerebral Initiative and the Role of Conscious Will in Voluntary Action." *Behavioral and Brain Sciences* 8: 529–39.

Lieberman, Matthew. 2013. *Social: Why Our Brains Are Wired to Connect*. Crown.

Litman, Jordan A. 2005. "Curiosity and the Pleasures of Learning: Wanting and Liking New Information." *Cognition and Emotion* 19(6): 793–814.

Lucchelli, F., and H. Spinnler. 2007. "The Case of Lost Wilma: A Clinical Report of Capgras Delusion." *Neurological Science* 28: 188–95.

Lutz, Antoine, John Dunne, and Richard Davidson. 2007. "Meditation and the Neuroscience of Consciousness." In Philip Zelazo, Morris Moscovitch, and Evan Thompson, eds., *Cambridge Handbook of Consciousness*. Cambridge University Press.

Lutz, Antoine, Heleen Slagter, John Dunne, and Richard Davidson. 2008. "Attention Regulation and Monitoring in Meditation." *Trends in Cognitive Sciences* 12(4): 163–69.

Maner, Jon, Douglas Kenrick, D. Vaughn Becker, Theresa Robertson, Brian Hofer, Steven Neuberg, Andrew Delton, Jonathan Butner, and Mark Schaller. 2005. "Functional Projection: How Fundamental Social Motives Can Bias Interpersonal Perception." *Journal of Personality and Social Psychology* 88(1): 63–78.

Mars, Roger B., Franz-Xaver Neubert, MaryAnn P. Noonan, Jerome Sallet, Ivan Toni, and Matthew F. S. Rushworth. 2012. "On the Relationship between the 'Default Mode Network' and the 'Social Brain.'" *Frontiers in Human Neuroscience* 6: 189.

McDonald, Michele. 2015. "R.A.I.N.D.R.O.P." *Dharma Seed*. Lecture, True North Insight, August 28. http://dharmaseed.org/teacher/126/talk/29234/.

Mendis, N. K. G., trans. 2010. "Anatta-Lakkhana Sutta: The Discourse on the

Not-Self Characteristic." (Samyutta Nikaya 22:59) *Access to Insight: Readings in Theravada Buddhism.* http://www.accesstoinsight.org/tipitaka/sn/sn22/sn22.059.mend.html.

Mezulis, Amy H., Lyn Abramson, Janet Hyde, and Benjamin Hankin. 2004. "Is There a Universal Positivity Bias in Attributions? A Meta-analytic Review of Individual, Developmental, and Cultural Differences in the Self-Serving Attributional Bias." *Psychological Bulletin* 130(5): 711–47.

Michaelson, Jay. 2013. *Evolving Dharma: Meditation, Buddhism and the Next Generation of Enlightenment.* Evolver Editions.

Miller, Timothy. 1994. *How to Want What You Have.* Henry Holt & Co.

Nanamoli, Bhikkhu, and Bhikkhu Bodhi, trans. 1995. *The Middle Length Discourses of the Buddha: A Translation of the Majjhima Nikaya.* Wisdom Publications.

Nisker, Wes. 1998. *Buddha's Nature: A Practical Guide to Enlightenment through Evolution.* Bantam Books.

Oppenheimer, Mark. 2013. *The Zen Predator of the Upper East Side.* Atlantic Books.

Parfit, Derek. 1984. *Reasons and Persons.* Oxford University Press.

Pessiglione, Mathias, Liane Schmidt, Bogan Draganski, Raffael Kalisch, Hakwan Lau, Ray Dolan, and Chris Frith. 2007. "How the Brain Translates Money into Force: A Neuroimaging Study of Subliminal Motivation." *Science* 316: 904–6.

Pessoa, Luiz. 2013. *The Cognitive-Emotional Brain: From Interactions to Integration.* MIT Press.

Pinker, Steven. 1997. *How the Mind Works.* W. W. Norton.

Plassmann, Hilke, John O'Doherty, Baba Shiv, and Antonio Rangel. 2008. "Marketing Actions Can Modulate Neural Representations of Experienced Pleasantness." *Proceedings of the National Academy of Sciences* 105(3): 1050–54.

Preston, Carolyn, and Stanley Harris. 1965. "Psychology of Drivers in Traffic Accidents." *Journal of Applied Psychology* 49(4): 264–68.

Pronin, Emily, Thomas Gilovich, and Lee Ross. 2004. "Objectivity in the Eye of the Beholder: Divergent Perceptions of Bias in Self versus Others." *Psychological Review* 111(3): 781–99.

Pronin, Emily, Daniel Y. Lin, and Lee Ross. 2002. "The Bias Blind Spot: Perceptions of Bias in Self versus Others." *Personality and Social Psychology Bulletin* 28(3): 369–81.

Rahula, Walpola. (1959) 1974. *What the Buddha Taught.* Grove Press.

Romanes, George John. 1884. *Mental Evolution in Animals.* D. Appleton and Co.

Roney, James R. 2003. "Effects of Visual Exposure to the Opposite Sex: Cognitive Aspects of Mate Attraction in Human Males." *Personality and Social Psychology Bulletin* 29: 393–404.

Sabini, John, Michael Siepmann, and Julia Stein. 2001. "The Really Fundamental Attribution Error in Social Psychological Research." *Psychological Inquiry* 12(1): 1–15.

Salzberg, Sharon. 2002. *Lovingkindness: The Revolutionary Art of Happiness.* Shambhala Classics.

———. 2003. *Faith: Trusting Your Own Deepest Experience.* Riverhead Books.

Salzberg, Sharon, and Robert Thurman. 2013. *Love Your Enemies: How to Break the Anger Habit and Be a Whole Lot Happier.* Hay House.

Sample, Ian. 2014. "Curiosity Improves Memory by Tapping into the Brain's Reward System." *Guardian,* October 2. http://www.theguardian.com/science/2014/oct/02/curiosity-memory-brain-reward-system-dopamine.

Sapolsky, Robert. 2005. "Biology and Human Behavior: The Neurological Origins of Individuality." Audio lecture. *The Great Courses.* 2nd ed.

Sayadaw, Mahasi. 1965. *The Progress of Insight.* Trans. Nyānaponika Thera. Buddhist Publication Society.

Schultz, Wolfram. 2001. "Reward Signaling by Dopamine Neurons." *Neuroscientist* 7(4): 293–302.

Schultz, Wolfram, Paul Apicella, Eugenio Scarnati, and Tomas Ljungberg. 1992. "Neuronal Activity in Monkey Ventral Striatum Related to the Expectation of Reward." *Journal of Neuroscience* 12(12): 4595–610.

Sedikides, Constantine, and Mark D. Alicke. 2012. "Self-Enhancement and Self-Protection Motives." In Richard M. Ryan, ed., *The Oxford Handbook of Human Motivation.* Oxford University Press.

Sedikides, Constantine, Lowell Gaertner, and Jack L. Vevea. 2005. "Pancultural Self-Enhancement Reloaded: A Meta-analytic Reply to Heine." *Journal of Personality and Social Psychology* 89(4): 539–51.

Seligman, Martin. 2002. *Authentic Happiness: Using the New Positive Psychology to Realize Your Potential for Lasting Fulfillment.* Free Press.

Siderits, Mark, Evan Thompson, and Dan Zahavi, eds. 2001. *Self, No Self? Perspectives from Analytical, Phenomenological, and Indian Traditions.* Oxford University Press.

Sidgwick, Henry. 1884. *The Methods of Ethics.* MacMillan and Co.

Smith, Rodney. 2014. *Awakening: A Paradigm Shift of the Heart.* Shambhala.

Stein, Rob. 2013. "Gut Bacteria Might Guide the Workings of Our Minds." NPR. November 18.http://www.npr.org/blogs/health/2013/11/18/244526773 /gut-bacteria-might-guide-the-workings-of-our-minds.

Thanissaro Bhikkhu, trans. 1997. "Bahuna Sutta: To Bahuna" (Anguttara Nikaya 10:81). *Access to Insight: Readings in Theravāda Buddhism.* http://www.ac cesstoinsight.org/tipitaka/an/an10/an10.081.than.html.

———, trans. 2012. "Cula-Saccaka Sutta: The Shorter Discourse to Saccaka" (Majjhima Nikaya 35). *Access to Insight: Readings in Theravāda Buddhism.* http://www.accesstoinsight.org/tipitaka/mn/mn.035.than.html.

———. 2013. "The Not-Self Strategy." *Access to Insight: Readings in Theravāda Buddhism.* http://www.accesstoinsight.org/lib/authors/thanissaro/notself strategy.pdf.

Thera, Nyānaponika, trans. 2007. "Freed of Fivefold Fear" (Anguttara Nikaya 9:5). *Access to Insight: Readings in Theravāda Buddhism.* http://www.accessto insight.org/lib/authors/nyanaponika/wheel238.html.

Thera, Soma, trans. 2013. "The Way of Mindfulness: The Satipatthana Sutta and Its Commentary." *Access to Insight: Readings in Theravāda Buddhism.* http:// www.accesstoinsight.org/lib/authors/soma/wayof.html.

Wall, R., J. F. Cryan, R. P. Ross, G. F. Fitzgerald, T. G. Dinan, and C. Stanton. 2014. "Bacterial Neuroactive Compounds Produced by Psychobiotics." *Advances in Experimental Medicine and Biology* 817: 221–39.

Weber, Gary. 2007. *Happiness Beyond Thought: A Practical Guide to Awakening.* iUniverse.

Wilson, Margo, and Martin Daly. 2004. "Do Pretty Women Inspire Men to Discount the Future?" *Proceedings of the Royal Society of London B (Suppl.)* 271: S177–79.

Wright, Dale S. 2016. *What Is Buddhist Enlightenment?.* Oxford University Press.

Wright, Robert. 1994. *The Moral Animal: Evolutionary Psychology and Everyday Life.* Pantheon.

———. 2000. *Nonzero: The Logic of Human Destiny.* Pantheon.

Yongey Mingyur, Rinpoche, and Eric Swanson. 2007. *The Joy of Living.* Three Rivers Press.

Zajonc, R. B. 1980. "Feeling and Thinking: Preferences Need No Inferences." *American Psychologist* 35(2): 151–75.

Index